SpringerBriefs in Psychology

SpringerBriefs present concise summaries of cutting-edge research and practical applications across a wide spectrum of fields. Featuring compact volumes of 55 to 125 pages, the series covers a range of content from professional to academic. Typical topics might include:

- A timely report of state-of-the-art analytical techniques
- A bridge between new research results as published in journal articles and a contextual literature review
- A snapshot of a hot or emerging topic
- An in-depth case study or clinical example
- A presentation of core concepts that readers must understand to make independent contributions

SpringerBriefs in Psychology showcase emerging theory, empirical research, and practical application in a wide variety of topics in psychology and related fields. Briefs are characterized by fast, global electronic dissemination, standard publishing contracts, standardized manuscript preparation and formatting guidelines, and expedited production schedules.

Robert Wegener • Tamara Garcia
Nicky Terblanche • Till Grossrieder
Editors

Coaching in the Age of AI

Perspectives on Opportunities, Challenges, and Future Directions

Springer

Editors
Robert Wegener
Fachhochschule Nordwestschweiz FHNW
Hochschule für Soziale Arbeit
Olten, Schweiz

Nicky Terblanche
Stellenbosch Business School
Cape Town, South Africa

Tamara Garcia
Institute of Applied Psychology
ZHAW Zurich University of Applied Sciences
Zürich, Zürich, Switzerland

Till Grossrieder
Institute of Applied Psychology
ZHAW Zurich University of Applied Sciences
Zürich, Switzerland

ISSN 2192-8363 ISSN 2192-8371 (electronic)
SpringerBriefs in Psychology
ISBN 978-3-032-23331-8 ISBN 978-3-032-23332-5 (eBook)
https://doi.org/10.1007/978-3-032-23332-5

This work was supported by ZHAW Zurich University of Applied Sciences and Fachhochschule Nordwestschweiz.

This Springer imprint is published by the registered company Springer Nature Switzerland AG
The registered company address is: Gewerbestrasse 11, 6330 Cham, Switzerland

Foreword[1]

We are living through a historic transformation, one in which artificial intelligence is no longer a distant possibility but an active force reshaping the way we live, work, and relate to one another. Nowhere is this more apparent than in the world of coaching, where the integration of AI technologies presents both profound opportunities and critical challenges. *Coaching in the Age of AI* arrives at exactly the right moment to help us navigate this evolving landscape.

This volume brings together a diverse group of international scholars and practitioners who explore the dynamic interplay between human coaching and AI. Rather than offering simplistic answers or advocating for a wholesale replacement of human coaches, the authors thoughtfully map the terrain of possibility, identifying where AI can extend human potential—and where it must be approached with caution.

The book begins by addressing the boldest question: Can AI simulate human coaching? Through studies of chatbot-based coaching and initiatives like StudiCoachBot and Ephoria, the authors reveal both the promise and pitfalls of AI-driven interactions. AI tools can offer accessible, scalable support and even foster rapport, goal attainment, and self-disclosure. However, they also introduce serious ethical concerns—especially around bias, transparency, and the dilution of human presence. These tensions surface repeatedly in chapters on ethics, relationship-building, and self-regulation.

Yet AI is not simply a substitute—it is, at least potentially, a collaborator. Several chapters in this book explore how AI can *enhance* human coaching rather than replace it. Triadic coaching models, generative AI as a "sparring partner," and AI-supported diagnostics exemplify hybrid approaches that enrich the coaching dialogue without undermining the coach–client relationship. These models reflect a growing recognition: the power of AI lies in amplifying the uniquely human capacities that coaching is built upon—empathy, deep listening, meaning-making, values discernment, and presence.

[1] Edited by ChatGPT.

Equally important is how AI can be used to strengthen coaching education and supervision. With tools like Ovida and Meaning@Work, coaches now have access to performance metrics, video analysis, and feedback systems previously available only in fields like sports or psychotherapy. Used wisely, these tools can promote leadership development—contrary to the fear that AI must necessarily dehumanize or de-emphasize what makes coaching an essentially human enterprise.

The final section of the book does not shy away from hard questions. What does real intelligence mean in a coaching context? Can standards, ethics, and professional frameworks keep pace with accelerating innovation? Through thought-provoking contributions from leaders like Tatiana Bachkirova and David B. Drake, readers are invited to reflect not just on tools and techniques, but on the philosophical and ethical foundations of the coaching profession itself.

In short, this is not just a book about coaching *with* AI. It is a call to coach *through* AI—using it as a lens to better understand ourselves, our clients, and the evolving nature of human development in a digital world. As AI continues to advance, the coaching field must evolve with it—boldly and wisely. This book is an essential guide for that journey.

Executive Director
Institute of Coaching
Lecturer, Harvard Medical School
McLean Hospital, Mass General Brigham

Jeffrey Hull

Contents

About the Contributors

Tatiana Bachkirova is Professor of Coaching Psychology in the International Centre for Coaching and Mentoring Studies at Oxford Brookes University, UK. As an academic, she supervises doctoral students, teaches coaching supervisors, and tries to create more time for academic writing. As a practitioner, she supports coaches through individual and group supervision. In her over 70 research articles, book chapters, and books and in her many speaking engagements, she aims to explore the most challenging issues of coaching as a service to individuals, organizations, and wider societies.

James Bridgeman is an executive and team coach and leadership consultant and is co-editor of the Association for Coaching's *Coaching Perspectives* magazine. He is director of Bridgford Consultancy, providing executive coaching alongside people skills and leadership development. He holds a Master's in Applied Positive Psychology and Coaching Psychology from the University of East London.

Joel A. DiGirolamo is Vice President of Research and Data Science at the International Coaching Federation. Joel leads a research team whose goals are to advance the understanding of how coaching works as well as how coaching is evolving and enhancing society. One of his most recent publications is: "The potential for artificial intelligence in coaching."

E-mail: joel.digirolamo@coachingfederation.org

Sandra J. Diller is a Professor of Organizational Psychology at the Seeburg Castle University (SCU), a Research Affiliate at Harvard Medical School's Institute of Coaching, and an Affiliate at the Ludwig-Maximilian-University's Center for Leadership and People Management. She researches leadership and personnel development and is responsible for the MBA in Coaching at SCU.

David B. Drake David Drake is CEO of The Moment Institute in Amsterdam, which offers professional development programs, personal development retreats, advisory services, coaching, and publications. He has been a pioneer in coaching for over 25 years, most notably as the founder of Narrative Coaching. He is a Thought Leader for the Institute of Coaching, a 9x WBECS Summit speaker, and a member of the inaugural class of Coaches50 in recognition for his contributions. David is the Head of Ovida Labs, which uses his work and AI to enrich the feedback process, accelerate growth, and improve outcomes. He advises Viva la Coaching Academy on AI and coaching. He is the author of The Five Maturities: A new paradigm for developing coaches; he uses this work in facilitating retreats and advising projects for the evolution of coaching and coach education.

Tamara Garcia is a work and organizational psychologist, a BSO-certified coach, and an organizational consultant. She is the director of the Centre for Coaching and Organizational Change at the IAP (Institute for Applied Psychology). She also leads the MAS in Coaching, Supervision, and Organizational Consulting. Her work focuses on organizational development, coaching, team development, and leadership development. Her teaching portfolio includes courses such as CAS Coaching in Practice, MAS Organizational Consulting, and Coaching with AI and VR. In addition, she works on consulting mandates with companies from various industries, as well as with public institutions and NGOs. Tamara Garcia has contributed to several applied publications, including as the editor of the foundational book Coaching – Angewandte Psychologie für die Beratungspraxis published by Springer.

Harald Geißler was a university professor until his retirement in 2015. His research focuses on organizational learning and business coaching, with particular emphasis on the use of modern media.

Drawing on his many years of experience as a coaching practitioner, he offers an AI coaching education program. Recent publications: Bedeutsame Momente und Erfolgsfaktoren im Online-Coaching (2022), Handbuch professionelles Online-Coaching (2023, co-authored with S. Rödel), and KI-Coaching (2025).

E-mail: dr.h.geissler@t-online.de

Andrea Giraldez-Hayes is an experienced chartered psychologist, coach, psychotherapist, supervisor, academic, and consultant with an international reputation. She is currently the Course Director for the MSt in Coaching at the University of Cambridge. Andrea has published several peer-reviewed papers and books, including Arts-Based Coaching: Using Creative Tools to Promote Better Self-Expression and The Routledge International Handbook of Wellbeing Arts.

Till Grossrieder studied psychology and specialized in relationship building in counseling settings and effectiveness research during his studies. He currently works as a research assistant at the Centre for Coaching and Organizational Change at the IAP (Institute for Applied Psychology), where he is involved in coaching and leadership training as well as service mandates with various clients from diverse industries. He led the project for the fourth edition of the textbook Coaching – Angewandte Psychologie für die Beratungspraxis and continues to serve as project manager for the current publication.

Sam Isaacson is an award-winning coaching thought leader and consultant specializing in the impact of cutting-edge technologies on the coaching profession, and the strategic use of coaching within organizations. He is the founder of the Coachtech

Collective and co-founder of AIcoach.chat. His work has been featured in both mainstream and specialist press, and he has served on advisory boards for a range of organizations, including the EMCC and the ICF. He was the Chair of the Coaching Professional apprenticeship trailblazer group, which developed the standard that now underpins England's most popular coaching qualification. He has contributed widely to the coaching literature, including in particular editing The Digital and AI Coaches' Handbook, writing How to Thrive as a Coach in a Digital World, and co-writing the chapter on Internal Coaching in The Complete Handbook of Coaching.

Gregor J. Jenny is a senior researcher and lecturer at the Institute for Mental and Organisational Health, FHNW. He currently focuses on the experience of meaning at work and the digitalization of health-promoting interventions, hereby developing and researching web applications, such as the Crafting Playbook (https://crafting-playbook.net/).

Eva Jonas is head of the Department of Social Psychology at the University of Salzburg and is a trained coach, supervisor, mediator, and certified PSI competence advisor. In addition, she has significant experience directing postgraduate programs at PLUS. Her research focuses on processes in social interaction, particularly on how individuals respond to psychological threats. A central emphasis lies in deriving interventions to strengthen individuals, promoting cooperative interaction, and exploring the role of consulting formats in enhancing self-regulation.

E-mail: eva.jonas@plus.ac.at

Jan Juchli is a clinical psychologist, counselor, lecturer at ZHAW, and a psychotherapist in training. His expertise lies in psychotherapy, psychological counseling, and supervising counselors in training. In the spin-off project "ephoria," he was responsible for programming the app's solution-based brief therapy (SFBT) content and served as a consultant.

Vanessa Mai is leader of the research group "Smart Technologies in Coaching & Learning" at Cologne Cobots Lab and board member of the Center for Teaching Development at TH Köln/University of Applied Sciences. She is a certified systemic coach and supervisor. In 2024 she published her dissertation on "Chatbots in (student) coaching," exploring relationship-building factors in AI-based human–machine coaching (https://doi.org/10.57684/COS-1287). She developed the StudiCoachBot (www.th-koeln.de/studicoachbot), which provides low-threshold support to students on the topic of exam anxiety. Vanessa studied linguistics, communication sciences, psychology, and works as a freelance business coach.

Olivier Malafronte is a Professional Coach in individual coaching (2015), team and organizational coaching (2021), pioneer in AI Coaching through co-founder roles in PocketConfident.com, Rypple.ai, Magify.fun, member of the ICF Global AI Coaching Standards working group and the Coaching and Mentoring research group of the French Association of HR Management (AGRH), and PhD on AI Coaching and Leader Development at Université Côte d'Azur (2021–2025).

E-mail: Olivier_2203@hotmail.fr

Christina Mühlberger is a postdoctoral researcher in Social Psychology at the University of Salzburg. She is a certified coach, ZRM® trainer, and PSI competence advisor. In her research, she investigates how individuals cope with discrepancies—especially when facing threats to psychological needs. Her current research focuses on how formats like coaching, supervision, training, and mentoring support need fulfillment and personal development.

E-mail: christina.muehlberger@plus.ac.at

Anja Richert is Dean of the Faculty of Process Engineering, Energy and Mechanical Systems at TH Köln/University of Applied Sciences, Professor of Innovation Management, founder and head of the Cologne Cobots Lab & Cologne TrainING Center. She supervised the doctoral thesis of Vanessa Mai. She researches digital learning and working environments, social robotics, and data-driven innovation management.

Rebecca Rutschmann is a tech and AI coaching entrepreneur and innovator specializing in the intersection of coaching and artificial intelligence. She is co-founder of Viva la Coaching Academy, Viva la Coaching Academy—the world's first AI literacy movement tailored to coaching and corporate learning. She co-founded evoach in 2019, creating the AI Coach Alpina, one of the first generative AI-integrated coaching tools. An accredited coach with the International Coaching Federation (PCC) and the European Mentoring & Coaching Council (Senior Practitioner), she serves as VP Accreditation for EMCC Germany and advises on global initiatives to advance AI literacy in coaching. Her mission is to make coaching accessible through innovative AI solutions that combine ethical design, technological sophistication, and human-centered practice. Recent publications include "Evaluating Student Acceptance of an AI-based Coaching Chatbot for Virtual Reflection in Interdisciplinary Project Teams," "'Getting better all the time': using professional human coach competencies to evaluate the quality of AI coaching agent performance", and "Top Bot: Comparing User Preferences for Interacting with GROW, Solution Focused and Cognitive Behavioral AI Coaching Chatbots."

Rebecca Rutschmann, Viva la Coaching Academy, rebecca@vivalacoaching.com

Marcel Schär-Gmelch is a psychotherapist and works at the Institute of Mental Health at the ZHAW School of Applied Psychology. He is Co-Director of the MAS in Psychotherapy and teaches in higher education and continuing education programmes at various other universities. Recent publications include Liebe ist mehr, als wir denken: Von der Kunst, an Konflikten in der Partnerschaft zu wachsen (Schär, M., & Gmelch, S., 2019, Springer).

E-mail: shma@zhaw.ch

Marc Schreiber is a professor of vocational and personality psychology at the IAP Institute of Applied Psychology at the ZHAW Zurich University of Applied Sciences. He provides counseling to both private individuals and companies on career development matters. His primary areas of expertise in education and research include career counseling in the context of Work 4.0, vocational and personality psychology. He has developed the online platform “Laufbahndiagnostik” (www.laufbahndiagnostik.zhaw.ch).

Wendy-Ann Smith founded the Coaching Ethics Forum, Journal of Coaching Ethics, Ethical Edge Insights and Champions of Courage Awards. A coaching psychologist, author, and researcher, she works at the intersection of positive psychology, coaching, and ethics to foster courageous leadership, professional integrity, and well-being.

Adina Tarry is a polymath thinker and practitioner who combines international business delivery experience with talent, leadership, and management development of people and organizations in corporations and SMEs across industries and cultures. A Master coach, supervisor, team coach, and business psychologist, Adina’s practice is informed by business, technology, philosophy, and ethics as they come together in work, life, society, and the environment. Adina is also an author, speaker, and visiting lecturer and enjoys sharing knowledge and contributing pro bono time in academic and practitioner circles.

Nicky Terblanche is an academic, researcher, leadership coach, and entrepreneur. He has a master’s degree and PhD in Leadership Coaching and a master’s degree in electronic and software engineering. He is Associate Professor of Leadership Coaching and Research Methodology at Stellenbosch Business School, South Africa. His research interests include leadership coaching with a focus on Artificial Intelligence Coaching. He also runs an executive and leadership coaching practice. Nicky has published more than 40 peer-reviewed research articles and book chapters and regularly presents at international conferences as a keynote speaker. He is also the founder and CEO of CoachVici.com that creates AI Coaches for organizations.

Robert Wegener is an executive and team coach with extensive expertise in coaching research, education, and practice. He is co-responsible for the Coaching Studies program at the University of Applied Sciences Northwestern Switzerland and leads Das Coaching Haus, a Swiss coaching and supervision company. For 12 years, Dr. Wegener organized the international conference Coaching meets Research in Olten. Holding a PhD in Coaching from the Helmut-Schmidt University and master’s degrees in Communication Psychology and Political Science, Dr. Wegener combines academic knowledge and writing on coaching with practical expertise.

Part I
Introduction

Chapter 1
And the Journey of Coaching Continues

Robert Wegener, Tamara Garcia, Nicky Terblanche, and Till Grossrieder

Abstract This introduction sets the stage for the edited volume *Coaching in the Age of AI* by exploring the conceptual foundations and guiding questions that shape the book. It addresses the growing ambiguity surrounding both "coaching" and "artificial intelligence" (AI), proposing a framework to understand how these domains intersect in practice and theory.

The chapter outlines three scenarios for how coaching and AI can be integrated: (1) AI as a means to enhance human coaching, (2) AI as a potential substitute for human coaches, and (3) AI as a tool for training and supervising coaches. These scenarios inform the book's overall structure and thematic sections.

In addition to mapping these perspectives, the introduction defines coaching as a professional developmental approach that emphasizes self-regulation, personal congruence, and goal-oriented learning. It highlights the relevance of coaching in an AI-driven world, where human judgment, ethical reflection, and adaptability are increasingly vital.

Ultimately, this chapter provides a conceptual and ethical grounding for the book's contributions and invites readers to engage critically with the evolving relationship between coaching and AI.

Keywords Coaching · Artificial intelligence · AI-based coaching · Human-AI collaboration · Coaching skills · Self-regulation · Generative AI in coaching · Ethical principles in AI coaching · Digital coach training and supervision · Working alliance in human-AI interaction

---

R. Wegener
Fachhochschule Nordwestschweiz FHNW, Hochschule für Soziale Arbeit, Olten, Schweiz
e-mail: robert.wegener@fhnw.ch

T. Garcia · T. Grossrieder (✉)
Institute of Applied Psychology, ZHAW Zurich University of Applied Sciences, Zürich, Switzerland
e-mail: tamara.garcia@zhaw.ch; till.grossrieder@zhaw.ch

N. Terblanche
Stellenbosch Business School, Cape Town, South Africa
e-mail: nickyt@sun.ac.za

R. Wegener et al. (eds.), *Coaching in the Age of AI*, SpringerBriefs in Psychology, https://doi.org/10.1007/978-3-032-23332-5_1

In a way, the terms coaching and artificial intelligence have a lot in common. Both have the potential to raise questions in society about what exactly the phenomena referred to by these terms actually mean. What exactly does artificial intelligence stand for, and what exactly artificial intelligence? We want to counter this double ambiguity with this book. And what's more, with this book we also want to contribute to the discourse on how coaching and artificial intelligence already go together and will do so even more in the future. Because one thing is clear: both coaching and artificial intelligence are spreading rapidly, as are attempts to establish a productive relationship between the two.

With the aim of contributing to the above-mentioned discourse, we have examined various basic positions and have come to the conclusion that there are basically three possible scenarios for how coaching and artificial intelligence (hereinafter referred to as AI) can be conceived and brought together. First: coaching as a human practice that can be specifically expanded and improved with the help of artificial intelligence. The fantasy here is perhaps that coaches will one day have a button in their ear that, as a gently persuasive voice, will help them make the coaching process even more effective or efficient for their clients. Second, coaching as a human practice that will be completely replaced in the future by services based purely on artificial intelligence. The mental association here is, for example, a humanoid robot that, like a professional coach, helps people to deal with their concerns effectively and efficiently, perhaps even more effectively and efficiently than a human coach can do. Third, coaching as a human practice that must be learned and trained by humans, and where artificial intelligence can contribute in the future, especially in the education, training, and further development of coaches. An example of this would be AI-supported training in dealing with "difficult" clients or coaching supervision guided directly by artificial intelligence. Furthermore, there are also a wealth of important overarching issues in this emerging relationship between coaching and AI, such as the question of the ethical basis for the use of AI in coaching, or fundamentally critical arguments that advocate a more cautious use of AI in coaching.

The three scenarios and the level of the aforementioned cross-cutting issues of AI and coaching form the basis for the structure of this book. Accordingly, this book contains contributions from renowned experts on all four areas. But before we delve deeper into the content of this book, it is necessary to clarify the terms used and define what is meant by coaching as a human practice, on the one hand, and artificial intelligence, on the other. This is important because only contributions based on a clear understanding of coaching and artificial intelligence can make a truly substantial contribution to the discourse mentioned above. Contributions based on vague terms are of no help here.

1.1 Coaching in Transition: A Contemporary Understanding

Coaching has become a widely adopted practice. In almost every area of society, from leadership development to education, sports, and health to lifestyle and career planning, coaching is used. However, its growing popularity has also led to conceptual ambiguity. What do we mean when we talk about coaching? And how can professional coaching be distinguished from other forms of consulting, training, or instruction?

In a world of acceleration, increasing complexity, and technical disruption—for example, through artificial intelligence (AI)—coaching faces a double challenge: on the one hand, it must maintain its clarity and effectiveness; on the other hand, it must respond flexibly and with an eye to the future to the changing conditions of human development.

1.1.1 Coaching as a Particular Professional Developmental Approach and not a Method

Coaching is not a defined catalog of methods, but a particular professional developmental approach. The focus is on providing individual support to people with the aim of successfully promoting their self-regulation and thus enabling both successful action and personal development. Coaching should enable people to learn to develop and implement solutions themselves (Wegener, 2022). Thus, coaching is a professional developmental approach that supports individuals in particular in their organizational roles (see also "the role concept" in Lippmann et al., 2006).

Sir John Whitmore, a pioneer in coaching, described coaching as unleashing human potential with the aim of maximizing performance (Whitmore, 1992). He emphasized that coaching should support people in learning, not give them instructions. German coaching researcher Siegfried Greif (2008) puts it similarly: coaching is aimed at promoting results-oriented problem-solving and self-reflection in order to better achieve the so-called self-congruent goals. This goal orientation is therefore not arbitrary: it is always a combination of goal orientation and personal fit—in other words, a match between goals and the values, interests, and potential of the client (Wegener, 2022).

1.1.2 Coaching as a Systematic Developmental Process

Professional coaching follows a systematic process that can be divided into phases (Loebbert & Bruni, 2025): contact, contract, hypothesis formation, intervention, and evaluation. In the contact phase, a trusting working relationship is established, and in the contract phase, the framework is defined. The hypothesis phase serves to reflect on the initial situation and why a person is not (yet) able to successfully address their concerns despite having the necessary resources. In the intervention phase, appropriate methods are used—dialogical, exploratory, and individually tailored. Finally, the evaluation phase checks whether the desired progress has been achieved and to what extent the chosen path can be maintained or needs to be adjusted (Schmidt, 2004). These phases do not proceed linearly but in systemic loops; within any given phase, the whole cycle can reappear in miniature, which makes process-oriented coaching practice complex.

This structure also allows coaching to integrate specialist advice on a selective basis—provided that it follows the developed hypothesis framework and is clearly used as an intervention in the sense of coaching—namely as an offer that the client can decide whether or not to take advantage of and what to do with it. All without any risk of losing face. Coaching thus remains flexible and open to learning without abandoning its basic principles (2022).

1.1.3 Coaching Between Self-realization and Performance

The central dialectic of coaching consists in the connection between individual development and contextual success. Coaching that is exclusively focused on achieving goals risks self-exploitation. Coaching that focuses only on self-congruence can remain ineffective. It is the interplay of both poles—performance and meaning—that makes coaching such a special and relevant developmental approach.

This also highlights the difference between purely cognitive learning approaches or technically oriented consulting: coaching always asks about the "why" of the goal, about inner consistency, and about long-term benefits. This orientation is all the more relevant in a world that is becoming increasingly technologized by AI—because it puts people and their self-efficacy at the center (Wegener, 2022).

1.1.4 Relevance in a World Shaped by AI

At a time when algorithms prepare decisions and automated systems are changing entire areas of work, coaching is taking on a new meaning: it helps to promote human judgment, ethical reflection, and creative problem-solving skills. At the same time, AI is also changing coaching itself: behavioral analysis tools, AI-based feedback systems, and digital coaching platforms open up new possibilities, but also place new demands on the profession and ethics.

1.1.5 Conclusion: Coaching as an Attitude and Skill

Coaching is much more than just a trend. It is a professional attitude toward promoting human development and growth. The central question is: How can we support people in their self-regulation so that they can make effective, coherent, and sustainable decisions and successfully achieve their desired goals and performances?

As a professional developmental approach, coaching thus contributes not only to individual development, but also to the further development of teams, organizations, and societies. Especially in the age of AI, formats such as coaching are needed that do not replace people, but empower them—and thus contribute to the humanization of technology.

1.2 What Is Artificial Intelligence?

Artificial Intelligence (AI) refers to a broad set of technologies such as computer vision, natural language processing, robotics, robotic process automation, and virtual agents. AI aims to mimic aspects of human cognition, including perception, reasoning, and decision-making. From a functional perspective, AI can be seen as computer programs trained on real-world data to perform specific tasks, improving performance through iterative interaction and learning from user input. More broadly, AI is the study and creation of systems that, from an observer's perspective, appear to act intelligently (Bughin & Hazan, 2017).

AI is commonly classified into three categories: Artificial Narrow Intelligence (ANI), which performs highly specialized tasks (e.g., speech recognition, virtual assistants); Artificial General Intelligence (AGI), which would match human-level intelligence across multiple domains; and Artificial Super Intelligence (ASI), which would surpass human intelligence across most dimensions. While AGI and ASI remain theoretical, ANI is widely deployed and continues to advance rapidly, particularly with breakthroughs in natural language processing (Siau & Yang, 2017).

Recent advances introduced generative AI through transformer-based large language models (LLMs) like ChatGPT and Bard. This step-change has revolutionized human–computer interaction. These generative AI systems process and produce human-like language, enabling sophisticated, contextually adaptive conversations. Generative AI is a game changer for dialogue-heavy fields such as coaching as will be evident from the content of this book (Terblanche, 2025).

1.3 What Can You Expect from This Book?

This edited volume explores the evolving relationship between coaching and artificial intelligence through diverse disciplinary perspectives. Organized into four thematic sections—AI simulating human coaching, AI enhancing human coaching, AI used for training and supervision, and fundamental questions about AI in coaching, the book brings together empirical studies, design-based insights, and critical reflections. Together, these contributions aim to foster a differentiated understanding of how AI is reshaping the landscape of professional coaching.

The first section, AI simulating human coaching, focuses on the extent to which AI can imitate or replace (substitute) human coaching processes. Rebecca

Rutschmann is critically examining coaching chatbots in terms of trust, bias, and transparency. She highlights the ethical risks of delegating coaching to AI and calls for professional standards and regulatory frameworks to guide development. Vanessa Mai and Anja Richert follow by analyzing how chatbot-based coaching systems can create perceived connection and rapport. Using the StudiCoachBot as a case study, they show that empathy, conversational tone, and thoughtful design help simulate relational quality in digital coaching.

Christina Mühlberger and Eva Jonas are investigating whether AI coaching can promote self-regulated behavior—a key outcome in coaching. Their findings suggest that the absence of interpersonal judgment in AI contexts can foster emotional openness and sustained engagement. In their chapter about the Ephoria project, Jan Juchli and Marcel Schär-Gmelch present a mental health app using a solution-focused coaching model. Their chapter illustrates how AI can increase access to psychological support while maintaining ethical safeguards. Finally, Nicky Terblanche examines the effectiveness of chatbot coaches and argues that AI should not replicate human behavior but develop an interaction logic that respects autonomy and fosters reflection.

The second section, AI enhancing human coaching, explores how AI can support rather than substitute the coach. Sam Isaacson highlights the opportunities for AI to expand coaching capacity, improve feedback, and deepen insight. At the same time, he warns that ignoring AI development could marginalize the profession. Harald Geissler introduces a model where AI acts as a third voice in the coaching dialogue, offering prompts and structure while preserving ethical coaching standards.

Sandra Diller and Wendy Ann Smith build on this idea of AI as a Third Party in Coaching, exploring how trust and human-centered values can be maintained when AI enters the relational space. They argue that ethical reflection must guide the integration of AI into coaching. Marc Schreiber and Gregor Jenny offer a narrative-based contribution around Social Constructionist Counselling, describing a platform where generative AI serves as a reflective companion for career identity work. AI in this setting acts as a sparring partner, not a solution provider—encouraging meaning-making without undermining autonomy.

In the third section, AI used for training and supervisory purposes, the authors examine how AI can support professional development in coaching and leadership. Olivier Malafronte's chapter provides a multidisciplinary view of how AI supports leadership supervision. He outlines both its potential and its limits, particularly regarding psychological safety. Andrea Giraldez-Hayes and James Bridgeman present Ovida, a tool combining video feedback with AI-generated analytics to improve coach reflection. They highlight both the benefits and emotional challenges of receiving AI-based feedback, stressing the need for ethical use and reflective practice.

The final section, Fundamental questions about AI in coaching, addresses deeper philosophical and normative concerns. Tatiana Bachkirova argues that coaching is grounded in moral reasoning, presence, and human insight—qualities that AI cannot reproduce. She warns against a technocratic view of coaching that reduces it to procedures. David Drake contributes by applying the Five Maturities framework, proposing a developmental model that supports coaches and organizations in evolving alongside AI while safeguarding ethical integrity.

Joel Di Girolamo reinforces this call for guidance. He advocates for clear standards, transparency, and professional responsibility in the use of AI systems. His contribution stresses that widespread adoption must be accompanied by education and ethical oversight. Concluding the section, Adina Tarry offers a broader systemic perspective. She argues that coaches need to engage actively with technological transformation—not only to stay relevant, but also to shape it in ways that uphold human agency and learning.

Taken together, these chapters suggest that AI is neither an existential threat nor a ready-made solution for coaching. Rather, it is a complex and evolving set of tools and systems whose impact depends on how thoughtfully and ethically they are implemented. This book invites readers—whether practitioners, educators, or researchers—to develop informed, critical, and creative responses to coaching in the age of AI.

1.4 What Do We Hope to Achieve with This Book?

With this book, we want to contribute to the discussion on how coaching and AI can be brought into a meaningful relationship. To this end, we provide insight into various positions, current research findings, and essayistic perspectives. Overall, our aim is to provide readers interested in this topic with a basis for developing their own differentiated positions on the subject of coaching and AI. We wish you every success in reading this book.

References

Bughin, J., & Hazan, E. (2017). *The new spring of artificial intelligence: A few early economies*. VoxEU.org. [Internet]. August 21. Available from: https://cepr.org/voxeu/columns/new-spring-artificial-intelligence-few-early-economies

Greif, S. (2008). *Coaching und ergebnisorientierte Selbstreflexion: Theorie, Forschung und Praxis des Einzel- und Gruppencoachings*. Hogrefe.

Lippmann, E., Garcia, T., & Klink, T. H. (2006). *Coaching: Angewandte Psychologie für die Beratungspraxis* (4th ed.). Springer. Available at: https://doi.org/10.1007/978-3-662-71516-1

Loebbert, M., & Bruni, Z. (2025). *Coaching Theorie: Eine Einführung* (3rd ed.). Springer.

Schmidt, G. (2004). *Liebesaffären zwischen Problem und Lösung: Hypnosystemisches Arbeiten in schwierigen Kontexten*. Carl-Auer-Systeme Verlag.

Siau, K. L., & Yang, Y. (2017). Impact of artificial intelligence, robotics, and machine learning on sales and marketing. In *Midwest United States Association for Information Systems 12th annual conference, 18–19 May 2017, Springfield, Illinois*. Available at: http://aisel.aisnet.org/mwais2017/48

Terblanche, N. H. (2025). Smooth talking: Generative versus scripted coaching chatbot adoption and efficacy comparison. *International Journal of Human–Computer Interaction, 41*(14), 9109–9122.

Wegener, R. (2022). Die Zukunft des Coachings: Auf der Suche nach einer Definition. *BSO Journal, 2*, 4–8.

Whitmore, J. (1992). *Coaching for performance: A practical guide to growing your own skills.* Nicholas Brealey Publishing.

Part II
AI Simulating Human Coaching

Chapter 2
Navigating Bias and Ethics in Practical Applications

Rebecca Rutschmann

Abstract AI-driven chatbots functioning as coaching tools are no longer hypothetical; they have arrived and are actively reshaping the profession. This raises important questions not only about what coaching actually means to those applying AI in coaching or AI coaching companions on a broader scale, but also about their scope, ethical implications, and potential biases. This chapter critically examines the role of chatbots in coaching, considering their benefits and limitations with regard to coaching applications as understood by professional coaching bodies. The discussion draws on real-world applications and empirical findings to assess AI-assisted coaching in practice, covering both AI in coaching (AI used to enhance human coaching) and AI coaching (AI applied to substitute human coaching). Key considerations include user trust, chatbot adaptability, and the limitations of AI-generated coaching responses. Additionally, the chapter explores when chatbots best function as standalone coaching tools and when they are best suited to complement human-led coaching engagements. A dedicated section examines bias in large language models (LLMs) and its implications for AI-driven coaching conversations. Drawing on ethical frameworks such as UNESCO's AI Ethics Guidelines and the Global Code of Ethics in Coaching, Mentoring, and Supervision, this chapter explores strategies for possible mitigation of bias and strategies to align AI conversations to make them safe to use for the client, ensuring AI-driven coaching aligns with principles of integrity, respect for diversity, transparency, and human oversight. Ultimately, this chapter argues that while chatbot-based coaching offers significant opportunities, it must be developed and implemented within strong ethical guardrails. Responsible AI coaching and AI in coaching requires continuous oversight, transparency, and a commitment to create safe environments for both client and coach. Looking ahead, a robust ethical framework will be essential to maintaining coaching as a profession that prioritizes a human-centered approach, confidentiality, and trust.

R. Rutschmann (✉)
Viva la Coaching, Karlsruhe, Germany
e-mail: rebecca@vivalacoaching.com

R. Wegener et al. (eds.), *Coaching in the Age of AI*, SpringerBriefs in Psychology, https://doi.org/10.1007/978-3-032-23332-5_2

Keywords AI coaching · AI coach · Chatbot coach · Chatbot coaching · Ethical AI in coaching · Responsible AI coaching · Large language models in coaching · Human–AI collaboration · Human–machine interaction · AI coaching ethics · AI transparency and accountability in coaching · Conversational AI in coaching

2.1 Introduction

The rapid evolution of AI coaching tools has shifted the boundaries of what coaching can be. Today, AI companions not only support human coaches but also in some cases function autonomously, guiding clients through structured conversations. Based on this growing presence in the coaching space challenges traditional assumptions about what defines coaching, raising questions about ethics, trust, and professional standards.

This chapter focuses on the ethical dimensions and potential biases inherent in AI-driven coaching, with particular attention to large language models. It examines how these technologies can expand access while also introducing new complexities that must be navigated with care.

2.2 AI (in) Coaching: Applications, Capabilities, and Limitations

The integration of AI technologies into coaching has been accelerated by advancements in natural language processing over the last decades and even more through the broad availability of Large Language Models such as ChatGPT by OpenAI since their first launch to the public in 2022. While AI-empowered applications have supported coaches in various capacities for some time, modern autonomous AI Coaching has now reached a level of remarkable human-like responses that can engage in extended conversations, mirror human empathy, and even adapt to different communication styles.

2.2.1 Applications of AI in Coaching

As outlined in the ICF AI Coaching Framework (2024), coaching applications can be distinguished between "coach assisting applications" and "coaching service applications." Based on experience teaching AI literacy to coaches, mentors, and learning professionals, we can further categorize these applications into more specific use cases:

AI Coaching: The use of AI systems to deliver coaching conversations, either as a complement to human-led coaching or as a fully autonomous and independent coaching solution. AI in Coaching: The use of AI systems enhancing the coaching process between coach and coachee.

2.3 AI in Coaching: Enhancing Human-to-Human Coaching

AI in Coaching refers to the integration of AI tools to assist human coaches, including ideation, content creation, session analysis, and learning path design. These tools mainly enhance human coaching into:

Ideation & Innovation: Using AI for strategic positioning, creating business strategies, new signature programs, innovating on products and services, and challenging the status quo. Human coaches can leverage AI to expand their creative thinking and offer clients fresh perspectives.

Content Creation: Using AI to develop brand voice, brand design, ghostwrite emails, messages, articles, newsletters, and other text-based content, as well as creating images, videos and other visual and audio content to support coaching programs.

Meeting Assistants & Insights: Using AI to analyze data from coaching session transcripts, emails, messages, assessments, etc., to generate insights about clients' situations and development, helping coaches design personalized learning paths.

Session Support: Deploying AI as a session assistant for further ideation around client topics, generating visual representations of client situations, or creating soothing background sounds and music that reflect certain themes during sessions.

2.4 AI Coaching: Interactive Conversational Companions & Agents

These applications function more independently in the coaching role delivering actual AI-driven coaching conversations, either as a complement to human-led coaching or as a fully autonomous and independent coaching solution:

AI Coaching Assistants: AI systems that support specific coaching functions such as onboarding, session preparation, follow-up assistance, and role-play practice. These tools operate with limited autonomy within clearly defined parameters.

AI Coach: Fully autonomous AI-powered coaching companions that can address specific topics by integrating different coaching approaches, interventions, and techniques, mirroring human coaching methodologies.

2.4.1 Empirical Findings on AI Coaching Effectiveness

Research on AI coaching effectiveness still remains limited but promising and is growing strongly. Terblanche et al. (2022) found that while human coaches outperform AI systems, the margin was smaller than expected. Participants working with AI coaches reported significant progress toward their goals, suggesting AI systems can facilitate meaningful development.

The gap appears most pronounced in areas requiring emotional intelligence, cultural nuance, and detection of subtle cues. For goal-setting, accountability, and structured reflection, AI coaches demonstrated stronger capabilities. Interestingly, Malafronte and Loufrani-Fedida (2023) found some clients reported being more candid with AI systems than with human coaches about sensitive topics, echoing findings from Lucas et al. (2014) about reduced fear of judgment with AI systems.

Kouros and Papa's study (2024) reveals users often form emotional attachments to AI companions, viewing them as safe spaces for identity exploration. This raises important questions about whether such interactions constitute genuine coaching relationships. They found that "AI companions provide a safe space for self-expression and identity exploration, often without fear of judgment, offering a backstage setting in Goffmanian terms." This aligns with coaching's aim to create psychologically safe environments for personal development. But what does this mean for the future of human coaching?

2.4.2 Capabilities and Limitations

In the "Communicating Effectively" domain of coaching competencies, AI chatbots excel at linguistic analysis and can maintain perfect recall of previous conversations, but struggle with subtle emotional cues and contextual understanding that aren't explicitly verbalized. In the "Cultivating Learning" domain, AI can systematically track progress and reinforce insights but lacks the creative intuition and adaptive presence that human coaches bring to transformational learning (International Coaching Federation, 2024).

Several technical limitations constrain AI coaching effectiveness. The "hallucination problem"—where AI systems generate plausible but incorrect information—remains a concern in coaching contexts where factual accuracy matters (Sun et al., 2024). Additionally, AI's pattern-matching approach to conversation fails to capture the nuanced understanding of complex human situations, particularly when these involve cultural contexts, organizational dynamics, or interpersonal relationships not explicitly stated.

Perhaps most significantly, AI systems lack genuine empathy and moral agency—qualities central to traditional coaching relationships. While they can simulate empathetic responses based on pattern recognition, they cannot experience the emotional resonance that allows skilled human coaches to connect with clients at a deeper level.

2.4.3 User Experiences and Expectations

Research shows mixed user experiences with AI coaching. Many appreciate the accessibility, 24/7 availability, and non-judgmental nature of AI interactions, while others note limitations in depth and personalization (Laestadius et al., 2022). Users with realistic expectations about AI capabilities generally report more positive experiences than those expecting human-equivalent coaching (Malafronte & Loufrani-Fedida, 2023).

The limitations of AI coaching raise important questions about how these systems should be positioned, as standalone coaching solutions or as complements to human coaching. A complementary approach recognizes the unique strengths of both AI and human coaches, leveraging AI for consistency, unlimited availability, and freedom from judgment, while human coaches provide genuine empathy, intuitive understanding, and creative adaptation to complex situations.

As the EMCC Ethics Guidance (2023) suggests, technology and AI "can provide solutions which, when implemented well, can enable the wider use of coaching, mentoring, and supervision," highlighting a view of AI as expanding coaching practice rather than simply replacing human coaches.

These mixed experiences highlight the importance of positioning AI coaching tools thoughtfully within the coaching ecosystem. Understanding where AI excels and where it falls short sets the stage for a deeper examination of the underlying biases that shape AI-driven coaching interactions—and the ethical considerations necessary to address them effectively.

2.4.4 Bias in Large Language Models (LLMs) and Its Implications for AI-driven Coaching

Bias in large language models (LLMs), like ChatGPT, Claude, Gemini, Mistral, Llama and many others, is not a theoretical problem; it's an embedded feature of how these systems are trained and operate. Since LLMs are trained on vast datasets scraped from the internet, including books, social media networks, forums, and academic content, they inevitably reflect the dominant views, cultural assumptions, and exclusions present in that data. But this is not the only bias we need to look at.

Bias in AI in Coaching can appear in several forms. LLMs powering AI chatbots face various forms of bias that can impact coaching conversations. Liu (2024) categorizes these biases as stemming from training data quality, algorithm design, and user interaction dynamics:

2.4.4.1 Data Bias

Since LLMs are trained on large-scale, publicly available data—much of which reflects dominant cultural norms—they absorb and reproduce those perspectives. This affects the kinds of values, metaphors, and assumptions embedded in coaching conversations, such as individualistic approaches to success or standardized views on emotional expression.

2.4.4.2 Algorithm Bias

Beyond the training phase, models are fine-tuned and aligned by developers to behave in ways deemed "safe," "helpful," or "appropriate." These judgments are made by human teams who bring their own cultural backgrounds, values, and blind spots into the process. If the development team is not diverse, or if the alignment process lacks ethical oversight, these biases can become reinforced at a structural level.

2.4.4.3 Interaction Bias

LLMs interpret user input through attention mechanisms that weigh some words or phrases more heavily than others in shaping responses. This means the structure, tone, and vocabulary of a user's message can significantly influence the quality and depth of the AI's reply. Users with more aligned linguistic styles, such as fluent, confident, or culturally dominant language, may receive more coherent or supportive coaching input. Conversely, those who use less common phrasing, indirect speech, or non-standard grammar may experience less relevant or even dismissive responses. Studies have shown that attention mechanisms can amplify biases already present in the training data by overemphasizing dominant patterns and underrepresenting marginal ones (Bommasani et al., 2021; Vaswani et al., 2017). In a coaching context, this dynamic can subtly reproduce power imbalances or exclude non-dominant perspectives.

These biases matter because coaching relies on fairness, inclusion, and the ability to challenge unhelpful assumptions. If an AI coaching tool subtly reinforces stereotypes or fails to recognize the coachee's context, it can do harm while appearing helpful. For example, in a career reflection prompt, an AI might inadvertently suggest leadership paths that align with gendered expectations present in its training data.

2.5 The Black Box Problem

AI-driven coaching chatbots often operate as "black boxes," meaning their internal decision-making processes are opaque even to their developers (IBM, 2024; Rudin, 2019). This lack of transparency complicates efforts to identify and mitigate biases, validate outputs, or explain recommendations to users (Molnar, 2020). For instance, an AI coach might generate culturally insensitive feedback due to hidden biases in its training data, but the complexity of neural networks makes tracing the root cause nearly impossible (Leverege, 2025). The so-called Clever Hans effect—where models arrive at correct conclusions for flawed or spurious reasons—is particularly risky in coaching, as chatbots might mimic effective human coaching patterns without understanding their contextual nuances (IBM, 2024).

2.6 Ethical Frameworks and How to Identify Technologies "Safe to Use" in Coaching

In the coaching field, bias and intransparency is not just a technical glitch; it strikes at the heart of the profession's ethical commitments. Coaching frameworks emphasize respect for individual uniqueness, non-discrimination, and sensitivity to power dynamics. Any system that claims to replicate or support coaching must be held to the same standard.

To address this, developers and deploying organizations must invest in bias mitigation strategies: diverse and inclusive training data, regular auditing, clear limitations in user interfaces, and human supervision. Without these safeguards, AI-driven coaching runs the risk of reinforcing the very barriers that coaching aims to dismantle.

Several ethical frameworks guide responsible AI coaching development (Fig. 2.1). UNESCO's AI Ethics Guidelines (2021) emphasize human rights, fairness, transparency, and oversight.

All these frameworks emphasize transparency, bias mitigation, privacy, and accountability, which are critical for the responsible development and deployment of AI-driven coaching tools. The UNESCO recommendation, in particular, provides a globally endorsed, actionable foundation for ethical AI in sensitive domains such as coaching.

Meanwhile, we can also draw from industry frameworks already in place such as the Global Code of Ethics for Coaches, Mentors and Supervisors (EMCC, 2016), which outlines principles including integrity and respecting diversity. Building on this, the EMCC Global Ethics Guidance for Technology and AI (2023) specifically addresses transparency, confidentiality, and prioritization of client interests for those providing coaching services through technology.

Privacy and confidentiality, at the very heart of every coaching code of ethics, present unique challenges in AI coaching. Unlike human coaches bound by

Summary Table: Key Ethical Frameworks for Responsible AI Coaching

Framework/Guideline	Key Principles/Features	Relevance to AI Coaching
UNESCO Recommendation on the Ethics of AI	Human rights, do no harm, privacy, transparency, accountability, inclusiveness, sustainability, multi-stakeholder participation	Globally recognized, holistic, actionable; ensures AI coaching is human-centered, fair, transparent, and accountable
IEEE Ethically Aligned Design	Human rights, well-being, accountability, transparency, privacy	Industry standard for ethical AI; supports robust, safe, and explainable AI coaching
EU Trustworthy AI Guidelines	Human agency, robustness, privacy, fairness, accountability	Widely adopted in policy and practice; comprehensive checklist for ethical AI coaching
General Responsible AI Principles	Fairness, transparency, accountability, privacy, continuous review	Adaptable to specific coaching contexts; encourages ongoing improvement and oversight

Fig. 2.1 Summary of ethical frameworks for responsible AI coaching (generated by the author with Claude.ai)

professional ethics, AI systems typically store and process conversation data—this is part of their existence.

The ICF AI Coaching Standards (2024) address these concerns by requiring systems to inform clients about data management practices and obtain explicit consent for data processing. Thus, most of what they refer to is already well regulated through Key Ethical Frameworks on Responsible AI and Software Certification Standards such as ISO. The other part is how it matches their competency framework, which is more a part of the discussion of who actually owns how coaching is defined.

The most relevant and up-to-date ISO standard to consider when looking for safe technology to use in Coaching is ISO/IEC 42001:2023IEC certifying software and especially AI-driven coaching applications against ethical, responsible, and transparent development practices. This standard specifically mandates risk assessment for bias, privacy, and societal impact, aligning with global ethical frameworks such as UNESCO, IEEE, and the EU AI guidelines. In the United States, the most relevant standards for software—especially AI-driven coaching tools that may handle sensitive data—are HIPAA and SOC 2 (not "SOCK"), but they are nowhere near as protective with regard to user data handling as ISO.

To comply with the Global Coaching Code of Ethics, we should always aim for the highest possible standard protecting user data, which are both the client and coach data. Thus, looking out for certification to ISO/IEC 42001 signals to clients, regulators, and partners that the AI system you are using, including AI coaching chatbots, meets the highest standards for ethical and responsible development and deployment.

2.7 Conclusion

AI-driven chatbots and AI companions are already influencing coaching practices, offering scalable support and new tools for reflection. Yet, the promise of accessibility must not obscure the ethical and relational complexities these tools introduce. This chapter has argued that coaching chatbots, while useful in structured or low-risk contexts, cannot replace the human depth, presence, and adaptive intelligence that define coaching as a profession.

As large language models shape more coaching interactions, the risks of embedded bias, lack of transparency, and erosion of trust grow. The very mechanisms that make these tools appear "intelligent" can mask normative assumptions and reinforce exclusion, especially when development lacks diverse perspectives and ethical guardrails.

The Manifesto for AI in Coaching, released on 30th April 2025 by the Viva la Coaching Academy (Viva la Coaching, 2025), provides a values and principles-based foundation for moving forward. Its emphasis on ethical integrity, human dignity, and client empowerment sets the standard for how AI should be integrated into coaching. Principles like informed consent, bias mitigation, and human oversight are not optional; they are necessary preconditions for any responsible AI application in this field.

The path forward requires more than regulation or design fixes. It calls for collective leadership, transparent practices, and a commitment to continuous learning. As AI becomes more capable, the coaching community must shape its development, not just react to it, to ensure that human flourishing remains at the center. Therefore, we need to understand how AI in Coaching works and is applied in order to make informed decisions for the well-being of AI users.

By addressing this thoughtfully and adhering to strong ethical principles, we can work toward a future where AI enhances coaching practice while maintaining the profession's commitment to human dignity, growth, and ethical integrity.

References

Bommasani, R., Hudson, D. A., Adeli, E., Altman, R., Arora, S., von Arx, S., et al. (2021). *On the opportunities and risks of foundation models*. Stanford Center for Research on Foundation Models. https://arxiv.org/abs/2108.07258

EMCC. (2016). *Global code of ethics for coaches & mentors*. https://www.emccglobal.org/quality/ethics/

EMCC. (2023). *Ethics guidance for providers of coaching, mentoring and supervision using technology and AI*. https://www.emccglobal.org/quality/ethics/

IBM. (2024). *What is AI transparency?* IBM.com. https://www.ibm.com/think/topics/ai-transparency
International Coaching Federation. (2024). *The International Coaching Federation artificial intelligence coaching framework and standards*. https://coachingfederation.org/wp-content/uploads/2025/01/icf-research-ai-coaching-framework-standards.pdf
Kouros, T., & Papa, V. (2024). Digital mirrors: AI companions and the self. *Societies, 14*(10), 200. https://doi.org/10.3390/soc14100200
Laestadius, L., Bishop, A., Gonzalez, M., Illenčík, D., & Campos-Castillo, C. (2022). Too human and not human enough: A grounded theory analysis of mental health harms from emotional dependence on the social chatbot Replika. *New Media & Society, 26*(21–22), 5923–5941. https://doi.org/10.1177/14614448221142007
Leverege. (2025). *The Clever Hans effect: How AI can be fooled*. Retrieved August 18, 2025, from https://www.leverege.com/blogpost/the-clever-hans-effect-how-ai-can-be-fooled
Liu, Z. (2024). Cultural bias in large language models: A comprehensive analysis and mitigation strategies. *Journal of Transcultural Communication*. https://doi.org/10.1515/jtc-2023-0019
Lucas, G. M., Gratch, J., King, A., & Morency, L. P. (2014). It's only a computer: Virtual humans increase willingness to disclose. *Computers in Human Behavior, 37*, 94–100. https://doi.org/10.1016/j.chb.2014.04.043
Malafronte, O., & Loufrani-Fedida, S. (2023). *Developing leader competence with coaching questions and artificial intelligence-based tools: Change of schemas and multilevel impacts.*
Molnar, C. (2020). *Interpretable machine learning: A guide for making black box models explainable*. Leanpub. https://christophm.github.io/interpretable-ml-book/
Rudin, C. (2019). Stop explaining black box machine learning models for high-stakes decisions and use interpretable models instead. *Nature Machine Intelligence, 1*(5), 206–215. https://doi.org/10.24384/b7gs-3h05
Sun, Y., Sheng, D., Zhou, Z., et al. (2024). AI hallucination: Towards a comprehensive classification of distorted information in artificial intelligence-generated content. *Humanities and Social Sciences Communications, 11*, 1278. (2024). https://doi.org/10.1057/s41599-024-03811-x
Terblanche, N., Molyn, J., de Haan, E., & Nilsson, V. O. (2022). Comparing artificial intelligence and human coaching goal attainment efficacy. *PLoS One, 17*(7), e0270255. https://doi.org/10.1371/journal.pone.0270255
UNESCO. (2021). *Recommendation on the ethics of artificial intelligence*. https://unesdoc.unesco.org/ark:/48223/pf0000380455
Vaswani, A., Shazeer, N., Parmar, N., Uszkoreit, J., Jones, L., Gomez, A. N., Kaiser, Ł., & Polosukhin, I. (2017). Attention is all you need. In *Advances in neural information processing systems* (Vol. 30). https://doi.org/10.48550/arXiv.1706.03762
Viva la Coaching. (2025). *The manifesto for AI in coaching*. https://vivalacoaching.com/manifesto/

Chapter 3
Building Relationships with AI Coaches: Insights from Chatbot Coaching Research

Vanessa Mai and Anja Richert

Abstract This chapter explores the potential of chatbot-based coaching to foster meaningful relationships between coach and coachee. Drawing on an interdisciplinary research project at the intersection of human–machine interaction and coaching effectiveness research, it investigates what conversational strategies help establish a trustful relationship—defined through rapport, working alliance, and social presence—between humans and machines. Through a design-based research approach, key relational elements such as coachbot self-disclosure, empathic feedback, and generative AI's paraphrasing capabilities were found to enhance users' perception of social presence and strengthen the working alliance. Practical recommendations address both structural and linguistic dimensions of coaching chatbot interaction, while also underscoring ethical considerations and design implications for generative AI. The findings offer guidance for the responsible integration of AI in coaching contexts. The chapter concludes with future-oriented theses on the role of AI-based chatbots in coaching and highlights emerging research avenues.

Keywords Chatbots · Chatbot coaching · AI-based coaching · Working alliance · Rapport · Social presence · Self-disclosure · Empathy · Ethics in AI coaching · Students

3.1 Introduction: Exploring the Foundations of Relationship Building in AI Coaching

Professionals frequently face emotionally demanding situations—important presentations, critical decisions, or evaluations—prompting organizations to seek tools that foster self-reflection and solution-focused thinking. AI-based technologies like

V. Mai (✉) · A. Richert
Cologne Cobots Lab, TH Köln/University of Applied Sciences, Köln, Germany
e-mail: vanessa.mai@th-koeln.de; anja.richert@th-koeln.de

R. Wegener et al. (eds.), *Coaching in the Age of AI*, SpringerBriefs in Psychology, https://doi.org/10.1007/978-3-032-23332-5_3

coaching chatbots offer low-threshold access to self-coaching in a confidential, non-judgmental space (Graßmann & Schermuly, 2021; Terblanche, 2020). In academic contexts, they support students in addressing challenges like exam anxiety without fear of stigma (Lee et al., 2020). When individual coaching isn't scalable, such tools complement traditional support systems. Many low-threshold coaching models and interventions can already be implemented in chatbots, enabling fully digital coaching processes (Graßmann & Schermuly, 2021; Mai & Rutschmann, 2023; Terblanche, 2020). Coaching chatbots are categorized as digital self-coaching tools (Kanatouri, 2020).

Despite rapid advancements in text-based generative AI, large language models (LLMs), and chatbot interfaces like ChatGPT, research on relationship building in AI coaching remains limited (Graßmann & Schermuly, 2021). While existing studies show user acceptance depends on perceived clarity and benefit (Terblanche & Cilliers, 2020), and chatbot therapy has shown promise (e.g., Fitzpatrick et al., 2017), further exploration is needed. This article draws on Mai's (2024) dissertation, which examined coaching interactions between chatbots and students, with a focus on relationship-building factors in the coaching process.

3.1.1 Key Factors in Chatbot Coaching: Relationship Building

A trusting working alliance is considered essential for coaching success. Drawing from Bordin's (1979) model, this therapeutic alliance is defined by three components: agreement on goals, clarity of tasks, and a bond characterized by trust and appreciation. Numerous studies confirm the link between a strong working alliance and coaching effectiveness (e.g., Graßmann et al., 2020). However, whether such an alliance can also form in chatbot coaching is still under active investigation. The bond component of the alliance aligns with the concept of rapport (Sharpley, 1997). Originally from psychology, rapport refers to a sense of trust and connection. Leach (2005) suggests that rapport, therapeutic alliance, and therapeutic relationship can be used interchangeably to describe this connection.

Rapport in human–machine contexts, often termed "virtual rapport," refers to feelings of harmony, synchronicity, and ease during interaction. Current research investigates how dialog systems must be designed to foster such rapport (e.g., Gratch et al., 2007; Huang et al., 2011). Additionally, other concepts for studying relationship building in human–machine interactions focus on low-threshold aspects of interaction, such as social presence—the extent to which a conversation with a machine feels natural and responsive (Harms & Biocca, 2004).

3.1.2 Key Factors in Chatbot Coaching: Relationship-Building Strategies

Research on relationship-building factors in chatbot coaching is still limited. Therefore, insights from human-to-human coaching and human–machine interaction are valuable: What conversational strategies help establish a trustful relationship/rapport between humans and machines—conceptualized through the interrelated constructs of working alliance and social presence?

A key verbal factor is self-disclosure. It describes "verbal behaviour, through which individuals truthfully, sincerely and intentionally communicate novel, ordinarily private information about themselves to one or more addressees" (Fisher, 1984, p. 278). In psychotherapy, self-disclosure supports deeper understanding and trust. It can take various forms, including facts, feelings, strategies, or immediacy (Knox & Hill, 2003) and does not always require revealing private details—authenticity alone can suffice. In human–machine interaction, studies show that a machine's self-disclosure can enhance rapport-related outcomes like copresence, trust, and relationship quality (e.g., Kang & Gratch, 2011; Lee et al., 2020).

Empathy is another key factor. While understudied in chatbot coaching, findings suggest that empathetic responses improve user experience. E.g., empathetic chatbots in health contexts are preferred over emotionally neutral ones (Liu & Sundar, 2018), and emotional intelligence—such as empathy—positively impacts relationship-building (Chaves & Gerosa, 2021).

3.1.3 Supporting Exam Anxiety: Development of the StudiCoachBot

To investigate the research question: what conversational strategies help establish a trustful relationship between humans and machines, a text-based coaching chatbot was designed. The StudiCoachBot @TH Köln is grounded in systemic coaching—a resource- and solution-oriented approach—and supports students' self-reflection on learning and work strategies, using exam anxiety as a use case (www.th-koeln.de/studicoachbot). The coachbot and coachee collaboratively define concerns and goals, forming the basis for structured interventions with open-ended, reflective prompts to encourage self-reflection. The system is based on the Conversational AI Rasa and has been integrating generative AI and LLMs since 2023 to enable more natural interactions.

At the time of development, few systematic guidelines for effective conversation design were available (e.g., Diederich et al., 2022). However, key design principles include transparent onboarding—clarifying goals, tasks, and limitations—and a consistent, credible chatbot personality (Diederich et al., 2022). Additionally, natural and intuitive dialog flow, including user guidance and handling of unexpected inputs, is critical for user engagement.

3.1.4 Experimental Investigation of Relationship-Building Factors

A design-based research approach was adopted to explore relationship building in chatbot coaching, combining application- and knowledge-oriented inquiry. In Phase 1, literature from coaching and human–machine interaction was analyzed to identify relevant relational factors. In Phase 2, these were operationalized into guidelines and tested in iterative experimental cycles using a mixed-methods approach—including qualitative, quantitative, and psychophysiological measures.

Iteration 1 focused on concept development and validation of the StudiCoachBot through a Wizard-of-Oz study (Mai et al., 2021). An experimental study with 201 participants examined the impact of coachbot self-disclosure on working alliance using standardized measures (Mai et al., 2022). *Iteration 2* involved a 10-week field study ($N = 242$) with a second coachbot prototype (Mai et al., 2023), followed by an experiment ($N = 284$) testing additional factors—such as the coachbot's empathic responses—on rapport (measured via working alliance and social presence. *Iteration 3* advanced evaluation methods and coachbot capabilities: In Iteration 3.1, the impact of a coachbot's self-disclosure on the working alliance was examined using psychophysiological metrics (electrodermal activity, EDA, and heart rate variability, HRV) in an explorative study with 20 participants (Mai et al., 2024). Iteration 3.2 focused on advancing the coaching chatbot by integrating generative AI. A hybrid chatbot was developed to implement paraphrasing as a coaching technique and its effect on rapport (measured via working alliance and social presence) was examined in a comparative study with 83 participants (Bauer et al., 2026). As part of this proof of concept, the study also tested the integration of two large language models (LLaMA2 and GPT-4) to assess their influence on relationship quality—conducted during the early public adoption phase of generative AI.

A final phase synthesized findings on effective relationship-building strategies and evaluated their transferability to future research and practice. Across all studies, self-disclosure and empathy were systematically varied. For example, in the self-disclosure condition, the coachbot shared relatable exam-anxiety experiences from its own "perspective" (e.g., delays during updates), while empathetic responses acknowledged user input (e.g., "Thank you for your openness"). An example reads: "Did you know that sometimes you can tell that I'm nervous, even though I'm a machine? My developers notice this before updates, as I sometimes take a little longer to respond. What do you think? Do others sometimes notice when you are nervous before exams?"

3.2 Results: Relationship Building in Chatbot Coaching Is Possible

The results show that rapport building (measured via working alliance and social presence inventories) is possible in chatbot coaching (Mai, 2024): (1) *Iteration 2.2* showed with statistical significance that—at least in terms of social presence—self-disclosure of a coaching chatbot leads to stronger rapport than when a coachbot does not disclose any information. Significant differences were found in the Perceived Affective Understanding (PAU) subscale ($F(2.278) = 21.98$; $p = 1.35E–9$; $p < 0.001$). With a mean value of $M = 3.43$ (SD = .79), the self-disclosure chatbot has a significantly higher PAU than the no-disclosure chatbot with $M = 2.74$ (SD = .73).

(2) *In iteration 2.2*, it was furthermore shown with statistical significance that empathic reactions of a coachbot lead to more social presence than no empathic reactions. Significant differences were found in the Perceived Message Understanding (PMU) subscale ($W = 12{,}004$; $p = 0.0049$; $p < 0.005$). With a mean value of $M = 4.1$ (SD = .62), the empathy chatbot showed significantly higher PMU than the chatbot that did not show empathy ($M = 3.86$, SD = .76). *Iteration 2.2* also showed a relationship-building effect of a self-disclosure coachbot that shows empathy, in terms of the perception of social presence. Significant differences were found in the PMU subscale of social presence (X2(5) = 18.349; $p = 0.0025$; $p < 0.005$). The self-disclosure chatbot, which showed empathy, had a significantly higher mean ($M = 4.15$, SD = .62) than the self-disclosure chatbot, which did not show empathy ($M = 3.7$, SD = .78).

Finally, (3) in *iteration 3.2*, statistically significant differences in relationship building between different LLMs (GPT-4 and Llama2) were measured. The implementation of the LLM GPT-4 compared to the LLM Llama2 leads to a higher perception of social presence (Bauer et al., 2026). Here, both subscales showed significant differences in PMU (X2(2) = 20.213; $p = 4.08E–05$; $p < 0.001$) and PAU (X2(2) = 8.2592; $p = 0.01609$; $p < 0.05$). The direction of this significance could be determined based on the mean values of the two subscales. On the PMU subscale, the experimental group with GPT-4 ($M = 4.19$, SD = 0.87) achieved a higher value than the experimental group with Llama2 ($M = 3.08$, SD = 0.94). Similarly, GPT-4 ($M = 3.13$, SD = 0.53) achieved a higher mean value on the PAU subscale than Llama2 ($M = 2.62$, SD = 0.77). The results from the psychophysiological measurements were not significant (*Iteration 3.1*), but showed potential for future studies (Mai et al., 2023).

A comparison of the results of the experimental studies across all three iterations revealed differences in the strength of the working alliance: Compared to iteration 1, the values of the working alliance increased significantly in iterations 2 and 3. In iterations 2 and 3, the StudiCoachBot showed mean values in the bonding subscale of $M = 3.63$ (SD = .57) compared to $M = 2.73$ (SD = 1.21) in iteration 1 (on a five-point Likert-scale). Thus, cautious positive statements can be made about the effectiveness of chatbot coaching for students and can be integrated into the existing literature on the effectiveness of chatbots in other domains such as therapy and health care (Fitzpatrick et al., 2017) and social chatbots (Skjuve et al., 2022).

3.3 Contribution to the Ethical and Responsible Use of AI-Based Coaching: Four Concrete Conclusions for Practical Application

Coaching chatbots are still at the beginning of their potential applications. The digital coaching market is evolving rapidly, and blended or hybrid coaching will continue to grow (Clutterbuck, 2022; Terblanche, 2024). AI-based coaching will support and complement human-to-human coaching in various ways and at different levels. Therefore, ongoing scientific research on these developments is crucial. The research presented here by Mai (2024) contributes to this by exploring the opportunities and limitations of AI-based systems in emotionally sensitive areas such as coaching. It examines where human coaches and coaching chatbots can collaborate as hybrid teams, where a coaching chatbot may be more helpful than a human may, and where human coaches remain indispensable. It also explores how generative AI can be used responsibly, incorporating the ethical dimension of chatbot coaching. The results provide recommendations for research and practice. These are aimed at chatbot designers, developers, researchers, and experts in coaching and counseling. This contribution concludes with four concrete recommendations for the development and use of AI-based coaching chatbots.

3.3.1 Hybrid Chatbots to Manage Hallucinations

The lack of consistency and reliability in LLM-generated responses (so-called "hallucinations") remains a significant challenge, even with advancing technology. In the research project, it was demonstrated through a proof of concept that developing a hybrid chatbot appears to be a promising approach to addressing these challenges. Such hybrid chatbots consist of rule-based/scripted, and AI-based elements. This allows better control over the conversation flow and ensures the quality and reliability of responses. E.g., user messages are handed off to a Dialog Management that acts as initial gatekeeper, ensuring incoming messages are filtered and anonymized before reaching the generative part of the architecture. In addition, in this rule-based stage, the conversation flow can be altered. E.g., a limit for follow-up questions for a conversation can be set. Hybrid chatbots also offer better data protection than purely generative AI (Bauer et al., 2026).

3.3.2 Effective Conversation Design and Prompting

The research presented here by Mai (2024) has shown that chatbot design should include clear expectation management and a consistent chatbot concept for users to perceive coaching chatbots as helpful. During onboarding, the chatbot should clearly communicate its goals, tasks, limitations, as well as safety and privacy considerations. Concrete recommendations for conversation design can be derived from the studies on both structural and linguistic levels: varying between click- and text-based interactions, text and images, as well as information and self-reflection, can make chatbot coaching more engaging (Mai et al., 2022a). On the linguistic level, self-disclosure statements should be integrated, and empathetic chatbot responses should be incorporated (Mai et al., 2022b).

Furthermore, Mai (2024) highlights the importance of proper prompting. Defining role, context, task, and conversation strategies has significant intersections with the "classic" conversation design. This means that the conversation design must be expanded to include elements of prompting. It also underscores that conversation design and prompting are crucial aspects of chatbot development.

3.3.3 Shared Responsibility and AI Literacy

The increased use of generative AI across various societal domains raises questions about responsibility for content and expectation management. By examining initial use cases of chatbot coaching in universities, we provide recommendations for different stakeholders on the responsible integration of AI in coaching.

For human coaches and coachees, this requires something like *AI Literacy*, meaning the willingness to engage with new technologies as well as the competence to explore potentials and limits and weigh their own usage possibilities. In this process, researchers and experts can support with knowledge and discourse offerings. Universities and coaching associations are called upon to responsibly and openly accompany and moderate these discourses and to provide guidance. This can be done through the organization of conferences and symposia or the discussion and development of standards. Providers and companies are called upon to address ethical and legal aspects. Their task is to develop something like *AI Leadership*, meaning the ability to use AI as a strategic tool to transform an organization. This requires both technological understanding and consideration of strategic and ethical aspects. In the field of education, the relationship between learners and teachers will continue to change, particularly for schools and universities. Lecturers are expected to take on a role as informed experts regarding the use of AI in general and (coaching) chatbots in particular.

3.3.4 Understanding Social Impact and Coaching Redefinition

As part of the research on relationship building in chatbot coaching, statements can also be made about typical processes and interaction patterns in AI-based coaching: Which topics are addressed? Where are there similarities or differences to human-to-human coaching? This contributes to the refinement of the coaching concept (in human-to-human coaching) in relation to the concept of AI-based coaching and the question of how societal communication is changing as a result of the increasing presence of AI in our everyday and work lives. As one of the first researchers, Bachkirova offers a decidedly critical perspective on the use of AI in coaching (Bachkirova & Kemp, 2024).

3.4 Conclusion: Toward Responsible and Relational AI in Coaching

The research presented here contributes to the responsible integration of generative AI in education and counseling contexts. The iterative development of a coaching chatbot demonstrates that well-thought-out conversation design can enhance the effectiveness of AI-based coaching. This work convincingly addresses key scientific and societal discussions on the responsible use of generative AI. It highlights both the potential and the risks and offers detailed solutions: AI-based coaching chatbots can establish low-threshold contact and show their great strength in pattern recognition. In this area, they are certainly superior to human coaches—as we know from the use of AI as an assistance system in medical diagnosis. However, today's AI-based coaching chatbots cannot (yet) demonstrate anything like empathy and emotional intelligence. They lack the ability to empathize with the coachee's emotional state and to create a space. Therefore, AI-based coaching chatbots are currently not being designed as a human replacement, but rather as a supplement and support. Blended or hybrid coaching (Kanatouri, 2020) will therefore be the future, in which AI-based coaching will support and complement human-to-human coaching at various levels and in various ways.

References

Bachkirova, T., & Kemp, R. (2024). 'AI coaching': Democratising coaching service or offering an ersatz? *Coaching: An International Journal of Theory, Research and Practice.* https://doi.org/10.1080/17521882.2024.2368598

Bauer, A., Mai, V., Neef, C., & Richert, A. (2026). Smarter Coaching Chatbots: Leveraging Hybrid Architectures for Deeper Context Awareness. In: *HCI International 2025 – Late Breaking Papers : 27th International Conference on Human-Computer Interaction, Gothenburg, Sweden, June 22–27, 2025*, Proceedings, Part XV, pp. 3–22. https://doi.org/10.1007/978-3-032-13184-3_1

Bordin, E. S. (1979). The generalizability of the psychoanalytic concept of the working alliance. *Psychotherapy: Theory, Research & Practice, 16*(3), 252–260. https://doi.org/10.1037/h0085885

Chaves, A. P., & Gerosa, M. A. (2021). How should my chatbot interact? A survey on human-chatbot interaction design. *International Journal of Human–Computer Interaction, 37*(8), 729–758. https://doi.org/10.1080/10447318.2020.1841438

Clutterbuck, D. (2022). The future of AI in coaching. In S. Greif, H. Möller, W. Scholl, J. Passmore, & F. Müller (Eds.), *International handbook of evidence-based coaching* (pp. 369–379). Springer.

Diederich, S., Brendel, A. B., Morana, S., & Kolbe, L. (2022). On the design of and interaction with conversational agents: An organizing and assessing review of human-computer interaction research. *Journal of the Association for Information Systems, 23*(1), 96–138. https://doi.org/10.17705/1jais.00724

Fisher, D. (1984). A conceptual analysis of self-disclosure. *Journal for the Theory of Social Behaviour, 14*(3), 277–296. https://doi.org/10.1111/j.1468-5914.1984.tb00498.x

Fitzpatrick, K. K., Darcy, A., & Vierhile, M. (2017). Delivering cognitive behavior therapy to young adults with symptoms of depression and anxiety using a fully automated conversational agent (Woebot): A randomized controlled trial. *JMIR Mental Health, 4*(2), e19. https://doi.org/10.2196/mental.7785

Graßmann, C., & Schermuly, C. C. (2021). Coaching with artificial intelligence: Concepts and capabilities. *Human Resource Development Review, 20*(1), 106–126. https://doi.org/10.1177/1534484320982891

Graßmann, C., Schölmerich, F., & Schermuly, C. (2020). The relationship between working alliance and client outcomes in coaching: A meta-analysis. *Human Relations, 73*(1), 35–58. https://doi.org/10.1177/0018726718819725

Gratch, J., Wang, N., Gerten, J., Fast, E., & Duffy, R. (2007). Creating rapport with virtual agents. In C. Pelachaud (Ed.), *Lecture notes in computer science: Vol. 4722. Intelligent virtual agents* (pp. 125–138). Springer. https://doi.org/10.1007/978-3-540-74997-4_12

Harms, C., & Biocca, F. (2004). Internal consistency and reliability of the Networked Minds Measure of Social Presence. In M. Alcaniz & B. Rey (Eds.), *Seventh annual international workshop: Presence 2004*. Universidad Politecnica de Valencia. https://web-archive.southampton.ac.uk/cogprints.org/7026/1/Harms_04_reliability_validity_social_presence_(Biocca).pdf

Huang, L., Morency, L.-P., & Gratch, J. (2011). Virtual rapport 2.0. In H. H. Vilhjálmsson (Ed.), *Lecture notes in computer science lecture notes in artificial intelligence: Vol. 6895. Intelligent virtual agents: 11th international conference, IVA 2011, Reykjavik, Iceland, September 15–17, 2011; Proceedings* (pp. 68–79). Springer. https://doi.org/10.1007/978-3-642-23974-8_8

Kanatouri, S. (2020). *The digital coach*. Routledge. https://doi.org/10.4324/9780429022753

Kang, S.-H., & Gratch, J. (2011). People like virtual counselors that highly-disclose about themselves. In *Annual review of cybertherapy and telemedicine 2011* (pp. 143–148). IOS Press. https://doi.org/10.3233/978-1-60750-766-6-143

Knox, S., & Hill, C. E. (2003). Therapist self-disclosure: Research-based suggestions for practitioners. *Journal of Clinical Psychology, 59*(5), 529–539. https://doi.org/10.1002/jclp.10157

Leach, M. J. (2005). Rapport: A key to treatment success. *Complementary Therapies in Clinical Practice, 11*(4), 262–265. https://doi.org/10.1016/j.ctcp.2005.05.005

Lee, Y.-C., Yamashita, N., Huang, Y., & Fu, W. (2020). "I hear you, I feel you": Encouraging deep self-disclosure through a chatbot. In R. Bernhaupt, F. Mueller, D. Verweij, J. Andres, J. McGrenere, A. Cockburn, I. Avellino, A. Goguey, P. Bjørn, S. Zhao, B. P. Samson, & R. Kocielnik (Eds.), *Proceedings of the 2020 CHI conference on human factors in computing systems* (pp. 1–12). ACM. https://doi.org/10.1145/3313831.3376175

Liu, B., & Sundar, S. S. (2018). Should machines express sympathy and empathy? Experiments with a health advice chatbot. *Cyberpsychology, Behavior, and Social Networking, 21*(10), 625–636. https://doi.org/10.1089/cyber.2018.0110

Mai, V. (2024). *Chatbots im (Studierenden-)Coaching: Einfluss beziehungsbildender Faktoren auf die Beziehungsgestaltung im KI-basierten Mensch-Maschine-Coaching*. Kölner Schriften zur Ingenieur- und Naturwissenschaftlichen Forschung. https://nbn-resolving.org/urn:nbn:de:hbz:832-cos4-12875

Mai, V., & Rutschmann, R. (2023). Chatbots im Coaching: Potenziale und Einsatzmöglichkeiten von digitalen Coaching-Begleitern und Assistenten. *Organisationsberatung, Supervision, Coaching, 30*(1), 45–57. https://doi.org/10.1007/s11613-022-00801-3

Mai, V., Wolff, A., Richert, A., & Preusser, I. (2021). Accompanying reflection processes by an AI-based StudiCoachBot: A study on rapport building in human-machine coaching using self-disclosure. In C. Stephanidis et al. (Eds.), *Lecture notes in computer science: Vol. 13096. HCI International 2021* (pp. 439–457). Springer. https://doi.org/10.1007/978-3-030-90328-2_29

Mai, V., Neef, C., & Richert, A. (2022a). "Clicking vs. writing": The impact of a chatbot's interaction method on the working alliance in AI-based coaching. *Coaching | Theorie & Praxis, 8*(1), 15–31. https://doi.org/10.1365/s40896-021-00063-3

Mai, V., Bauer, A., Deggelmann, C., Neef, C., & Richert, A. (2022b). AI-based coaching: Impact of a chatbot's disclosure behavior on the working alliance and acceptance. In J. Y. C. Chen et al. (Eds.), *Lecture notes in computer science: Vol. 13518. HCI International 2022* (pp. 391–406). Springer. https://doi.org/10.1007/978-3-031-21707-4_28

Mai, V., Bauer, A., Deggelmann, C., & Richert, A. (2023). Acceptance and user needs of coaching chatbots: An empirical analysis of a StudiCoachBot's conversation histories. In P. Zaphiris et al. (Eds.), *Lecture Notes in Computer Science: Vol. 14060. HCI International 2023* (pp. 176–190). Springer. https://doi.org/10.1007/978-3-031-48060-7_14

Mai, V., Richert, A., Savanevska, N., Preusser, I., & Heisenberg, G. (2024). Relationship building in human-machine interaction: A proof of concept on the influence of self-disclosure on rapport in chatbot coaching using psychophysiological measurements. *Journal kommunikation. medien*, 1–27. https://doi.org/10.25598/JKM/2024-16.2

Sharpley, C. F. (1997). The influence of silence upon client-perceived rapport. *Counselling Psychology Quarterly, 10*(3), 237–246. https://doi.org/10.1080/09515079708254176

Skjuve, M., Følstad, A., Fostervold, K. I., & Brandtzaeg, P. B. (2022). A longitudinal study of human–chatbot relationships. *International Journal of Human-Computer Studies, 168*, 102903. https://doi.org/10.1016/j.ijhcs.2022.102903

Terblanche, N. (2020). A design framework to create artificial intelligence coaches. *International Journal of Evidence Based Coaching and Mentoring, 18*(2), 152–165. https://doi.org/10.24384/B7GS-3H05

Terblanche, N. (2024). Artificial intelligence (AI) coaching: Redefining people development and organizational performance. *The Journal of Applied Behavioral Science, 60*(4), 631–638. https://doi.org/10.1177/00218863241283919

Terblanche, N., & Cilliers, D. (2020). Factors that influence users' adoption of being coached by an artificial intelligence coach. *Philosophy of Coaching: An International Journal, 5*(1), 61–70. https://doi.org/10.22316/poc/05.1.06

Chapter 4
Exploring Self-Regulation and Self-Access in AI-Based Coaching: The Impact of the Coaching Relationship and Self-Disclosure

Christina Mühlberger and Eva Jonas

Abstract While AI-based coaching matches human coaching in goal attainment, its impact on clients' self-regulation and self-access—core capacities for self-development—remains unclear. These abilities have so far only been studied in the context of human coaching. Thereby, the coach plays a vital role, supporting the coachee's self through a strong relationship. This raises an important question: Can AI-based coaching, which lacks a traditional coaching relationship, still support the coachee's self-development effectively? On the one hand, studies suggest that clients of AI-based coaching mention the absence of personal interaction and report a lower working alliance compared to clients of human coaching. On the other hand, research indicates that coachees can form meaningful relationships with AI agents, benefiting from reduced inhibition and increased self-disclosure due to the non-judgmental nature of AI. This chapter explores the role of AI-based coaching in fostering proximal outcomes such as goal attainment and, more importantly, in influencing distal outcomes, including self-regulation and self-access. We address underlying mechanisms such as the coaching relationship, self-disclosure, and inhibition and present findings from our own studies investigating AI-based coaching.

Keywords Coaching · Self-regulation · Self-access · Self-disclosure · AI-based coaching · Coaching relationship quality · Working alliance with chatbots · Digital coaching outcomes · Psychological self-development · Large language model coaching

---

C. Mühlberger (✉) · E. Jonas
Paris Lodron University of Salzburg (PLUS), Department of Psychology, Social Psychology, Salzburg, Austria
e-mail: christina.muehlberger@plus.ac.at; Eva.Jonas@plus.ac.at

R. Wegener et al. (eds.), *Coaching in the Age of AI*, SpringerBriefs in Psychology, https://doi.org/10.1007/978-3-032-23332-5_4

4.1 Introduction

The growing influence of artificial intelligence (AI) in the coaching world is reflected in headlines such as "AI is Changing the Coaching Landscape" (Gopalan, 2022), "The New Era of Coaching with ChatGPT!" (Rutschmann, 2023), or "When Everyone Gets a Coach: The AI-Powered Revolution in Learning" (Tavis, 2024). Tools like iThrive and Wysa have made significant progress in enhancing coaching practices (Kanatouri, 2021). Although skepticism regarding the use of AI in coaching persists, research suggests that coachees are open to engaging with a variety of AI-driven methodologies—including voice-, text-, script-, and conversation-based approaches (Passmore et al., 2025). Nonetheless, a central question remains: What impact can AI-based coaching generate and how does it work? The current chapter examines the outcomes of AI-based coaching, focusing on the key outcome of self-regulation and the mechanisms that drive it.

4.1.1 Human- and AI-Based Coaching

Coaching is recognized as a method for supporting individuals in achieving goals across professional, organizational, and personal contexts (e.g., Sonesh et al., 2015). When entering a coaching relationship, the coach consistently supports clients in clarifying and working toward self-congruent goals, i.e., goals aligned with the individual's self (Greif, 2022). This focus on the self is often emphasized in coaching definitions. For instance, coaching is described as a process of self-reflection that enhances the achievement of self-congruent goals, self-change, and self-development (Greif, 2022). Some mention that coaching stimulates self-awareness (Passmore & Fillery-Travis, 2011) and others speak of coaching, developing self-regulatory skills to support continuous self-directed learning and personal growth (Grant, 2012). Even if the terms used differ, all of these coaching definitions convey the same core idea: In coaching, coachees become aware of their self and discover it. They set and pursue self-congruent goals to support their personal development. Therefore, they are deeply engaged with their sense of self throughout the coaching process.

Meta-analyses on coaching have shown that coaching with human coaches is effective (Burt & Talati, 2017; De Haan & Nilsson, 2023; De Meuse et al., 2009; Jones et al., 2016; Nicolau et al., 2023; Sonesh et al., 2015; Theeboom et al., 2014; Wang et al., 2022). Goal attainment and satisfaction often emerge alongside self-efficacy as key proximal indicators of coaching success. Distal outcomes that have been investigated in human coaching include career satisfaction, stress management and well-being, work–life balance, life satisfaction, self-development, and self-regulation (Greif & Jonas, 2021).

AI coaching refers to coaching delivered by a computer instead of a human coach. An AI coachbot generates responses either by following a predetermined script or via large language models (Passmore & Diller, 2024). In this chapter, AI-based coaching includes both spoken and text-based interactions with such systems. As empirical research on AI-based coaching is still in its infancy, only a limited number of studies have examined its effectiveness. One such study by Terblanche et al. (2022) used a chatbot designed to support goal achievement and found that, over ten months, individuals coached by AI achieved goal levels comparable to those coached by humans. Despite these promising results, evidence on other outcomes—especially those with benefits beyond immediate satisfaction or goal attainment—is scarce. There is one study where banking employees reported increased self-resilience after they engaged with a coaching chatbot for eight weeks. This was evidenced by increased expressions of hope, positivity, and motivation (Ellis-Brush, 2021). In this study, AI-based coaching appeared to affect the self in some way. An interview study with nine graduate employees who used a goal-attainment AI chatbot coach over a four-week period to help with their career goals revealed that the chatbot encouraged reflection on their personal development, thereby strengthening their self-awareness (Terblanche & Tau, 2025). Nevertheless, further research is needed to examine such distal outcomes.

Previous research has suggested that self-regulation, an ego-powering competence enabling individuals to set and pursue self-congruent goals with flexibility and prudence (Baumann & Kuhl, 2021), is a particularly important distal outcome in human coaching (Mühlberger et al., 2024a).

4.1.2 Self-Regulation and Self-Access

According to the Theory of Personality Systems Interactions (PSI; Kuhl, 2001), the self is "a complex knowledge structure comprising personal traits, needs, emotions, and values, integrating positive and negative self-representations" (Quirin & Kuhl, 2018, p. 1). It is rooted in the Extension Memory (EM), an unconscious system that stores personal experiences, needs, values, and strengths, and fosters serenity by making these resources accessible. The EM, along with three other affect-regulated functional systems, shapes how a person perceives the world, guides their behavior, and influences their emotional state (Fig. 4.1). The Object Recognition System (ORS) processes discrepancies and anxiety; the Intuitive Behavioral Control (IBC) supports spontaneous action under positive affect; and the Intention Memory (IM) enables planned action in a low-emotion, focused state.

Self-regulation draws its impulses from the EM and interacts with the other three systems. When individuals act in a self-regulated manner, they strive toward goals that align with their core self, a self that considers and integrates both their own and others' needs, emotions, and values (Baumann & Kuhl, 2021). Self-regulated individuals plan and act in accordance with their motives and values, identify with their goals, and perceive them as self-chosen (*self-determination*). To pursue these goals effectively, they require motivation fueled by positive affect, which provides the energy necessary for action (*self-motivation*). When perception shifts to worries and anxiety, behavior can become impulsive and disorganized. Then, the ability to *self-soothe* is crucial for balanced, goal-directed action. In coaching, all three are key: identifying with goals, staying motivated, and regulating anxiety.

Under stress, individuals may become trapped in negative thought spirals and lose connection to their inner self. Coping with this requires *self-access*, i.e., the

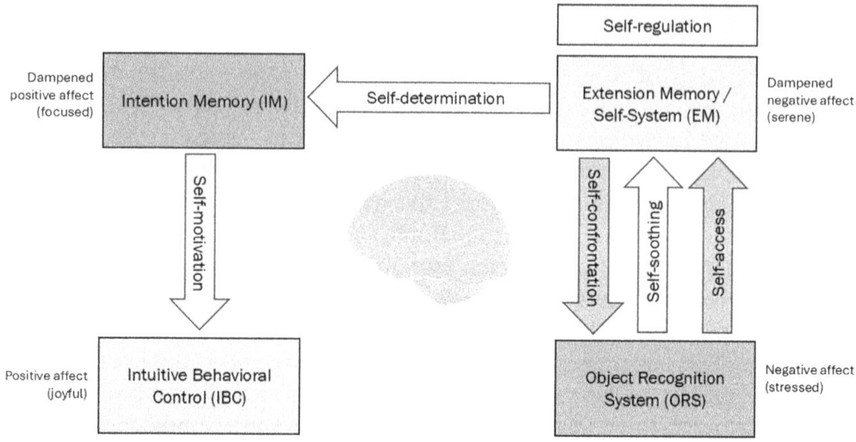

Fig. 4.1 The four cognitive systems of PSI theory and the positioning of self-regulation and self-access within them

ability to access one's emotions, needs, goals, and values. This enables individuals to perceive what they want and feel even under threat (*self-awareness*), to reconcile perceived contradictions within themselves and integrate them (*integrating contradictions*), and to overcome failure (*letting go rather than ruminating*). Self-access thus forms a core foundation for effective self-regulation (Kuhl, 2001; Quirin & Kuhl, 2018).

Empirical studies show that self-regulation and self-access are fundamental variables in coaching. In a study on caregivers working as managers, a five-month coaching program increased both their self-regulation and self-access, with self-regulation predicting goal attainment (Mühlberger et al., 2024a). Another study involving 298 coaching sessions found that the self-regulation and self-awareness (an important component of self-access) achieved through coaching were positively associated with goal attainment, coaching satisfaction, and need fulfillment. (Mühlberger et al., 2024b). Even a single 90-min coaching session improved both abilities (Diller et al., 2021). Thus, human coaching can indeed foster self-regulation and self-access. But what exactly drives this self-development?

4.1.3 Fostering Self-Development Through the Coaching Relationship

Coaches play a crucial role in supporting coachees' self-development. Central to this is a strong coaching relationship, which fosters openness and the sharing of personal thoughts, concerns, and emotions (Wasylyshyn, 2019), thereby enabling access to underlying motives and values. In 298 coaching sessions, coaches' self-rated relational factors—particularly the bond they established and their perspective-taking—contributed to coachees' self-regulation and self-awareness (Mühlberger et al., 2024b). Another key relational factor is the coach's activation of the coachee's personal resources. Empathy also plays a central role in this process: When coaches conveyed genuine understanding, clients reported higher levels of self-regulation. This effect was mediated by the clients' perception of the coach's empathy (Diller et al., 2021; Schiemann et al., 2019). These findings underscore that a strong coach–coachee relationship is pivotal for fostering self-development in human coaching.

This raises the question of whether a relationship can also emerge in AI-based coaching, where the traditional interpersonal connection is absent. And if such a relationship can indeed be established, can it promote the client's self-development in a similar way?

4.1.4 Building a Relationship with an AI Coach?

While it is often assumed that a relationship cannot be formed in AI coaching, findings are mixed. Quantitative and qualitative analyses found that most users of a coaching chatbot developed no working alliance (Ellis-Brush, 2021). However, other studies report moderate to moderately high working alliance levels with AI coaches (Mai et al., 2022), though still lower than the consistently high alliance ratings reported in human coaching (e.g., Gessnitzer & Kauffeld, 2015). In interviews, coachees criticized chatbot interactions as impersonal and robotic, lacking facial expressions and physical presence (Terblanche et al., 2024; Terblanche & Tau, 2025). Likewise, experienced coaches noted the absence of meaningful connection when using chatbots and emphasized the importance of personal sharing in strengthening the human coaching relationship (Bruning & Boak, 2025).

At the same time, some clients value the anonymity and non-judgmental nature of AI-based coaching, which reduces inhibition and helps them open up more easily (Terblanche et al., 2024). Coaches also see potential in chatbots outperforming humans in tasks like analyzing body language or physiological data (Bruning & Boak, 2025). While machines lack emotions, they can still deliver emotionally responsive interactions, suggesting that a data-driven cognitive empathy may be possible (Passmore et al., 2025). This is relevant, as cognitive empathy—especially perspective-taking—has been shown to enhance coachees' self-regulation in human coaching (Diller et al., 2021; Mühlberger et al., 2024a).

Research from clinical and health psychology supports the idea that clients can form meaningful relationships with AI agents. More human-like systems tend to be rated more positively. For instance, participants engaging with an animated virtual human that used relational behaviors, such as empathetic feedback, humor, name usage, and gestures, reported stronger bonds and greater willingness to continue using the system compared to those interacting with a non-relational version (Bickmore et al., 2005). Furthermore, chatbots that shared emotional experiences prompted users to disclose more and report stronger relationships than those that shared few emotional experiences (Kang & Gratch, 2011; Lee et al., 2020). However, another study did not find such a difference (Mai et al., 2022). Studies also show that AI interactions are sometimes rated more positively than human ones. In health-screenings, participants showed lower resistance to self-disclosure and lower impression management when they believed a virtual human was automated rather than human-controlled (Gratch et al., 2014). Similarly, participants who thought they were alone with a virtual human communicated more openly, while those who believed they were being observed feared negative evaluation and expressed a preference for more privacy (Lucas et al., 2014).

In summary, research on relationship building with AI shows mixed results. While such relationships are often perceived as weak and insufficiently human, AI-based coaching offers an anonymous, non-judgmental space and can exhibit cognitive empathy. Relationship strength and self-disclosure increase when AI displays human-like traits such as empathy or self-disclosure. Clients also show less inhibition in sharing personal information and report lower fear of negative evaluation when they feel alone with the AI. In this way, AI-based coaching may still support self-development. But how?

4.1.5 Self-Development Within AI-Based Coaching

In coaching, coachees often face discrepancies between their needs, goals, or intentions and reality. Such discrepancies can trigger uncertainty and anxiety (Jonas et al., 2014), highlighting the need for coping with such threat. This coping process can be supported when the coach offers timely and empathetic reassurance (Engel & Kuhl, 2022). Relationship behaviors such as empathy, trust, and a strong working alliance enable coachees to disengage from ORS and reconnect with their inner self (EM), thereby promoting self-access. This was shown in a study in which the coaches' relationship behavior positively affected the coachees' self-regulation and self-awareness (Mühlberger et al., 2024a).

As discrepancies often cause discomfort, especially when coping resources are limited (Jonas et al., 2014), many individuals seek to avoid them. Confronting such discrepancies can offer valuable opportunities for personal development. In coaching, addressing discrepancies is key. This requires *self-confrontation*—the ability to tolerate negative affect (Kuhl, 2001). Self-confrontation involves leaving the calm state of EM, engaging with negative affect via ORS, and ultimately achieving self-access, where the discrepancy can be integrated into the self. Yet, realizing that one can tolerate negative affect through self-confrontation and consequently regaining self-access shows individuals that they can deal with stress in a self-growing way that is not defensive such as euphemism, denial, or impulsive action (Engel & Kuhl, 2022). In summary, self-development also requires confronting discomfort.

Human coaches support self-confrontation and self-access through a strong relationship. Here, AI-based coaching may fall short of what human coaching can offer. While AI-based coaching may foster self-regulation by giving clients the opportunity to plan in accordance with their self (*self-determination*) and use this to realize their intentions (*self-motivation*), we suggest that AI coaches may fail to fully activate the ORS or do so only superficially, limiting opportunities for self-confrontation and thus, self-access. While AI coaches may be able to address discrepancies, they lack the relational depth of human coaches, particularly warmth, empathy, and situational flexibility. However, these qualities are crucial for helping coachees tolerate discrepancies, manage distress, access the self, and thereby regain inner balance. Without them, coachees may remain stuck in familiar patterns, avoiding deeper exploration of obstacles.

In summary, AI-based coaching may be capable of supporting proximal outcomes such as goal attainment. It may also foster distal outcomes such as self-regulation by promoting self-determination and self-motivation. However, it may be less effective in facilitating self-access. In the following, we present two studies investigating these hypotheses.

4.2 Empirical Studies on AI-Based Coaching

In a pilot study, participants engaged in a 30-min goal-setting conversation based on the SMART principle—either with a real person (n = 28) or with a chatbot (ChatGPT-4; n = 32). Human conversation partners were psychology students following a step-by-step guide with example questions; chatbot prompts mirrored the same structure. Although neither condition increased goal attainment, participants in the human conversation reported greater satisfaction and perceived the conversation as more empathetic. Both formats, however, led to short-term gains in self-efficacy.

In a follow-up randomized controlled trial (RCT) study in collaboration with Delphi Artificial Agents GmbH (Oliver Wüntsch), we examined the effects and mechanisms of a coaching chatbot. The chatbot combines various psychological approaches (including person-centered communication, solution-focused brief therapy, and Appreciative Inquiry) into a structured, resource-oriented coaching process. Over the course of three weeks, it guided 60 participants through weekly sessions, while a control group (n = 51) worked with a self-coaching online booklet during the same period. Participants completed questionnaires assessing changes in goal attainment, self-efficacy, well-being, intrinsic motivation to work on their goal, self-regulation, and self-access. As potential working mechanisms, we assessed self-disclosure and inhibition. For the chatbot condition, we also examined empathy and working alliance.

Findings show that both formats improved coachees' goal attainment and well-being. However, only the chatbot users reported a significant increase in self-efficacy and intrinsic motivation to work on their goals. The chatbot as well as the self-coaching booklet was able to increase coachees' self-regulation, with the chatbot achieving a higher increase. There was no increase in self-access in the chatbot group but a slight increase was observed in the self-coaching group. Regarding our assessed working mechanisms, chatbot users felt less inhibited although both groups reported similarly high levels of self-disclosure. The relationship with the chatbot was also rated surprisingly positive, especially in terms of empathy and the working alliance (means above 5 on a 1–7 scale). Moreover, in the chatbot group, working alliance task was positively correlated with increased goal attainment, self-efficacy, and well-being. This suggests that the more participants perceived a collaborative alliance with the chatbot, the more they benefited. These results support earlier evidence in human coaching, where task and goal agreement predicted outcomes. The hypothesis that AI-based coaching appears capable of fostering clients' self-regulation, but not their self-access, should be examined in more detail. Further research is needed to identify possible mechanisms that could explain this assumption.

4.3 Conclusion

Empirical research on AI-based coaching is still in its early stages. A recent review identified 16 peer-reviewed studies, with only three using RCT—the gold standard for evaluating coaching effects (Passmore et al., 2025). While findings on AI-based coaching are mixed, studies suggest that coachees benefit from low inhibition and a willingness to share personal thoughts. AI-based coaching can support goal attainment and self-regulation, but may lack the emotional depth needed to foster self-access, which is key for deeper growth. Understanding coaching through the theoretical framework of PSI theory helps explain how and why certain coaching processes—particularly those involving self-regulation and self-access—are effective. In summary, we need more and strong empirical research using RCT to test the effectiveness of AI-based coaching as well as the mechanisms underlying its effects.

References

Baumann, N., & Kuhl, J. (2021). PSI theory in action: The assessment of self-competences as an aid in counseling and therapy. In J. F. Rauthmann (Ed.), *Handbook of personality dynamics and processes* (1st ed.). Elsevier.

Behrendt, P., Mühlberger, C., Göritz, A. S., & Jonas, E. (2021). Relationship, purpose, and change—An integrative model of coach behavior. *Consulting Psychology Journal: Practice and Research, 73*(2), 103–121.

Bickmore, T., Gruber, A., & Picard, R. (2005). Establishing the computer–patient working alliance in automated health behavior change interventions. *Patient Education and Counseling, 59*, 21–30.

Bruning, F., & Boak, G. (2025). Artificial intelligence coach bots: Coaches' perceptions of potential future impacts on professional coaching, a qualitative study. *Journal of Work-Applied Management*.

Burt, D., & Talati, Z. (2017). The unsolved value of executive coaching: A meta-analysis of outcomes using randomised control trial studies. *International Journal of Evidence Based Coaching and Mentoring, 15*(2), 17–24.

De Haan, E., & Nilsson, V. O. (2023). What can we know about the effectiveness of coaching? A meta-analysis based only on randomized controlled trials. *Academy of Management Learning & Education, 22*, 641–661.

De Meuse, K. P., Dai, G., & Lee, R. J. (2009). Evaluating the effectiveness of executive coaching: Beyond ROI? *Coaching, 2*(2), 117–134.

Diller, S. J., Mühlberger, C., Löhlau, N., & Jonas, E. (2021). How to show empathy as a coach: The effects of coaches' imagine-self versus imagine-other empathy on the client's self-change and coaching outcome. *Current Psychology*, 1–19.

Ellis-Brush, K. (2021). Augmenting coaching practice through digital methods. *International Journal of Evidence Based Coaching & Mentoring, 15.*

Engel, A. M., & Kuhl, J. (2022). Affective change for action control and self-growth in coaching. In S. Greif, H. Möller, W. Scholl, J. Passmore, & F. Müller (Eds.), *International handbook of evidenced based coaching: Theory, research and practice* (pp. 27–38). Springer.

Gessnitzer, S., & Kauffeld, S. (2015). The working alliance in coaching: Why behavior is the key to success. *Journal of Applied Behavior Science, 51*(2), 177–197.

Gopalan, R. (2022). *AI is changing the coaching landscape*. Simply Coach Newsletter. https://www.linkedin.com/pulse/ai-changing-coaching-landscape-heres-how-prepare-simplycoach/

Grant, A. M. (2012). An integrated model of goal-focused coaching: An evidence-based framework for teaching and practice. *International Coaching Psychology Review, 7*, 146–165.

Gratch, J., Lucas, G. M., King, A. A., & Morency, L. P. (2014). It's only a computer: The impact of human-agent interaction in clinical interviews. In *Proceedings of the 2014 international conference on autonomous agents and multi-agent systems* (pp. 85–92).

Greif, S. (2022). Motivation, volition, and implementation in coaching. In *International handbook of evidence-based coaching* (pp. 649–664). Springer.

Greif, S., & Jonas, E. (2021). Evaluation von Coaching-Prozessen und-Ergebnissen [Evaluation of coaching-process and results]. *Handbuch Coaching, 1*, 347–374.

Jonas, E., McGregor, I., Klackl, J., Agroskin, D., Fritsche, I., Holbrook, C., & Quirin, M. (2014). Threat and defense: From anxiety to approach. In J. M. Olson & M. P. Zanna (Eds.), *Advances in experimental social psychology* (pp. 219–286). Academic Press.

Jones, R. J., Woods, S. A., & Guillaume, Y. R. F. (2016). The effectiveness of workplace coaching: A meta-analysis of learning and performance outcomes from coaching. *Journal of Occupational and Organizational Psychology, 89*, 249–277.

Kanatouri, S. (2021). Digitales coaching. *Handbuch Coaching, 4*, 131–162.

Kang, S.-H., & Gratch, J. (2011). People like virtual counselors that highly-disclose about themselves. *Annual Review of Cybertherapy and Telemedicine, 167*(143–148).

Kuhl, J. (2001). *Motivation und Persönlichkeit. Interaktionen psychischer Systeme*. Hogrefe.

Lee, Y. C., Yamashita, N., Huang, Y., & Fu, W. (2020). "I Hear You, I Feel You": Encouraging deep self-disclosure through a chatbot. In *Proceedings of the 2020 CHI conference on human factors in computing systems* (pp. 1–12). ACM.

Lucas, G. M., Gratch, J., King, A., & Morency, L. P. (2014). It's only a computer: Virtual humans increase willingness to disclose. *Computers in Human Behavior, 37*, 94–100.

Mai, V., Bauer, A., Deggelmann, C., Neef, C., & Richert, A. (2022). AI-based coaching: Impact of a chatbot's disclosure behavior on the working alliance and acceptance. In *International Conference on Human-Computer Interaction* (pp. 391–406). Springer Nature Switzerland.

Mühlberger, C., Zerle, G., Möller, J., Diller, S. J., Greif, N., Kinder, N., & Jonas, E. (2024a). Zooming in on the self in workplace coaching: Self-regulation and its connection to coaching success. *Journal of Occupational and Organizational Psychology*.

Mühlberger, C., Behrendt, P., Greif, S., Diller, S., & Jonas, E. (2024b). *Guide, support, and activate resources – How relationship-oriented coach behavior fosters coaching success via self-development*.

Nicolau, A., Candel, O. S., Constantin, T., & Kleingeld, A. (2023). The effects of executive coaching on behaviors, attitudes, and personal characteristics: A meta-analysis of randomized control trial studies. *Frontiers in Psychology, 14*, 1089797.

Passmore, J., & Diller, S. J. (2024). Defining digital and AI coaching. In *The digital and AI coaches' handbook: The complete guide to the use of online, AI, and technology in coaching* (pp. 21–33).

Passmore, J., & Fillery-Travis, A. (2011). A critical review of executive coaching research: A decade of progress and what's to come. *Coaching: An International Journal of Theory, Research and Practice, 4*, 70–88.

Passmore, J., Olafsson, B., & Tee, D. (2025). A systematic literature review of artificial intelligence (AI) in coaching: Insights for future research and product development. *Journal of Work-Applied Management*.

Quirin, M., & Kuhl, J. (2018). The self-access form (SAF): Development and validation in the context of personality functioning and health. *Journal of Individual Differences, 39*, 1–17.

Rutschmann, R. (2023). *The new era of coaching with ChatGPT!* International Coaching Federtion. https://www.coachfederation.de/events/eventdetails.html?tx_news_pi1%5Bnews%5D=1432

Schiemann, S. J., Mühlberger, C., Schoorman, F. D., & Jonas, E. (2019). Trust me, I am a caring coach: The benefits of establishing trustworthiness during coaching by communicating benevolence. *Journal of Trust Research, 9*(2), 164–184.

Sonesh, S. C., Coultas, C. W., Lacerenza, C. N., Marlow, S. L., Benishek, L. E., & Salas, E. (2015). The power of coaching: A meta-analytic investigation. *Coaching, 8*(2), 73–95.

Tavis, A. (2024). *When everyone gets a coach: The AI-powered revolution in learning*. U.S. News & World Report. https://money.usnews.com/careers/articles/the-ai-powered-revolution-in-learning

Terblanche, N., Molyn, J., de Haan, E., & Nilsson, V. O. (2022). Comparing artificial intelligence and human coaching goal attainment efficacy. *PLoS One, 17*(6), e0270255.

Terblanche, N. H., van Heerden, M., & Hunt, R. (2024). The influence of an artificial intelligence chatbot coach assistant on the human coach-client working alliance. *Coaching: An International Journal of Theory, Research and Practice*, 1–18.

Terblanche, N. H. D., & Tau, T. (2025). Exploring the use of a goal-attainment, artificial intelligence (AI) chatbot coach to support first-time graduate employees. *Industry and Higher Education, 39*(3), 279–290.

Theeboom, T., Beersma, B., & van Vianen, A. E. M. (2014). Does coaching work? A meta-analysis on the effects of coaching on individual level outcomes in an organizational context. *Journal of Positive Psychology, 9*(1), 1–18.

Wang, Q., Lai, Y. L., Xu, X., & McDowall, A. (2022). The effectiveness of workplace coaching: A meta-analysis of contemporary psychologically informed coaching approaches. *Journal of Work-Applied Management, 14*(1), 77–101.

Wasylyshyn, K. M. (2019). The trusted leadership advisor: Defined, unpacked, encouraged. *Consulting Psychology Journal, 71*(1), 1–15.

Chapter 5
Digital Mental Health Coaching: Developing an LLM-Based Chatbot Application

Jan Juchli and Marcel Schär-Gmelch

Abstract This chapter presents the development, theoretical background, and application of "ephoria," a chatbot-based mental health coaching app using a solution-focused approach. Initial research results on the effect of the app will also be presented. The app's main objectives are to provide easy access to psychological support, reduce the risk of developing mental health issues and lower future healthcare costs, and explore the potential of AI in counseling and coaching from a scientific perspective. Powered by large language models and adaptive systems, the chatbot blends scripted and dynamic interactions. Users access tools like breathing exercises, gratitude journals, and mood tracking through an automatic needs detection system. While ephoria promotes well-being and self-reflection, it is not a replacement for psychotherapy and does not diagnose or treat mental illnesses. Instead, it follows a coaching-based approach aimed at fostering well-being, self-reflection, and problem-solving, but it does not diagnose or treat mental health conditions. This distinction ensures that users receive the right kind of guidance and are aware of the limitations of AI-driven interventions.

Keywords Coaching · AI-based coaching · Solution-focused digital mental health coaching · Large language model coaching chatbot · Psychological wellbeing · Ethics in AI coaching · Solution-focused chatbot · Solution-focused large language model

5.1 Introduction

The prevalence of mental health disorders is rising (Bundesamt für Gesundheit [BAG], 2024; World Health Organization [WHO], 2022). At the same time, there are very few low-threshold, preventive support services available. As a result,

J. Juchli (✉) · M. Schär-Gmelch
Institute of Mental Health (IMH), ZHAW Zurich University of Applied Sciences, Zürich, Switzerland
e-mail: jan.juchli@zhaw.ch; marcel.schaergmelch@zhaw.ch

R. Wegener et al. (eds.), *Coaching in the Age of AI*, SpringerBriefs in Psychology, https://doi.org/10.1007/978-3-032-23332-5_5

existing issues tend to worsen and become chronic, ultimately resulting in more mental health disorders, work-related problems and absences, and increased societal costs over time (BAG, 2025; WHO, 2022). Yet many psychological and occupational stressors could be mitigated—or even prevented—through early, low-threshold interventions. These might help individuals identify the stressors affecting them and develop functional coping strategies. This type of intervention has been described in the literature under the term "health coaching" (Todorova, 2022; Wolever et al., 2013). However, access to such support remains limited. Barriers include a lack of financial resources, fear of social stigma, or the general unavailability of appropriate services.

Against this backdrop, the idea emerged to develop a digital, low-threshold application using a Large Language Model (LLM) that could offer supportive guidance to individuals: the app "ephoria." The goal was to bridge existing gaps in care and provide an additional access point to mental health resources. At the same time, the development and evaluation of the app created an opportunity to explore the potential and limitations of AI-supported guidance—and to gain a deeper understanding of the differences between digital and human support.

This chapter begins with a brief theoretical background to the topic (Sect. 5.2), which serves as the foundation for presenting the app's content design (Sect. 5.3). This is followed by a discussion of the ethical and practical considerations surrounding the app (Sect. 5.4). Subsequently, initial empirical findings are explored (Sect. 5.5). The chapter concludes with a summary of key insights, a critical reflection, and an outlook on future developments (Sect. 5.6).

5.2 Theoretical Background

5.2.1 *Mental Health Coaching*

"Health coaching supports people's efforts to change health-related behaviors, prevent illness, and deal with symptoms and challenges of illness" (Todorova, 2022). Mental health coaching can thus be understood as a professional form of support aimed at strengthening psychological well-being and personal resilience. In contrast to psychotherapy, which focuses on the diagnosis and treatment of mental disorders, mental health coaching helps individuals manage stress, activate resources, and navigate personal or professional challenges. It emphasizes solution-oriented strategies, self-reflection, and behavior change to promote overall well-being.

5.2.2 *Solution-Focused Approach and Its Principles*

One approach that aligns well with the goals of coaching is the solution-focused approach. There are several reasons for this: first, it is a widely used method; second, it lends itself well to operationalization; third, it is consistently resource-oriented; and fourth, it is designed as a general problem-solving model—making it applicable across a wide range of content areas. Finally, the approach has a solid empirical foundation (Jerome et al., 2023). The solution-focused approach was developed in the 1980s by Steve de Shazer and Insoo Kim Berg (e.g., De Shazer, 1988). Inspired by systemic and constructivist traditions, they focused on what facilitates change in conversations and from this, developed a pragmatic form of intervention. The focus lies not on the problem, but on the solution. The method employs concrete, future-oriented questions to support the creation of a compelling and achievable goal. Scaling questions help make progress visible, and small, realistic action steps strengthen the sense of control and changeability.

Solution-focused approaches are successfully used in a wide variety of contexts—from outpatient psychotherapy to psychosocial counseling, coaching, education, leadership, and organizational development (O'Connell et al., 2013). It is ideal for those seeking quick, concrete change in limited time settings. Due to its structured and goal-oriented nature, the solution-focused approach offers an ideal theoretical foundation for the development of a coaching app supported by artificial intelligence.

5.2.3 *The Role of AI in Mental Health Coaching*

The foundation of today's AI systems lies in Large Language Models (LLMs). They are neural networks with attention mechanisms and are trained on extensive text corpora to recognize linguistic patterns and generate meaningful responses. These models have made tremendous progress in recent years, opening new possibilities for the implementation of coaching approaches. LLMs can not only respond reactively to user input but can also conduct structured, topic-driven conversations and steer targeted interventions in mental health coaching adaptively. We have leveraged these recent capabilities to combine the advantages of LLMs with evidence-based coaching strategies in our app.

5.3 The ephoria App: Features and Architecture

The following section presents the core features and structural design of the app "ephoria" (Ephoria, 2025), to illustrate how the conceptual considerations have been translated into practical implementation. The app's user interface is designed to support both guided, structured interventions and flexible, self-directed use. The platform offers three main modes of interaction:

- a dynamic chat and interaction interface (see Sect. 5.3.1),
- a menu-based content library for direct access to exercises (see Sect. 5.3.2), and
- a cockpit that functions as the home screen and central notification hub, where users receive suggestions for current tasks or reminders of important steps (see Sect. 5.3.3).

A seamless and dynamic transition between all elements of the app—notifications, exercises, and both structured and open chat—is possible. The following sections will present each feature in detail.

5.3.1 *The Interactive Chatbot Interface*

In the chat, you can engage with a digital mentor of your choice—through text or voice—for personalized guidance and conversation in multiple languages, including English, German, French, Italian, and simplified language.[1] The mentors differ in their communication styles (Fig. 5.1).

The app offers two types of interactive conversations: an open, unstructured AI-guided chat and structured guidance through the Quest program, based on the phases of the solution-focused approach. Both formats are interconnected.

5.3.1.1 The Quest: A Structured Solution-Focused Dialog

A "Quest" is a clearly defined, goal-oriented process that supports users in working step by step on a specific concern or desired change. Based on the principles of the solution-focused approach, this feature is designed to enable a resource-oriented form of guidance. The conversation structure helps clarify goals, explore possible solutions, and support users in building small, achievable steps toward their desired goal. A Quest is either initiated by the user or suggested by the chatbot when relevant cues emerge during a conversation. The course of a Quest follows a clear, sequential structure consisting of 12 phases:

1. Problem description
2. Goal clarification
3. Scaling
4. Resources
5. Past solutions
6. Exceptions
7. Fictional solutions

[1] Real-time conversations with a live-appearing digital figure are currently in development.

a

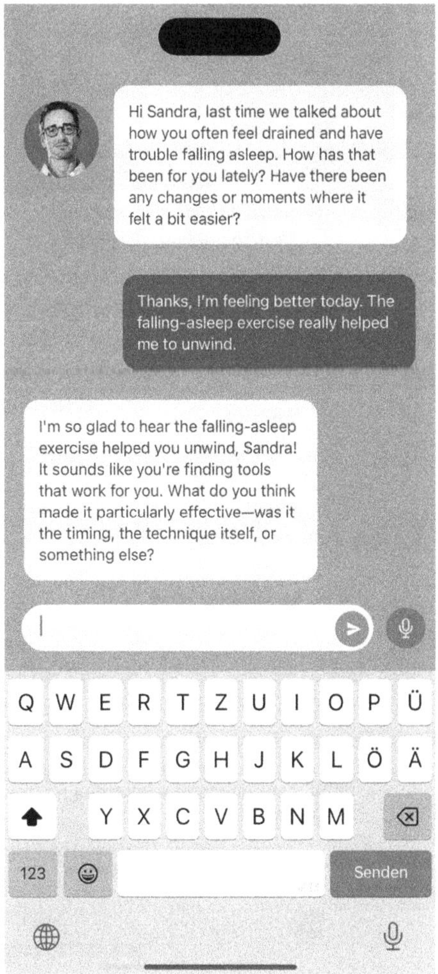

Fig. 5.1 Screenshots of the chatbot interface (**a**) and parts of the cockpit (**b**, in dark mode)

8. Universal solutions
9. First steps
10. Obstacles
11. Start
12. Evaluation

At appropriate points, the chatbot suggests pauses to allow time for real-life implementation of tasks. Completed responses—such as scaling values, formulated goals, or identified resources—are saved and referenced again in later phases.

5.3.4 Continuous Tracking

A fourth function of the app is the regular, voluntary assessment of the user's health status. The data is used exclusively to personalize the AI-assisted support. An initial assessment is aimed at defining the goals and focus of the support and influences the prioritization of recommended content on the homepage. If a person reports high levels of stress or sleep problems, the app will prioritize relevant exercises, such as breathing techniques or emotion tracking, as "daily goals." These suggestions appear both on the cockpit and contextually within the chat, such as when the bot detects stress indicators in the user's statements. The combination of self-reported symptoms and AI-driven dialogue analysis allows for finely-tuned support that remains committed to the principle of autonomy and self-determination.

5.4 Ethical and Practical Considerations of AI-Driven Coaching and Other Challenges

The integration and connection of artificial intelligence and mental health coaching bring a range of ethical and practical challenges that need to be considered both in the design and in the application (Diller, 2024). Unlike human coaches, an AI system cannot build emotional reciprocity and (yet) cannot interpret non-verbal cues. Above all, it cannot take responsibility for the consequences of its interventions. These limitations have far-reaching implications for the trust of users, their safety, and the responsibility we, as developers of the app, bear.

5.4.1 Transparency and User Autonomy

Transparency and autonomy are core ethical principles in the development of ephoria. Users are clearly informed that they are interacting with an AI system and that the app is not a substitute for professional mental health care—reinforced by a mandatory confirmation at first use. The app promotes self-reflection and personal responsibility, from setting goals to taking action. Unlike some AI platforms that can lead users into endless advisory loops, ephoria encourages regular breaks. Sessions are intentionally brief—about 10 min in open use and 30 min in the structured Quest program—after which users are prompted to act in the real world and reflect on the results. In line with the solution-focused approach: "Do something. If it works, do more of it. If not, try something else."

The chatbot follows a clearly defined, hardcoded coaching protocol based on the solution-focused method. This ensures it stays within its supportive, non-diagnostic role—using tools like scaling questions, goal setting, and resource activation.

5.4.2 Data Security and Privacy Considerations

The processing and storage of all user data is done in a way that would not allow inferences about the identity of the users and takes place exclusively on certified servers located in Switzerland. The app consciously avoids the collection of sensitive data such as addresses, or insurance numbers, except for a freely chosen name for personalized address in the chat. When using the integrated LLM, certain content generated during communication may leave Switzerland. However, this only concerns anonymized text inputs that cannot be traced back to a specific person or device. According to the contractual terms with the API provider, this data is not used for training or further development purposes of the model. Additionally, all communication between the end device, the server, and the LLM is secured through modern encryption methods. This ensures that, even in the event of an attack on external systems, no tracking or re-identification is possible. The data protection concept adheres to the applicable provisions of the Swiss Data Protection Act (FADP/DSG) and the European standards of the General Data Protection Regulation (GDPR).

5.4.3 Addressing Suicidal Ideation: Ethical and Technical Safeguards

The use of an LLM in the mental health field requires special caution when dealing with potentially acute crisis situations. Suicidal statements or suggestions pose an ethically sensitive challenge, which the system addresses with clearly defined safety mechanisms. If a potentially suicidal statement is recognized during a dialogue, an emergency protocol is triggered: the ongoing exercise or current dialogue flow is immediately interrupted, and the user receives a clearly structured overview with professional support services. This includes emergency numbers for crisis intervention services or telephone counseling offers. A button allows for a direct call to the relevant service. It relies on an advanced filtering mechanism that also captures implicit hints of suicidal thoughts (e.g. "sleeping forever sounds nice right now"). At the same time, no content evaluation or diagnostic classification is made by the language model—instead, responsibility is consistently delegated to human professionals. This addresses both the ethical obligation to protect vulnerable individuals and the technical limitations of an AI-supported system.

5.4.4 Challenges in Development

In addition to the classic challenges in app development, managing dynamic content and the limited predictability of the language model proved to be a central difficulty.

Unlike hardcoded functions, LLMs do not behave deterministically: their outputs vary even with identical prompts depending on the context, internal adjustments of the model, and the specific time of the query (Ouyang et al., 2025). While this inherent flexibility is advantageous for many applications, it posed a particular challenge in the context of structured coaching, as consistency, traceability, and methodological integrity are key quality criteria. Consequently, additional control mechanisms, stable prompt structures, and hybrid approaches had to be developed, where critical content is either controlled through well-defined processes or the language model is used only in a supporting role. This balance between flexibility and control was a central focus in the technical and content development of the application.

5.5 User Feedback and Outcomes

A central element in the evaluation and development of digital applications is the feedback from users as well as the systematic collection of their experiences and outcomes.

5.5.1 Study 1

During an earlier development phase of the app, the health questionnaires (PHQ-9) of 18 users were analyzed. They had an average score of $M = 11.72$, which indicates moderate symptom severity. After an average of 19 days, there was a significant reduction in depressive symptoms to $M = 9.33$ ($p = 0.016$). The decrease of 2.39 points is statistically significant and, according to Cohen's $d = 0.633$ and Hedges' $g = 0.604$, indicates a medium effect. Relative to other mental health apps assessed in meta-analyses, these effect sizes are notably strong (Linardon et al., 2024).

5.5.2 Study 2

In a larger study, the effect of the app on mental health (GHQ-12) was investigated. Data from 159 individuals could be analyzed in a pre-post design (without a control group) over 3 months. A significant improvement in mental health from the first to the second measurement point was observed (−1.23 points; $t(159) = 3.41, p < 0.001$). This corresponds to a standardized effect size (Cohen's d) of 0.27 and is comparable to other studies (Linardon et al., 2024).

Detailed analyses revealed two noteworthy findings: First, individuals experiencing psychological distress (with an initial GHQ score of 12 or higher; see also Comotti et al., 2023) benefited significantly more from the app (−2.13 points;

$t(132) = -5.04$, $p < 0.001$, Cohen's $d = 0.45$). Second, the effect of the app correlated with usage intensity. Users who completed more than 10 Quest chapters improved their GHQ score by an average of 3.08 points in the pre-post assessment. In contrast, users who did not complete any Quests (but only used the chat or other features) showed no relevant change (−0.23 points). This is an important finding, as it demonstrates that the app offers more than just a typical, unspecific chatbot experience.

User retention reflects how many users remain active after 30 days. For the ephoria app, this rate is 20.74%. Such a 30-day retention rate is considered exceptional. The median 30-day user retention for other mental health apps is 3.3% (Baumel et al., 2019).

5.6 Conclusion

5.6.1 Summary of Key Findings

This chapter demonstrates how current developments in artificial intelligence—particularly using LLMs—can be integrated into digital mental health coaching. Studies have shown that customers achieve their goals more easily with the support of a chatbot (Terblanche et al., 2022). The ephoria app was developed to help users transform challenges into achievable goals. Our study results show that the app improves overall well-being by providing personalized support that breaks goals down into smaller steps. This helps boost confidence, maintain motivation, and promote the long-term implementation of change.

The development of the system was shaped by challenges in controlling the LLM and the dynamics of its output but was overcome through a mix of hardcoded content and adaptive processing.

5.6.2 Limitations and Differences Compared to Live Coaching

There are some important limitations of a chatbot. Unlike a human coach, a chatbot can't easily recognize or respond to resistance. When users feel misunderstood or reject a task, they may skip it—or stop using the app entirely—making it easier to avoid challenging but important reflection and change. A key function of coaching and counseling is providing a safe space, even in extraordinary situations where central goals and values of the client may be radically questioned. In such cases, the focus cannot be on quick solutions; rather, it requires a space where slower thinking and emotional processes can be encouraged. These processes are characterized by the inability to clearly define goals and desired outcomes, and the client is accompanied in their helplessness and hopelessness without attempts to immediately resolve or dismiss these feelings. Creating and holding this open, non-goal-oriented space and guiding clients through deep (emotional) developments is something even the best AI systems cannot achieve. A chatbot, for instance, is unable to experience genuine empathy or personal concern. It also lacks the wisdom and sensitivity required to handle unclear, contradictory, or painful situations.

Of course, the app also has advantages that a real coach cannot offer. Real coaches are never available 24/7, while the app is always accessible. Further advantages are of course the much lower costs and consistency over time. Additionally, the app offers a form of low-threshold support by allowing users to reflect on and engage in short process steps that do not require the full scope of a live coaching session. It is particularly suited for clearly defined problem areas where relatively simple solution steps are possible.

5.6.3 Final Thoughts and Outlook

The integration of artificial intelligence, particularly LLMs, into mental health coaching opens new possibilities for psychological support, particularly in terms of accessibility, personalization, and scalability (Ong et al., 2024). At the same time, the use of LLMs also raises new questions—such as those concerning ethical guidelines. This chapter demonstrates that a responsible and methodologically sound use of LLM-based systems is possible when technical innovations are combined with psychological expertise, careful system architecture, and clear protective mechanisms. The approach of making traditional interventions, such as solution-focused coaching, accessible through a dialogical, adaptive system represents a concrete step toward future-proof care—without claiming to fully replace human support.

Future developments should focus on scientifically verifying the effectiveness of such systems, developing interfaces for regular healthcare provision, and defining regulatory standards for AI-powered coaching offerings in the healthcare sector. In this perspective, there is great potential—both for individual users and for a healthcare system that will increasingly rely on prevention, early detection, and digital support.

Acknowledgment Thanks to Gregor Waller and Simon Ducombe for their great work on the app.

References

Baumel, A., Muench, F., Edan, S., & Kane, J. M. (2019). Objective user engagement with mental health apps: Systematic search and panel-based usage analysis. *Journal of Medical Internet Research, 21*(9), e14567. https://doi.org/10.2196/14567

Bundesamt für Gesundheit. (2024). *Psychische Erkrankungen und Gesundheit.* https://www.bag.admin.ch/de/psychische-erkrankungen-und-gesundheit

Bundesamt für Gesundheit. (2025). *Psychiatrische Versorgung*. https://www.bag.admin.ch/de/psychische-gesundheit-und-psychiatrische-versorgung
Comotti, A., Fattori, A., Greselin, F., Bordini, L., Brambilla, P., & Bonzini, M. (2023). Psychometric evaluation of GHQ-12 as a screening tool for psychological impairment of healthcare workers facing COVID-19 pandemic. *La Medicina del Lavoro, 114*(1), e2023009. https://doi.org/10.23749/mdl.v114i1.13918
De Shazer, S. (1988). *Clues: Investigating solutions in brief therapy*. W. W. Norton & Company.
De Shazer, S., Dolan, Y., Korman, H., Trepper, T., McCollum, E., & Berg, I. K. (2021). *More than miracles: The state of the art of solution-focused brief therapy* (2nd ed.). Routledge.
Diller, S. J. (2024). Ethics in digital and AI coaching. *Human Resource Development International, 27*(4), 584–596. https://doi.org/10.1080/13678868.2024.2315928
Ephoria. (2025). *Dein mental health coach in der Hosentasche*. https://ephoria.ch/de/
Jerome, L., McNamee, P., Abdel-Halim, N., Elliot, K., & Woods, J. (2023). Solution-focused approaches in adult mental health research: A conceptual literature review and narrative synthesis. *Frontiers in Psychiatry, 14*, 1068006. https://doi.org/10.3389/fpsyt.2023.1068006
Linardon, J., Torous, J., Firth, J., Cuijpers, P., Messer, M., & Fuller-Tyszkiewicz, M. (2024). Current evidence on the efficacy of mental health smartphone apps for symptoms of depression and anxiety: A meta-analysis of 176 randomized controlled trials. *World Psychiatry, 23*(1), 139–149. https://doi.org/10.1002/wps.21183
O'Connell, B., Palmer, S., & Williams, H. (2013). *Solution focused coaching in practice*. Routledge.
Ong, Q. C., Ang, C., Chee, D. Z. Y., Lawate, A., Sundram, F., Dalakoti, M., Pasalic, L., To, D., Fox, T. E., Bojic, I., & Car, J. (2024). Advancing health coaching: A comparative study of large language model and health coaches. *Artificial Intelligence in Medicine, 157*, 103004. https://doi.org/10.1016/j.artmed.2024.103004
Ouyang, S., Zhang, J. M., Harman, M., & Wang, M. (2025). An empirical study of the non-determinism of ChatGPT in code generation. *ACM Transactions on Software Engineering and Methodology, 34*(2), 42. https://doi.org/10.1145/3697010
Terblanche, N., Molyn, J., De Haan, E., & Nilsson, V. O. (2022). Coaching at scale: Investigating the efficacy of artificial intelligence coaching. *International Journal of Evidence Based Coaching & Mentoring, 20*(2), 20–31. https://doi.org/10.24384/5cgf-ab69
Todorova, I. (2022). Health coaching research. In S. Greif, H. Möller, W. Scholl, J. Passmore, & F. Müller (Eds.), *International handbook of evidence-based coaching: Theory, research and practice* (pp. 429–445). Springer Nature Switzerland AG. https://doi.org/10.1007/978-3-030-81938-5_35
Wolever, R. Q., Simmons, L. A., Sforzo, G. A., Dill, D., Kaye, M., Bechard, E. M., Southard, M. E., Kennedy, M., Vosloo, J., & Yang, N. (2013). A systematic review of the literature on health and wellness coaching: Defining a key behavioral intervention in healthcare. *Global Advances in Health and Medicine, 2*(4), 38–57. https://doi.org/10.7453/gahmj.2013.042
World Health Organization. (2022). *World mental health report: Transforming mental health for all*. https://www.who.int/publications/i/item/9789240049338

Chapter 6
AI Coaching Chatbots: What We Know About How to Create Them, How Well They Work and What Coaches Think of Them

Nicky Terblanche

Abstract In our ongoing and inevitable quest to incorporate the rapidly evolving world of AI into coaching in a responsible manner, an important aspect is to understand how to create AI chatbot coaches that people want to use and that work. This new frontier in coaching begs many questions: can we simply replicate what human coaches do via AI? Or do AI chatbot coaches have hidden secrets that make it significantly different from human coaching? To answer this important question, it is necessary to do high-quality research to obtain empirical evidence, instead of relying on anecdotes. In this chapter, I will share insights from current research into the factors that influence users' adoption of AI chatbot coaching, as well as its influence on their efficacy. The answer is not as straightforward as we thought.

Keywords AI coaching · Artificial intelligence coaching · Artificial intelligence · Chatbots · Coaching · Working alliance · Goal attainment · Technology adoption · Human–AI interaction

6.1 Introduction

In many respects AI-based coaching is currently where human coaching found itself 20 years ago—in the Wild West. Back then, according to Sherman and Freas (2004), it was a free-for-all in terms of who called themselves executive coaches and how they went about their business with clients (executives), with none the wiser. The research guru at the time, the late Anthony Grant, determined that in 2003, there were only 131 peer-reviewed studies on coaching from 1937 to 2003. Only 57 of these were empirical, and of those, very few could be considered methodologically sound. Fast forward to 2025 and a Google Scholar search for executive/leadership/organisational coaching reveals thousands of peer-reviewed papers published in

N. Terblanche (✉)
Stellenbosch Business School, Cape Town, South Africa
e-mail: nickyt@sun.ac.za

R. Wegener et al. (eds.), *Coaching in the Age of AI*, SpringerBriefs in Psychology, https://doi.org/10.1007/978-3-032-23332-5_6

decent journals. There are, in fact, numerous meta-studies and systematic reviews that provide convincing proof that human coaching "works."

Where are we with AI-based coaching? Very much in the midst of a new Wild West. As of the time of this writing, there are fewer than five systemic reviews on AI-based coaching, each containing fewer than 20 papers, most of them written by the same few authors (see Plotkina & Sri Ramalu, 2024; Passmore et al., 2025). What then is known about AI-based coaching at this stage, not anecdotally or from commercial vendors, but from what we know through empirical research? Scanning through the published papers I derive three main themes that provide some insight into the current thinking and understanding around AI-based coaching: (i) AI coach design considerations; (ii) AI coach efficacy; (iii) Coach and client attitudes toward AI coaches.

In this chapter, when I refer to AI-based coaching (referred to as "AI Coaching" from here on in this text), it means the use of chatbots to simulate human coaching. There are of course other applications of AI in coaching as illustrated in Fig. 6.1.

The first application (Emulate human coaches) is what this chapter is about. This is the use of AI to fully or partially replace human coaches via AI entities such as chatbots. The second application refers to the use of AI to assist a human coach before, during, and after human-led coaching. This assistance could take many forms such as automated on-boarding, check-ins in between human coaching sessions by an AI coaching chatbot, or the use of reminders and chatbots to continue the learning after the coaching ends. Coaches can also use AI to provide summaries of their sessions to clients. The third application is using AI to educate coaches. This can be done via AI coach simulators and supervisors that help coaches practice their coaching skills and provide feedback by analysing coaching transcripts. The last

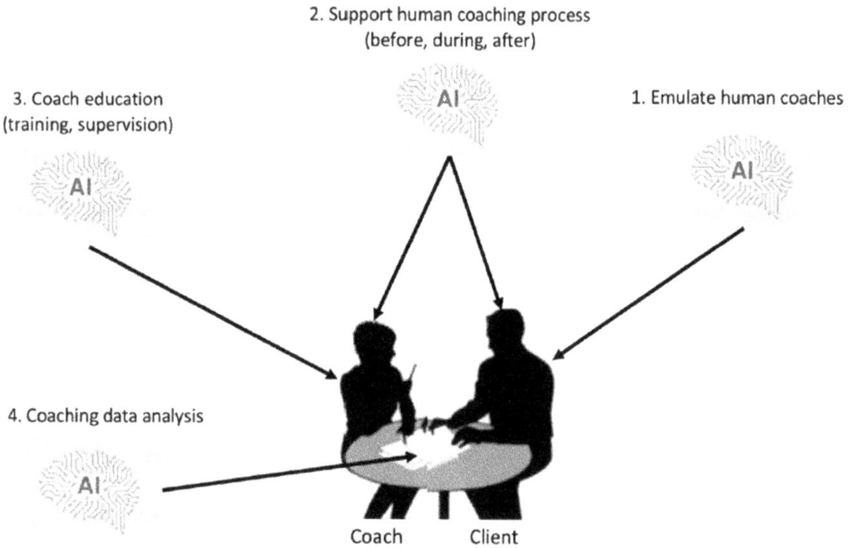

Fig. 6.1 Main applications of artificial intelligence (AI) in organisational coaching

application is using AI to analyse and search for patterns in human coaching sessions.

The purpose of this chapter is to disseminate the current research on AI coaching (the first application in Fig. 6.1) to lay a foundation for understanding what we currently know and to point to future areas of research.

6.2 AI Coach Design Considerations

One of the first attempts to put a stake in the ground on how to create AI coaches is my Designing AI Coach (DAIC) framework (Terblanche, 2020). This framework proposes a design philosophy that combines what we know is necessary for successful human coaching (strong relationships), with what is known to be good chatbot design principles. The result was a framework that contains eight human coaching attributes mapped to chatbot principles as shown in Fig. 6.2. This framework has been used by a number of AI coach creators and seems to be fairly robust, even though it was created before the arrival of generative.

In terms of design considerations, the notion of interaction modalities has received some interest in research. Researchers have investigated AI coaching chatbot aspects like talking or texting (Terblanche et al., 2023a); clicking or writing (Mai et al., 2022); scripted or generative AI (Terblanche, 2024); images and text or text only (Terblanche & Prywes, 2025). Some of the highlights and surprises of

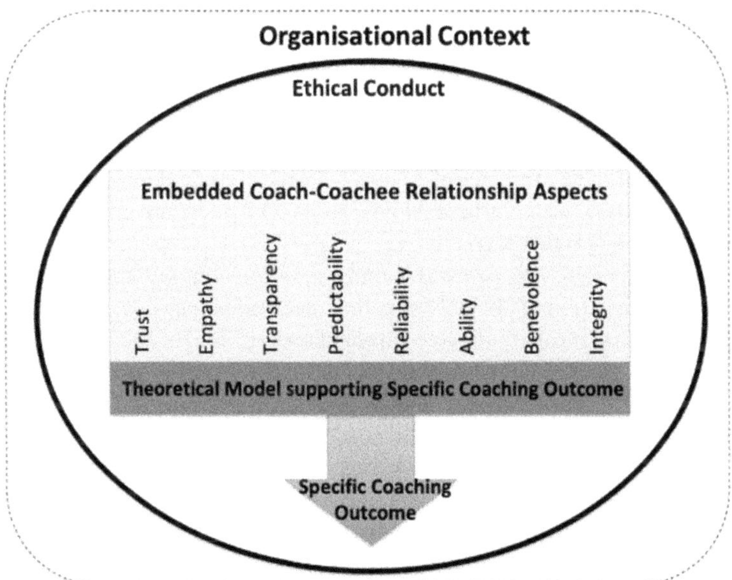

Fig. 6.2 The designing AI coach (DAIC) framework

these studies include the finding that introverts prefer to talk to an AI coach rather than typing (extroverts had no preference). People found click-based coaching chatbots to be easier to use; however, writing-based bots had a higher working alliance bond with the user. Generative AI-based bots outperformed old-school scripted bots in terms of how eager users were to use these bots, and the strengths of the working alliance between bot and user. However, interestingly, for goal attainment there was no difference between the scripted and generative AI-based coaching chatbots, which points to the fact that for highly structured coaching conversations like goal setting and tracking, using scripts instead of generative AI should be considered. This lowers the risks associated with generative AI such as hallucinations and data concerns. Finally, in terms of using images interspersed with text in coaching chatbots, it was found that it comes down to personal preferences. People who are pedantic about grammar find text-only bots less fun to use, while people with lower levels of imagination who find images interfere with their chatbot experience and prefer the text-only chatbot.

The conclusion I draw from these studies is that there are many aspects to consider when designing AI chatbot coaches and that people's personal preferences differ. This introduces the interesting concept of human and AI coach matching. Much has been written about human client and human-coach matching with some contradicting findings. For AI coaching we have a serious advantage—the AI coach can adapt itself and "shape-shift" to comply with what the client requires. For example, if the AI coach determines that a user is more introverted, it could change its interaction modality from text to voice. In fact, it could simply ask the user what it prefers and change into that mode. This is, of course, far more difficult for human coaches to do and points to the unique promise and potential of AI coaching.

6.3 AI Coaching Efficacy

Having reviewed some examples of AI coach design considerations, the next important question is, how well do these AI coaches work? There are unfortunately very few efficacy studies at this stage.

The most important one so far is a replication, randomised-controlled trial we conducted over a period of about 2 years that involved human coaching, AI chatbot coaching and two control groups (see Terblanche et al., 2022a, 2022b). The first part of this research involved a 10-month intervention where 94 people received six coaching sessions 1 month apart, with a 4-month waiting period at the end. The control group of 85 people received no coaching. The study measured goal attainment, resilience, psychological well-being, and perceived stress and the results revealed that the human coaching group showed improvements on all four measures compared to the control group. This study was repeated a year later with 75 people using a scripted AI coaching chatbot that was specifically programmed to do goal attainment, and a control group of 73 people who did not receive any coaching. The chatbot users had unlimited access to the AI coaching. The results showed that the chatbot group only improved their goal attainment, not the other three measures. This is not a surprise since the chatbot was specifically programmed for goal attainment. What was a surprise is when we compared the chatbot group's goal attainment to the human coaching group and found that they were comparable. This set the "cat lose among the pigeons" as it was the first-ever study to show the potential of AI coaching to rival human coaching in specific contexts.

There are other qualitative efficacy studies that found people responding positively to using a goal-attainment AI coaching chatbot. For example, Terblanche and Tau (2024) found that first-time graduate employees who used the chatbot for 4 weeks found that it was easy to use and that it helped to promote their autonomy and competence. In the Terblanche et al. (2023b) study, 11 final-year undergraduate students used the same chatbot for 12 weeks and reported that positive attitude and performance expectations played an important role in their chatbot engagement. Students perceived the AI coach as accessible, easy to use, intelligent and quick to respond. They also found the AI coach to pose minimal threat and would use it more if their friends did. In both cases, however, participants reported the need for more advanced conversation abilities of the chatbot to avoid a robotic interaction after several interactions. It must be pointed out that these studies were conducted before the availability of generative AI, which now adds a far more convincing conversational dimension.

More studies are underway to compare AI coaching to human coaching and AI coaching to control groups to try to understand for which people and in which circumstances AI coaching works best. Examples of these studies are investigating the ability of Cognitive-Behavioural AI coaches to promote resilience in middle managers and emotional intelligence in Generation Z employees. My hunch is that AI coaching will not work equally well for all people and in all situations. Our challenge is to understand where the AI coaching niche lies. Expect to be surprised as these studies are published.

6.4 Coach and Client Attitudes Towards AI Coaches

How do coaches and clients feel about AI coaching? The arrival of AI in the world of coaching has caused a major stir. Anecdotally from the conference and webinar talks I have done all over the world I get the sense that most coaches are cautiously optimistic (that could be sampling bias), but there are a significant number of coaches who have a strong negative reaction against AI coaching. One such example from the academic world is the opinion piece by Bachkirova and Kemp (2025) who state that "AI coaching" cannot be labelled coaching in the first place. A large-scale study involving 436 coaches from 50 different countries by Diller et al. (2024) investigated coaches' threat response when confronted with the notion of AI coaching. They found that coaches responded negatively to the idea of AI coaching showing a higher behavioural inhibition and lower behavioural activation. This leads to lower curiosity in and a more negative opinion of AI in coaching. The authors make a set of recommendations on how to remedy the situation, one being the increased knowledge and education about what AI is, how it works, and what its potential and limitations are. I wholeheartedly agree with this sentiment and I have seen profound shifts in coaches attending my talks after I explain some of these details. This is an area where the coaching bodies like ICF, EMCC, and others need to play a leading role.

In a qualitative study I was involved in, we investigated the influence of an artificial intelligence chatbot coach assistant on the human coach-client working alliance (Terblanche et al., 2024). Seven coaches and nine clients were exposed to an AI coaching chatbot assistant—a chatbot that checked in with clients between human coaching sessions. The findings show that coaches expressed concerns that the chatbot might negatively affect the coach–client relationship. In contrast, clients reported a more collaborative and psychologically safe experience—particularly when the chatbot was endorsed by their human coach. Both coaches and clients acknowledged the chatbot's value for tracking goals, enhancing accountability, and offering convenience. However, they emphasised that for the chatbot to be effective, it must be flexible, dependable, and display human-like qualities. The conclusion we drew from this study is the critical influence of the coach's attitude towards AI.

Based on these two studies, it becomes clear that clients value the potential of AI coaching and would engage with it more readily if human coaches endorse it; however, coaches are sceptical about AI. This is a slightly concerning situation that will hopefully change as human coaches come to terms with what is realistically possible with AI coaching.

Other studies have looked at the factors that influence user's decision to use AI coaches. One example is my study on technology adoption (Terblanche & Kidd, 2022). We asked 226 people to have a conversation with an AI coaching chatbot, after which they completed a technology adoption survey. The most important factors that contribute to their continued use of the AI coach were performance, social influence, and access to convenient technology platforms. We concluded that users place high value on the outcomes that the AI coach helps them achieve; it is important that people close to them also use it, and they consider convenience an important benefit. In contrast, they do not view the effort required or the potential risks of using the chatbot as significant concerns. This has important implications for the rollout of AI coaching in organisations. Making sure the AI coaching "works," appointing influencers or early adopters to promote the AI coach, and making sure you select the most appropriate user interaction platform (e.g. WhatsApp rather than a custom App) should be kept in mind.

6.5 What We Still Don't Know

We are making slow but steady progress in understanding what AI coaching is, how we should create it and where it would be most useful. There are many areas that need further investigation and this is a treasure trove for researchers in the field. Below I share a few suggestions on research areas.

In terms of AI coach design, an under-researched area is the optimal level of anthropomorphism (human likeness) of AI coaches. Do people prefer embodied AI coaching like avatars and robots rather than disembodied ones such as pure chatbots? And what qualities should these embodied AI coaches have? What role does AI coach gender, age, level of empathy and directiveness play in user adoption and coaching efficacy? The notion of directive versus non-directiveness in AI coaching is of particular interest. In "pure" human coaching we are taught that the coach should not provide answers but rather create a space through open questions for the client to find their own answers. Is this true for AI coaching? My suspicion based on anecdotal evidence is that users of AI coaches become impatient if they are asked an endless string of questions. This is perhaps because generative AI chatbots like ChatGPT have been designed to provide answers from the start and people have become used to this type of AI chatbot behaviour. I am currently busy with a research study where we are investigating people's preferences relative to directive versus non-directive AI coaching.

In terms of AI coach efficacy, we need more longitudinal studies that compare AI coaches to control groups and AI coaches to human coaches. These studies should focus on different settings and different audiences. My suspicion is that AI coaching is not for everyone, but that it could be highly effective for specific people. Unpublished data from a study we conducted recently show, for example, that the people who identify as females are far more likely to engage with AI coaches and consider them far more effective than males. In terms of age, younger people are less likely initially to engage with AI coaches than older people, but with more frequent use the gap disappears. Insights like these could help us design and deploy AI coaches more successfully.

Finally, one of the largest obstacles to wide-scale AI coach usage is initial adoption and continued use. How do we get people to keep engaging with their AI coach? Studies in this regard could look at ways to reward users, or the types of feedback they would value to continue engaging. AI is very powerful in providing summaries and extracting patterns in conversation data. The effect of these should be tested empirically.

6.6 Conclusion

In this chapter, I provided a brief overview of some of the research themes that have been studied in AI coaching. We are making progress in understanding what AI coaching is, how to design it, how well it works and what our attitudes are towards it. My hope is that more researchers will enter this field so that we can speed up the creation of empirical evidence that should drive our decisions around AI. Let's try to spend less time in the Wild West of AI coaching than we did in human coaching.

References

Bachkirova, T., & Kemp, R. (2025). 'AI coaching': Democratising coaching service or offering an ersatz? *Coaching: An International Journal of Theory, Research and Practice, 18*(1), 27–45. https://doi.org/10.1080/17521882.2024.2368598

Diller, S. J., Stenzel, L. C., & Passmore, J. (2024). The coach bots are coming: Exploring global coaches' attitudes and responses to the threat of AI coaching. *Human Resource Development International, 27*(4), 597–621. https://doi.org/10.1080/13678868.2024.2375934

Mai, V., Neef, C., & Richert, A. (2022). "Clicking vs. Writing"—The impact of a chatbot's interaction method on the working alliance in AI-based coaching. *Coaching | Theorie & Praxis, 8*, 15–31. https://doi.org/10.1365/s40896-021-00063-3

Passmore, J., Olafsson, B., & Tee, D. (2025). A systematic literature review of artificial intelligence (AI) in coaching: Insights for future research and product development, *Journal of Work – Applied Management. Pre-Publication*, https://doi.org/10.1108/JWAM-11-2024-0164

Plotkina, L., & Sri Ramalu, S. (2024). Unearthing AI coaching chatbots capabilities for professional coaching: a systematic literature review. *Journal of Management Development, 43*(6), 833–848. https://doi.org/10.1108/JMD-06-2024-0182

Sherman, S., & Freas, A. (2004). The wild west of executive coaching. *Harvard Business Review, 82*(11), 82.

Terblanche, N. (2020). A design framework to create artificial intelligence coaches. *International Journal of Evidence Based Coaching and Mentoring, 18*(2), 152–165. https://doi.org/10.24384/b7gs-3h05

Terblanche, N. H. (2024). Smooth talking: Generative versus scripted coaching chatbot adoption and efficacy comparison. *International Journal of Human–Computer Interaction, 41*(14), 9109–9122. https://doi.org/10.1080/10447318.2024.2423125

Terblanche, N., & Kidd, M. (2022). Adoption factors and moderating effects of age and gender that influence the intention to use a non-directive reflective coaching chatbot. *Sage Open, 12*(2). https://doi.org/10.1177/21582440221096136

Terblanche, N. H. D., & Prywes, J. (2025). An exploration of the role of visuals and users' imagery and verbal preferences on goal attainment and coaching chatbot adoption. *International Journal of Evidence Based Coaching and Mentoring*. https://doi.org/10.7916/53zd-8232

Terblanche, N. H. D., & Tau, T. (2024). Exploring the use of a goal-attainment, artificial intelligence (AI) chatbot coach to support first-time graduate employees. *Industry and Higher Education, 39*(3), 279–290. https://doi.org/10.1177/09504222241287090

Terblanche, N., Molyn, J., de Haan, E., & Nilsson, V. O. (2022a). Comparing artificial intelligence and human coaching goal attainment efficacy. *PLoS One, 17*(6), e0270255. https://doi.org/10.1371/journal.pone.0270255

Terblanche, N., Molyn, J., De Haan, E., & Nilsson, V. O. (2022b). Coaching at scale: Investigating the efficacy of artificial intelligence coaching. *International Journal of Evidence Based Coaching & Mentoring, 20*(2), 20–31. https://doi.org/10.24384/5cgf-ab69

Terblanche, N. H. D., Wallis, G. P., & Kidd, M. (2023a). Talk or text? the role of communication modalities in the adoption of a non-directive, goal-attainment coaching chatbot. *Interacting with Computers, 35*(4), 511–518.

Terblanche, N., Molyn, J., Williams, K., & Maritz, J. (2023b). Performance matters: Students' perceptions of artificial intelligence coach adoption factors. *Coaching: An International Journal of Theory, Research and Practice, 16*(1), 100–114. https://doi.org/10.1080/17521882.2022.2094278

Terblanche, N. H. D., van Heerden, M., & Hunt, R. (2024). The influence of an artificial intelligence chatbot coach assistant on the human coach-client working alliance. *Coaching: An International Journal of Theory, Research and Practice, 17*(2), 189–206. https://doi.org/10.1080/17521882.2024.2304792

Part III
AI Enhancing Human Coaching

Chapter 7
Leaning into the Digital World: Embracing Intelligent Opportunities in a Human-Centred Profession

Sam Isaacson

Abstract This chapter is designed to act as a catalyst to encourage coaches to increase in curiosity and experimentation with regard to what is possible using artificial intelligence (AI). By acknowledging that certain characteristics of a coaching interaction and relationship can be performed to a satisfactory—and in some cases enhanced—extent, we reflect on the perspectives a coach should hold towards AI, and identify opportunities in which AI could add value within a coaching engagement. We begin at a conceptual level by establishing that AI can expand our capacity as coaches by doing some of what we do but "better", enhance our competence by improving what we can already do, and extend our capability by making new opportunities possible. We conclude that there are opportunities for coaches who educate themselves and use AI in intelligent ways, and that we are exposing ourselves to risks by ignoring it. We consider what sort of attitudes towards AI is valid and helpful. We look at how our personal preferences towards the adoption of AI are informed by nature and nurture, and recognise that becoming more informed about what's possible is a positive step for all coaches. We investigate how attitudes towards AI gravitate towards the extremes, and notice how both risks and benefits have a tendency to be overstated or over-interpreted. We also explore some practical ideas around how coaches could embrace AI in their practice. This includes an overview of which aspects of a coach's practice AI could contribute towards, and deep dives into some practical uses. The chapter concludes with an encouragement to coaches to continue in being curious—intellectually and practically—to protect our professional future and serve clients better.

Keywords Artificial intelligence · Coaching · Chatbots · Anthropomorphism · Human–AI interaction · Technology adoption · AI coaching · Coaching efficacy · Ethical decision-making in AI · Digital coaching practice

S. Isaacson (✉)
Coachtech Ltd, London, UK
e-mail: sam@coachtech.uk

R. Wegener et al. (eds.), *Coaching in the Age of AI*, SpringerBriefs in Psychology, https://doi.org/10.1007/978-3-032-23332-5_7

7.1 Introduction

The coaching profession is a practice designed around humans interacting at its core, so spending time thinking about technology systems can feel unfamiliar for coaches, but it's critically important. Our clients are using, and thinking about, technology all the time, so being aware of it allows us to demonstrate the relevance of coaching in the way we speak and act. It also offers opportunities to bring clear benefits to our clients and wider systems, so the more we know and understand it the greater an impact we might be able to have.

Perhaps most importantly, however, we have an ethics-driven imperative to think about the topic of artificial intelligence (AI) as a coach. With so much attention on the commercial benefits presented by AI, it's no surprise that technologists and venture capitalists around the world are leaping on the bandwagon. The early 2000s saw many new entrants to the ill-defined world of coaching staking a claim on the practice without the right grounding (Sherman & Freas, 2004), and we are seeing an evolution of this as the commercial opportunities presented by AI make themselves clear. In fact, the potential scale offered by AI exacerbates this risk by making "AI coaching" (a term that is even more poorly defined than "coaching" was at the turn of the millennium) the most influential factor in a new Wild West of coaching (Terblanche, 2024) that some argue ought to not even bear the name (Bachkirova & Kemp, 2025).

The objective of this chapter is to increase our curiosity to experiment with AI in our own coaching practice, to become familiar with it. The benefits afforded by AI are much more tangible than other technologies that have made grand claims that turn out to be a thin veneer, but AI is not a panacea by any stretch of the imagination. Its dystopian ability to work semi-autonomously, at scale, and at an affordable price means that its downsides are amplified. First-hand experience of AI grounds our understanding of it in reality, rather than in overly evangelistic or catastrophised media narratives.

7.2 The Theory: How AI Can Help

At its heart, coaching could be argued as one of the most purely human professions in existence. It's possible to deliver coaching without technology being present at all. In fact, some of the most deeply powerful coaching moments come when all of the noise we're otherwise surrounded by is recognised as no more than exactly that.

In one coaching session, Martin (not his real name), a coaching client, started exploring his thoughts about how to delegate more fully. He continued speaking in uninterrupted silence for 40 min, embracing the opportunity to simply complete his thought process. Afterwards, he said that it was the most impactful coaching session he's ever had.

The "generative attention" (Kline, 2002) provided by coaching presence can sometimes be precisely what's needed, cutting through the incessant interference of the all-important context and unlocking latent breakthroughs that simply cannot be achieved any other way. There are reasons why ancient spiritual practices established patterns of community and silent meditation long before mobile phone notifications became ubiquitous.

When thinking about the topic of AI's impact on coaching it's important to begin by recognising that oftentimes adding technology into a coaching conversation would be an unhelpful and immature distraction, reducing its impact. Why might we ever want to even contemplate the idea?

One valid reason without any sort of satisfactory counter is the fact that almost everybody in the world doesn't have the privilege of access to a coach. If AI can offer even the tiniest fraction of the experience of high-quality, non-directive coaching (and it unarguably can), we have a moral responsibility to support this vision for those who will benefit the most from it, and at the very least not try to stand in its way (see Terblanche et al., 2022).

But using AI as a coach can also be attractive in offering efficiency, opportunities for scale and more. Marketers' wont is to inflate expectations and state best-case scenarios as if they're commonplace, but anyone who's used even the free versions of the most basic generative AI models knows that it offers *some* benefits, and when we as coaches use AI in an informed way we give ourselves the chance to capitalise on those. If AI offers us the chance to coach more people and do it better, the question as to *whether* we should be open to adopting it answers itself.

We can apply this to our coaching practice in the form of three lenses through which we might view AI as supporting us: AI expands our capacity, enhances our competence, and extends our capability (Isaacson, 2022).

7.2.1 AI Expands Our Capacity

Some opportunities that AI offers are transparent in their application, because they do something we're already able to do, taking it off our plate and opening up greater possibilities. Ignoring the important ethical considerations associated with sharing the so-called confidential data for a moment (see below), the time one might take to write up a transcript of a coaching session can be dramatically shortened through widely available AI products.

The benefits of this are so obvious that their impact can feel self-evident, when that is actually not at all the case. While the time we save could be consciously used to do something more impactful, it's at least as likely we'll unconsciously find ourselves passively pulled into simply doing something different. The choice to invest our newfound resources for business development, personal development, servicing clients, or doomscrolling is down to us.

7.2.2 AI Enhances Our Competence

The second contribution AI can make is to improve and augment the things we're already able to do. There are more mature examples of this, of course, but perhaps a good foundational example is in forming "good enough" next questions to ask, in the midst of a coaching session. A well-formed prompt, tailored for the client sitting in a video call with us, could generate half a dozen suggested lines of questioning, reducing the risk of our own blind spots limiting the direction of the conversation (Bozkurt, 2024).

When thinking about applying AI to our coaching practice, this should be our target. We're already effective enough to deliver coaching that is at least passable to a certain extent, so we should capitalise on that starting position. What AI offers us in our practice is to make the coaching experience and outcomes even better for all the stakeholders involved.

7.2.3 AI Extends Our Capability

The final category of benefit that AI can offer is the ability to do things that are impossible without it. While this is perhaps overstated by press outlets driven to maximise engagement more than accurately communicate nuance, it's this category that presents the most paradigm-shifting opportunities, and therefore presents the greatest threats to traditional coaching practices.

The obvious example is in the introduction of AI-enabled coaching conversations, like those offered by Coach Vici, which research suggests is as effective as a human coach (Terblanche et al., 2022), and AIcoach.chat, which has seen measurable increases in goal attainment and self-efficacy within a single month of use (Isaacson et al., 2024). Suffice it to say that this aspect of AI is the most disruptive of the three.

7.2.4 The Risk of Inaction

The deployment of AI and its associated benefits can no doubt be impactful, and therefore its very presence demands a response. One of the big problems with the topic of AI is that it doesn't exist in many people's minds as anything more than science fiction, and as a result the stories we tell ourselves are similarly not grounded in reality. We anthropomorphise the machines (Ibrahim et al., 2025), and find ourselves becoming polarised behind clickbait stories designed to communicate that AI is either the panacea we've been waiting for, or an existential threat (e.g., see Diller et al., 2024).

Any informed person can confidently bat these extreme positions away. AI has inherent limitations, like any technology. As an emergent piece of innovation, it offers significant possibilities for impact, but the future most likely will look like neither an age of leisure ushered in by infinitely helpful robots, nor a dystopian cyberpunk apocalypse in which we return to a pre-industrial era. The disappointingly predictable outcome is probably going to be that life will feel extremely similar to the way it has always been, but AI will be present in it (Capraro et al., 2024; Ferretti, 2024; Park, 2023; Valenzuela et al., 2024).

An appropriate response therefore would be to think, research, experiment and either actively resist or adopt particular applications of AI. Our choosing not to introduce an AI coaching supervisor into our practice prevents us from accessing its benefits, and also avoids the risks. But one response that surely is not open to us is to ignore AI and do nothing at all.

By acting as if AI is not present in the environment we operate within, we put ourselves at personal risk. The world that our clients inhabit is being shaken by AI innovations, and while we may have a professional identity rooted in tradition to an extent, there is never much appetite to engage with a coach who is intentionally out of touch. With AI increasingly a topic that boards are aware of (Abrash & Probst, 2024), it is naturally much more attractive to work with a coach who understands the opportunities and threats it presents than one who may as well have difficulty spelling "GPT".

More than this, however, is the fact that the wider coaching market is evolving, and client expectations along with it. During the initial COVID-19 lockdowns, some coaches put coaching engagements on hold until life "returned to normal", and it was those coaches who were already using video conferencing as a medium for delivery that pivoted most smoothly. The biggest winners from the (accelerated) change in client behaviours weren't those that were the best at the delivery of coaching, but those that were best able to capitalise on the technology, many of whom weren't coaches at all.

If coaches do not engage with the concept of AI—not necessarily in adopting it, but in establishing clear thinking around it that is not clouded by bias either for or against it—we position the profession such that a well-placed technologist or venture capitalist will shape what coaching clients of 5 years' time mean when they hear the term "AI coaching". For the benefit of every stakeholder engaged in coaching to whatever extent, coaches must take it upon themselves to grapple with AI.

7.3 Practical Applications: AI in a Coaching Practice

7.3.1 The Coach's Landscape

The reason that AI is so newsworthy is its wide applicability. While AI as a replacement for the human coach might feel like the single most significant AI-related topic for discussion in the coaching profession, our roles tend to be much wider than simply the delivery of individual coaching sessions, and AI has the potential to play a part across the entire lifecycle.

At a surface level, AI is accessible in the form of prompts sent to an AI model, such as in the way that ChatGPT accesses the OpenAI models. In this way, it's possible to rapidly interact with AI to produce something of worth, whether that's a piece of content (such as a structure for a coaching programme) or simply an approach to a conversation (such as questions framed using clean language). But AI models are significantly more straightforward to access in advanced ways than previous technologies.

"No-code" automation platforms allow coaches to activate highly customised AI interactions with a level of sophistication historically hidden from all but the most technically-minded of technologists. The sorts of tasks that are repeatable but which have needed a level of nuance in the past can now be given to a machine without that much effort, increasing scale and therefore impact.

We might therefore categorise the opportunities for making the most of AI by considering the following.

7.3.2 Pre-Session Preparation

Depending on one's coaching approach, a coach might like to prepare for a coaching session with something more content-full than a mindfulness exercise. Where that's the case, AI can be of use in shaping one's thinking and providing a level of curated direction.

Let's say, for example, I take notes throughout a coaching session. The notes are barely more than half-sentences, in no particular order, capturing the key moments in the conversation but nothing more than that. Copy-pasting those notes into a simple prompt could give me pointers to ensure an enriching discussion in the next session.

For example, here's a prompt I just sent to ChatGPT:

> I am a professional coach. I am preparing for a second coaching session with a client. Analyse the notes from my first session and provide five lines of enquiry that will increase the likelihood of blind spots being identified and make the session as impactful as possible. Keep your answer brief. The notes follow: Problems with line manager??? "Project Paris" under-resourced, aggressive timelines. Recent restructuring, not affected his team. TWO CHILDREN, son rebelling at school. "I don't know what I'm afraid of" Not giving freedom to own team, John should be responding on a Saturday afternoon? Will ask wife about working patterns and speak to boss. Next time focus on personal brand.

And here's the response I received back, within 2 s (ChatGPT, personal communication, 25 April 2025):

> Here are five powerful lines of enquiry to surface blind spots and deepen the impact of your next session:
>
> "What assumptions are you making about what your team should be doing—especially outside work hours?"

"What do you fear might happen if you gave your team more freedom?"

"How are your personal values aligning (or clashing) with your leadership style right now?"

"What patterns do you notice in how you're responding to both your son's behavior and your team's performance?"

"What would need to change for you to feel more comfortable owning your personal brand?"

This provides a level of direction that might help shape a coach's thinking as they approach a coaching session.

And pre-session preparation isn't only helpful for the coach. A well-formulated onboarding process might add significant value to an opening session and accelerate insights. A simple form asking for some relatively generic information could be analysed almost immediately using an automation platform and a generative AI model to, for example, articulate a coaching goal according to the coach's own intellectual property, identify potential limiting assumptions and blind spots, suggest a structure for a coaching engagement and, in truth, anything the prompt engineer can imagine. This analysis could be parsed and presented graphically within a report for the client's reflection, without the coach having invested any time at all.

7.3.3 *Coaching Augmentation*

In spite of the deep humanity of coaching, the very practice of which in many ways should not change regardless of the presence of technology, AI offers opportunities to augment our conversations from time to time.

The go-to use case for many coaches as far as this is concerned is the use of AI transcribers and notetakers, which remove the need for us to be manually taking notes in a session. This is a good example of AI doing something we otherwise would find ourselves doing, giving us the chance to focus our attention on something more impactful. In this case, that would simply be the client. The outsourcing of notetaking to the AI removes the need for those coaches who use notes in advance of coaching sessions from taking them, putting them at ease to simply be present in the moment. One ought to expect that the quality of the coaching would increase, thanks to the presence of AI. Where notetaking is being used as a practice to increase focus on what the client is saying, however, the inverse would be true, so maturity is required!

Another opportunity AI affords us is to lean into its creative capabilities. In the past, many coaches have enjoyed, for example, bringing a deck of picture cards into a coaching conversation. They sometimes seem to run the session by themselves. When a client is over-rationalising or simply getting stuck, a picture inviting them to explore a metaphor seems to accelerate insightful lines of questioning that can end up carrying deep meaning for them and unlocking new ways of thinking. The rise of AI-generated artwork offers us the opportunity to create entirely new images from a simple text-based prompt (Isaacson, 2022).

For example, I just used the AI artwork generator within ChatGPT with the prompt "I'm feeling frustrated because I was overlooked for a promotion at work, and I want to feel more fulfilment in my role."

The client cannot claim that the image (Fig. 7.1) has nothing to do with their topic, because *their topic was the prompt*. Instead, they need to explain how what they are looking at describes their topic, perhaps through drawing on the concept of the client's internal metaphor landscape (Lawley & Tompkins, 2000). In this example, they might see the spark in the centre of the image as a flame of passion that they want to rekindle, and the swirling brushstrokes representative of a tempestuous ocean. In exploring it with them, however, they might become aware of the fact that the colour of the flame appears among the swirls, indicating that the passion that they are searching for is already present somehow, just not as they were expecting it. Even if it doesn't resonate with their own perspective, the opportunity to explore how it doesn't ought to present the chance to increase awareness around interpretations.

AI could also be used in supporting the client between sessions. A well-engineered prompt could make for some "homework" that's more than reading an article or watching a video. It might be helpful, for example, for the client to put some time in a conversational format into clearly articulating an outcome for the next coaching session or the engagement as a whole. That time would otherwise be spent with the coach, opening up opportunities to focus the coaching conversations on something arguably more impactful, and perhaps even reducing the number of sessions needed, saving money for the sponsor.

Fig. 7.1 AI-generated image

7.3.4 *Post-Engagement Learning*

The challenge of evaluating coaching is very present, and AI can be used for adding value to clients and sponsors upon the conclusion of a coaching relationship. Generative AI is brilliant at extracting structured insights from unstructured data, so with a good prompt even the most unadulterated of streams of consciousness could be analysed for whatever insights a coach is looking to discover; a transcribed couple of off-the-cuff minutes describing what difference the coaching has made is likely to demonstrate more value than many of the evaluation forms typically in circulation.

And AI can be used to extend the learning opportunities beyond the coaching sessions themselves. A custom report designed for a client based on a coach's framework, perhaps playing back themes that have emerged and summarising insights, could provide a useful takeaway to facilitate future reflections. When introduced alongside a 360 process, there could be significant new moments of insight made possible, through automatically extracting themes that are present across multiple perspectives.

7.4 The Ethical Impacts of AI on the Coaching Relationship

One of the most important words when defining coaching is confidentiality. In a private physical meeting space, understanding this word was straightforward. My client is going to share information with me, the coach, and I am never going to disclose it unless I'm legally (or morally) required to do so. AI presents a challenge to this key concept because the provision of the AI inherently requires that same information to be transmitted across the Internet to a third party for processing, and potentially for indefinite storage, presenting a raft of new risks.

The ethical dilemma of this new lack of confidentiality is real, and presents an even more significant issue. A huge proportion of coaching is delivered remotely, relying on technology for the processing and storage of video, audio, and text-based communications. It is true that using AI impedes on traditional professional commitments to confidentiality, but this barrier was crossed long ago. Coaching conversations conducted via video conference already provide the full session to a third-party provider of video conferencing services, so any concerns about AI need to apply to technology already in use.

Associated, but distinct, considerations of information security controls and data privacy compliance are absolutely valid (Fouracres, 2024). Data privacy regulations differ from one jurisdiction to another, so coaches using AI products governed elsewhere should gain assurance that their own legal responsibilities are being properly fulfilled and not compromised. They should also ensure that they are holding themselves—and, by extension, the technology they use—to a higher standard (Isaacson, 2021). If coaching conversations are reasonably assumed to be *more* confidential than other conversations similarly described using that same word, coaches ought not to settle for AI products that are not more secure than others simply because they provide a level of convenience.

Aside from confidentiality, there are other ethical concerns raised by the use of AI, both within and outside of a coaching conversation. There are valid ethical reasons to not want to use AI, such as the risk of bias in datasets and the amount of carbon emissions produced by large language models, but it's a one-dimensional argument to suggest that these single issues outweigh every individual and systemic benefit. Instead, in line with the most fundamental of coaching principles, it's the responsibility of coaches to transparently empower their clients to make informed decisions about when and how to deploy AI in their own coaching engagement, co-creating an AI landscape that will best support and challenge them.

7.5 Critical Reflection

While the case for AI integration in coaching practice is unarguably compelling, it reveals a fundamental tension. The assumption that more efficiency, more data, and more options inherently lead to better coaching outcomes isn't self-evident. At times, coaching insights arise from a thought process that's free from interference rather than one that's full of content. The fundamental building blocks of good-quality coaching—psychological safety, undivided attention, the courage to press into the unknown, and the flexibility to work with what's emerging—are deeply human and risk being hampered by introducing AI into the picture.

While AI is capable of injecting creativity into a coaching session with skilful prompting, the nature of the technology is such that it is only capable of surface-level listening, laden with assumptions based on its original training data. Anyone who's experienced great coaching before will attest to the fact that some of the most transformative questions emerge from an approach to deep listening that notices—sometimes unconsciously—subtle shifts in energy. This is more than simply "reading in-between the lines"; it's an indefinable intuitive sense that leads a coach to voice something that they don't—can't—know, not from algorithmic pattern matching.

Some applications of AI for some coaches are clearly helpful because they speed things up that don't become more valuable through doing slowly, or because they introduce a level of consistency that wouldn't be present otherwise. Others positively contribute to the profession, through making coaching more accessible than ever before, providing a moral imperative for us to support in their adoption.

Others might feel like red herrings, threatening harm to an extent that the benefits are undermined. Introducing AI into a coaching session, for example, risks fragmenting our attention and reducing a sense of presence. Indeed, the fact that coaching ought to increase the quality of our thinking ought to mean that findings around AI leading to cognitive decline (Kosmyna et al., 2025) should be ringing alarm bells if we try outsourcing creative activities to it.

In the end, rather than wholesale adoption or rejection of AI, the coaching profession needs more nuanced thinking. The question isn't, "Can AI contribute to coaching?" because it's undeniable that it can. For some coaches and for some clients, AI will turn a transactional interaction into something fun and innovative, and for others AI will undo everything. Whether or not it's possible to incorporate AI without compromising the human elements that make coaching what it is is a much more valuable idea to reflect on. What remains true is that the vast majority of people in the world don't have access to a human coach, and the possibilities offered by AI are too great to overlook.

The future of coaching depends in part on coaches' attitudes and abilities in integrating AI in a seamless way, and also on our wisdom to know when and how to resist marketeers' promises. The most profound coaching moments will continue to come about not because of technological augmentation but because of the ancient human practice of creating space. Perhaps our responsibility is not to endlessly optimise this, but to protect and nurture it instead.

7.6 Conclusion

As the coaching profession navigates an emerging era defined by rapid technological change, the thoughtful integration of AI might offer opportunities for growing in maturity and maximising the impact of the practice. Coaches must continually learn to balance the deeply human essence of our practice with the strategic use of AI to enhance their impact and challenge habits we've fallen into. AI provides many tangible benefits that demand conscious ethical leadership, protecting the foundations on which the coaching profession was built on. Coaches who engage with AI thoughtfully and maturely will safeguard their relevance, provide increasing value to their clients, and help to shape a future where coaching remains a transformative, human-centred force.

References

Abrash, L., & Probst, A. (2024). *Governance of AI: A critical imperative for today's boards*. Deloitte Global Boardroom Program.

Bachkirova, T., & Kemp, R. (2025). 'AI coaching': Democratising coaching service or offering an ersatz? *Coaching: An International Journal of Theory, Research and Practice, 18*(1), 27–45. https://doi.org/10.1080/17521882.2024.2368598

Bozkurt, A. (2024). Tell me your prompts and I will make them true: The alchemy of prompt engineering and generative AI. *Open Praxis, 16*(2), 111–118. https://doi.org/10.55982/openpraxis.16.2.661

Capraro, V., Lentsch, A., Acemoglu, D., Akgun, S., Akhmedova, A., Bilancini, E., Bonnefon, J. F., Brañas-Garza, P., Butera, L., Douglas, K. M., Everett, J. A. C., Gigerenzer, G., Greenhow, C., Hashimoto, D. A., Holt-Lunstad, J., Jetten, J., Johnson, S., Kunz, W. H., Longoni, C., Lunn, P., Natale, S., Paluch, S., Rahwan, I., Selwyn, N., Singh, V., Suri, S., Sutcliffe, J., Tomlinson,

J., van der Linden, S., Van Lange, P. A. M., Wall, F., Van Bavel, J. J., & Viale, R. (2024). The impact of generative artificial intelligence on socioeconomic inequalities and policy making. *PNAS Nexus, 3*(6), pgae191. https://doi.org/10.1093/pnasnexus/pgae191

Diller, S. J., Stenzel, L. C., & Passmore, J. (2024). The coach bots are coming: Exploring global coaches' attitudes and responses to the threat of AI coaching. *Human Resource Development International, 27*(4), 597–621. https://doi.org/10.1080/13678868.2024.2375934

Ferretti, T. (2024). Value alignment without institutional change cannot prevent the societal risks of artificial intelligence. *LSE Public Policy Review, 3*(3), 2.

Fouracres, A. J. S. (2024). Managing cybersecurity. In J. Passmore, S. Diller, S. Isaacson, & M. Brantl (Eds.), *The digital and AI coaches handbook*. Routledge.

Ibrahim, L., Akbulut, C., Elasmar, R., Rastogi, C., Kahng, M., Morris, M. R., McKee, K. R., Rieser, V., Shanahan, M., & Weidinger, L. (2025, February). *Multi-turn evaluation of anthropomorphic behaviours in large language models*. arXiv.org. https://arxiv.org/abs/2502.07077

Isaacson, S. (2021). *How to thrive as a coach in a digital world: Coaching with technology*. Open University Press.

Isaacson, S. (2022). *Superhuman coaching: Ten technologies that expand coaching beyond what's humanly possible*. Hanwell Publishing.

Isaacson, S., Kong, S., Leech, D., & Tee, D. (2024, March 4). *Unlocking potential: AI coaching in the NHS*. NHS Elect & AIcoach.chat.

Kline, N. (2002). *Time to think: Listening to ignite the human mind*. Octopus Publishing Group.

Kosmyna, N., Hauptmann, E., Yuan, Y. T., Situ, J., Liao, X., Beresnitzky, A. V., Braunstein, I., & Maes, P. (2025, June). *Your brain on ChatGPT: Accumulation of cognitive debt when using an AI assistant for essay writing task*. arXiv.org. https://arxiv.org/abs/2506.08872

Lawley, J. D., & Tompkins, P. L. (2000). *Metaphors in mind: Transformation through systemic modelling*. Developing Company Press.

Park, Y. J. (2023). *Let me tell you, ChatGPT-like AI will not change our world*. Internet Policy Review. https://policyreview.info/articles/news/let-me-tell-you-chatgpt-ai-will-not-change-our-world/1694

Sherman, S., & Freas, A. (2004). The wild west of executive coaching. *Harvard Business Review, 82*(11), 82–90.

Terblanche, N. (2024). Artificial intelligence (AI) coaching: Redefining people development and organizational performance. *The Journal of Applied Behavioral Science, 60*(4), 631–638. https://doi.org/10.1177/00218863241283919

Terblanche, N., Molyn, J., de Haan, E., & Nilsson, V. O. (2022). Coaching at scale: Investigating the efficacy of artificial intelligence coaching. *International Journal of Evidence Based Coaching and Mentoring, 20*(2), 20–36. https://doi.org/10.24384/5cgf-ab69

Valenzuela, A., Puntoni, S., Hoffman, D., Castelo, N., De Freitas, J., Dietvorst, B., Hildebrand, C., Huh, Y. E., Meyer, R., Sweeney, M. E., Talaifar, S., Tomaino, G., & Wertenbroch, K. (2024). How artificial intelligence constrains the human experience. *Journal of the Association for Consumer Research, 9*(3), 241–256. https://doi.org/10.1086/730709

Chapter 8
Triadic and Quasi-Triadic AI Coaching: AI Agents and Their Professional Use in Coaching Through External Prompt Scripts

Harald Geißler

Abstract The ways in which artificial intelligence (AI) can be utilized in and for coaching are determined by two key factors: the internal properties of the AI systems used and the external tasks assigned to them by coachees and/or coaches. For the professional application of AI in coaching, this implies two core requirements: first, the development of AI agents equipped with coaching-relevant capabilities, and second, the professional optimization of their usage through external prompt scripts—that is, sequences of preformulated prompts grounded in established coaching methodologies. In this sense, the following contribution focuses, on the one hand, on AI agents equipped with coaching-diagnostic problem-solving knowledge, and on the other hand, on the necessity that this knowledge can only be activated through systematically structured task sequences (prompt scripts) based on coaching methodology.

Keywords Artificial intelligence · Coaching · Chatbots · Human–AI collaboration · Diagnostic reasoning in coaching · Structured prompt scripts · Triadic and quasi-triadic AI coaching · Single-loop and double-loop learning · Problem-solving orientations · Methodology of AI-supported coaching

8.1 AI Usage in Dyadic and Triadic Coaching Formats

Artificial intelligence (AI) can be utilized in or for coaching both in *dyadic and triadic formats* (Geißler, 2025). *Dyadic* usage occurs when only two parties are involved: a user and a specific AI system. This AI can either be a *general-purpose system*, such as ChatGPT or Perplexity, or a *coaching-specific AI* developed explicitly for professional coaching purposes (Bachkirova & Kemp, 2024; Graßmann & Schermuly, 2020; Passmore et al., 2025; Terblanche, 2024). Depending on their

H. Geißler (✉)
Online-Coaching-Lernen, Hamburg, Germany

R. Wegener et al. (eds.), *Coaching in the Age of AI*, SpringerBriefs in Psychology, https://doi.org/10.1007/978-3-032-23332-5_8

level of complexity, these systems are referred to as bots, AI assistants, or AI agents. For the sake of simplicity, the term *AI agents* will be used consistently throughout this text. The specific opportunities associated with these systems will be elaborated upon in the next section. However, it is crucial to highlight already at this point a fundamental question: namely, who *leads*—and must take *responsibility* for—the conversation: the AI (and by extension its developers) or the user, meaning either the client seeking support or the coach preparing or reviewing a coaching session.

In contrast to dyadic AI usage, *triadic* AI usage is characterized by the human coach and coachee jointly engaging with either a general-purpose AI or coaching-specific AI agents *within* their coaching dialogue, with the coach assuming primary responsibility for leading and managing the conversation (Geißler, 2025). For this reason, it is not advisable to employ AI agents with built-in conversational leadership capabilities in triadic AI coaching.

In addition to dyadic and triadic AI coaching formats, two hybrid forms can also be identified. The first is *semi-triadic AI coaching*, characterized by coachees engaging dyadically with AI agents that possess built-in conversational leadership capabilities. Coachees use these AI agents for self-coaching purposes and subsequently discuss their experiences and insights with their human coach—without the AI agent participating directly in the coach–coachee dialogue itself (Mai & Rutschmann, 2023).

Conceptually, semi-triadic AI coaching is thus more closely aligned with dyadic than with triadic AI coaching. This distinction marks the critical difference from the second hybrid form, *quasi-triadic AI coaching*, which will be introduced in Sect. 8.3.

On this basis, several ideal-typical modes of AI usage can be identified, and the specific positioning of the subsequent discussion within the broader context of this volume's contributions can be clarified (Fig. 8.1):

- The usage model that has thus far dominated the discourse in coaching research refers to coachees utilizing coaching-specific AI agents with autonomous conversational leadership, either dyadically or in a semi-triadic format.
- Since this model is the focus of the contributions by Rutschmann, Mai, and Terblanche in this volume, it will not be further elaborated here.
- Diametrically opposed to this model, and much more widespread in practice, is the usage pattern where coachees seeking support—or coaches preparing or reviewing coaching sessions—engage with *general-purpose AI systems* such as ChatGPT in a *dyadic format*, issuing specific task instructions to the AI and thereby *maintaining leadership of the conversation themselves* (Edenhausen, 2024). Since the formulation of such task instructions (prompts) has been scarcely examined in coaching science—and because *prompt design* is fundamental for triadic and quasi-triadic AI coaching—this aspect will be addressed in detail in Sect. 8.3.
- Positioned between these two usage models is the *triadic AI coaching* approach, which forms the central focus of this contribution. It is characterized by coachees communicating with AI agents under the leadership of their coaches, with the AI agents acting in a supportive co-coaching role (Geißler, 2025). As already indicated, the design and deployment of prompts play a critical role in this process.

	Technology-driven conversational guidance ⟵⟶			Human-driven conversational guidance
General-purpose AI systems				Coachees and/or coaches use general-purpose AI systems with the support of externally generated prompts in a dyadic or triadic setting
Coaching specific AI agents	In a dyadic setting, coachees use coaching specific AI agents with embeddeed conversational leadership skills as self-coaching tools	In a semi-triadic setting, coachees integrate the insights und experiences gained from AI-supported self-coaching into their conversation with human coaches	In a quasi-triadic setting, coachees use AI-external prompt scripts developed by coaches, to guide their interaction with coaching-specific AI agents	In a triadic setting, coaches embed coaching specific AI agents into their coaching dialogues using externally engineered prompts (scripts) that structure the AI's interventions

Fig. 8.1 Models of AI-based coaching use

- Finally, a newly developed usage model, *quasi-triadic AI coaching* (Geißler et al., 2025), will also be introduced. Although conceptually closely related to triadic AI coaching, it differs by enabling coachees to interact with AI agents without the immediate presence of a human coach. Instead, coachees are guided by a prompt script, which serves as a coaching medium—functioning as the "voice" of a virtual coach operating behind it.

8.2 Coaching AI Agents

To better understand the AI agents that can be utilized in or for coaching, this section first outlines the *technical* foundations and design possibilities underlying their development, followed by an exploration of the *conceptual* frameworks and *practical applications* enabled by their technical and conceptual configurations.

At the *technical* level, the most critical component of any AI agent is the underlying large language model (LLM), which defines the scope and nature of the *knowledge* accessible to both the AI and its users. While this knowledge base is impressively vast, it is not without limitations. It is shaped not only by the wealth of information embedded by developers during the AI's initial training phase but also by various *biases* and *ethically problematic* distortions that have—often unintentionally—been introduced (Baum, 2024).

The root cause of these shortcomings is, fundamentally, human fallibility. Addressing them requires the *human-in-the-loop* approach advocated by Harari (2024), which suggests two complementary strategies. First, users should be enabled to create customized AI agents. Second, users must actively shape AI outputs by crafting targeted task instructions (prompts) (see Sect. 8.3).

The *technical foundation* for the first strategy has been available since November 2023, with ChatGPT's introduction of customizable GPTs, here referred to as AI agents. These agents can be individually designed through detailed *instructions* that define their *roles and communication styles*, and through the uploading of documents that expand or refine the *knowledge base* of the underlying LLM (Edenhausen, 2024).

These technical capabilities can be combined with different coaching-conceptual frameworks, leading to the following typology of AI agents:

- AI agents equipped with built-in conversational leadership capabilities
- AI agents simulating personal character profiles
- AI agents embodying special expert knowledge and
- AI agents possessing coaching-diagnostic problem-solving knowledge

When developing *AI agents that simulate specific personality profiles*—intended to demonstrate to coachees how others might perceive their issues—the selection of a suitable character typology is necessary. Similarly, for AI *agents with special expert knowledge*, it must be decided which knowledge will underpin their interpretive approaches.

The most complex design and justification challenges arise with *AI agents possessing coaching-diagnostic problem-solving knowledge*—knowledge concerning the potential underlying causes of coaching issues and appropriate solution strategies. The provision and application of coaching-diagnostic knowledge is indispensable for effective coaching—yet it constitutes one of its greatest challenges. The aim is to achieve a profound understanding of the coachees, both in terms of their current state and their potential development. This often requires understanding the coachees more deeply than they are presently able to understand themselves.

To meet these challenges, it is advisable to focus not on static personal traits as causes of problems, but rather on the *problem-solving orientations* that individuals—often driven by affect—activate in *specific situations*, which may unintentionally stabilize or exacerbate their difficulties (Schmidt, 2004). Furthermore, it is conceptually valuable to integrate situational diagnostics with corresponding solution knowledge.

This approach is well illustrated by Schulz von Thun (1989, p. 42) using the example of a coachee who suffers from excessive, naïve trust toward certain individuals in specific situations. Resolving this issue requires recognizing the *positive core* of this orientation—the impulse toward interpersonal trust—which, through overextension, transforms into a problem of naïve credulity. To address this overextension, Schulz von Thun proposes identifying the conceptual *antipode*: caution, which, if exaggerated, can itself become problematic, manifesting as paranoid mistrust.

This example highlights that the central goal of the proposed solution strategy is the *situational balancing of polar yet dialectically interconnected problem-solving orientations* (Geißler, 2025). In order to understand a given coaching issue and the implicit solution options it entails, it is therefore useful to examine the problem-solving orientations currently preferred by the coachees. It is important to assess how well these orientations are balanced with regard to the specific characteristics of the situation at hand, and to consider how they might need to be rebalanced in order to enable the resolution of the issue.

8.3 External Prompts and Prompt Scripts

To utilize artificial intelligence effectively in or for coaching, it is necessary to issue task instructions to the AI—and to design these instructions in a manner consistent with professional coaching standards. As previously mentioned, two complementary approaches are available. The first involves prescribing communication behavior *internally within the AI system through embedded prompts*. The second concerns *external prompts*: instructions delivered by coaches or coachees from outside the AI system, which they can adapt flexibly to their needs.

Having examined internal AI prompts in the previous section, we now turn to *external prompts*. Their primary function is to assist or guide coaches and coachees in managing their dialogue with either general-purpose AI systems or coaching-specific AI agents—provided that these agents do not possess built-in conversational leadership capabilities.

A fundamental characteristic of all prompts is their twofold structure: they must combine factual information with a specific task instruction.

Regarding the types of task instructions that coachees or coaches might issue through prompts, two paradigmatic forms can be distinguished, drawing on the organizational psychology theory of single-loop and double-loop learning (Argyris & Schön, 1978): *Single-loop prompts* aim directly at achieving specific coaching goals, and *double-loop prompts* encourage reflection on these goals at a deeper level.

Typical *single-loop prompts* might instruct the AI to:

- Assess the completeness of information provided and identify any gaps
- Edit supplied texts in particular ways, such as summarizing them or transforming them into first-person experiential narratives

- Identify potential underlying causes of a described problem
- Generate solution proposals for particular problems or challenges
- Develop conceptual frameworks based on defined criteria for specific tasks

In contrast, *double-loop prompts* task the AI with self-reflection—that is, with analyzing the outputs generated in response to single-loop prompts by asking:

- What empirically verifiable assumptions underlie the output?
- What implicit values and norms are embedded within it?

Several options are available for the professional application of these prompt types in coaching contexts. The most demanding—and simultaneously the riskiest—option is *intuitive prompting*, that is, the situational creation of tasks in interaction with the AI that requires highly advanced coaching competencies.

The second option is the use of a *prompt repository*, a comprehensive collection of preformulated prompts that users can adopt—either directly or with modifications—in any order. This approach can significantly support coaches in triadic AI coaching by enhancing both the efficiency and effectiveness of AI usage.

The third option is the use of *prompt scripts*: structured sequences of prompts designed to be followed in a specific order, with or without modifications. The methodological design of prompt scripts concerns both the formulation of individual prompts and their sequencing. A further important dimension is that prompt scripts may not only contain instructions addressed to the AI but also include directives aimed at the coaches and coachees themselves.

Accordingly, five types of prompts can be distinguished:

- *A-Prompts*, addressed to coaches, *providing guidance* on:
  - How to manage the *coaching situation methodologically*, particularly concerning the specific characteristics of the coachees
  - Which *content areas* are of strategic importance for the ongoing coaching process
  - And the *intentional focus* to be maintained during coaching
- *B-Prompts*, addressed to coachees, guiding them in creating a *report* that will subsequently be sent to the AI, specifying which *content* elements should be included.
- *C-Prompts*, directed at the AI agent, specifying the *goals* or intentional perspectives it should apply in processing the submitted report.
- *D-Prompts*, addressed to coachees, offering *methodological guidance* on how to engage with and reflect upon the AI's response.
- *E-Prompts*, instructing coachees on how to *provide feedback* to the AI and indicating which aspects of the interaction should be emphasized in that feedback.

In concrete terms, this may involve, for example, the following:

- A-Prompt instructs the coach to ask the coachee how they are doing.
- B-Prompt guides the coachee, with the support of the coach, to describe their issue in writing to the AI agent.

- C-Prompt provides the AI agent with a precisely formulated task specifying how to process the coachee's problem description.
- D-Prompt invites the coachee to quietly reflect on the AI agent's response.
- E-Prompt prompts the coachee, with the coach's support, to provide feedback to the AI agent regarding its response.

These five types of prompts are methodologically interconnected and together form *mega-prompts*, typically starting with an A-Prompt and proceeding through B-, C-, and D-Prompts, culminating in an E-Prompt. Frequently, a renewed C-Prompt follows after the E-Prompt to facilitate continued dialogue.

The professional quality of these prompts can be evaluated and optimized using the framework of *coaching success factors,* i.e. the observable behaviors exhibited by coaches that increase the likelihood of successful coaching outcomes (Behrendt & Greif, 2022) (see also Geißler et al., 2025).

Building on this conceptual foundation, it is also possible to design A-Prompts that are addressed exclusively to coachees. These prompts can inform coachees about the intended target group, the coaching contexts and challenges the prompt script is designed to address, and the role of the subsequent B- and C-Prompts. In this way, prompt scripts can function as structured guides for *AI-supported self-coaching*.

Such an A-Prompt could be formulated as follows:

> *Dear Coachee, in order to make optimal use of the AI agent you have just activated, you need to provide it with well-formulated tasks. This prompt script is designed to assist you in doing so. It consists of various instructions. One of these, the A-Prompt, addresses you directly and provides orientation as to where you currently stand in the coaching process and what the next step is. In this sense, I would like to inform you that the next coaching step is for you to describe your issue in detail to the AI agent. The aspects you should consider in doing so are explained in detail in the following B-Prompt. You will then send this problem description to the AI agent along with the C-Prompt, which contains precise instructions on how the AI agent should process your problem description.*

This usage model may be termed *quasi-triadic AI coaching*, because the coach—constitutive in traditional triadic coaching—appears here in virtualized form through the medium of the written prompt script, guiding coachees on how to manage the dialogue with the AI agent autonomously. This model thus differs fundamentally from *semi-triadic AI coaching*, discussed in Sect. 8.1, where the AI independently leads the self-coaching conversation without structured human guidance.

8.4 Data-Secure Communication Spaces Using Delta Chat

One of the major challenges in AI-supported coaching is ensuring data security. Communication with AI agents developed via platforms such as ChatGPT typically occurs in environments that are not fully secure—at least when using OpenAI's standard front-end interface.

The situation is different, however, when AI agents are created in OpenAI's Playground and communication is conducted through Delta Chat. Delta Chat is an open-source messaging service that enables decentralized, end-to-end encrypted communication via anonymized email addresses.

An additional important advantage of Delta Chat is the ability to create dedicated communication spaces where coaches and coachees can interact—both synchronously and asynchronously—with each other and with multiple AI agents. Within these spaces, prompt scripts can be stored to guide the coaching processes, specifically in rooms designed for this purpose.

Moreover, group spaces for teams and project groups can also be established, facilitating both synchronous and asynchronous team and organizational coaching activities.

In this sense, my message is: If data security is important to you, you should by no means use the ChatGPT front end. Instead, you should work with suitable AI agents either in the Playground or integrate them into a DeltaChat room in order to interact with them there.

8.5 Conclusion

To utilize the potential of artificial intelligence (AI) within and for coaching in a professional and ethically sophisticated manner, it is necessary to develop AI agents equipped with coaching-relevant capabilities and to deploy these capabilities based on the human-in-the-loop principle, using coaching-methodologically grounded and sequenced task instructions (prompt scripts) within data-secure environments.

In contrast to AI agents with built-in conversational leadership capabilities—designed to be used dyadically by coachees as substitutes for human coaches—these standards can be met primarily by integrating AI agents with coaching-diagnostic problem-solving knowledge into the coaching dialogue. In doing so, a triadic AI coaching format emerges.

In this format, it is important that coachees and coaches are guided in shaping their relationships—with one another and with the AI agent—through coaching-methodologically structured prompt scripts. These scripts must be designed to include and interconnect different types of prompts: those directed at the AI agent and those providing orientation for coachees and coaches.

On this conceptual basis, prompt scripts can also be developed for quasi-triadic AI coaching. The distinctive feature of such scripts is that they are directed solely at coachees and their interaction with the AI agent, recommending contact with a human coach only in exceptional cases.

References

Argyris, C., & Schön, D. (1978). *Organizational learning: A theory of action perspective.* Addison-Wesley.

Bachkirova, T., & Kemp, R. (2024). 'AI coaching': Democratising coaching service or offering an ersatz? *Coaching: An International Journal of Theory, Research and Practice, 18*(1), 27–45. https://doi.org/10.1080/17521882.2024.2368598

Baum, D. (2024). *Generative AI and LLMs*. John Wiley & Sons.
Behrendt, P., & Greif, S. (2022). Success factors in the coaching process. In S. Greif, H. Möller, W. Scholl, J. Passmore, & F. Müller (Eds.), *International handbook of evidence-based coaching* (pp. 877–888). Springer.
Edenhausen, M. (2024). *Coaching und Beratung treffen auf KI: Der systemische Ansatz in Zeiten von ChatGPT*. Selbstverlag.
Geißler, H. (2025). *KI-Coaching - Wie man Künstliche Intelligenz in und für Coaching nutzen kann*. Springer.
Geißler, H., Metz, M., & Böning, U. (2025). The foundation of AI coaching. *OSC. Organisationsberatung, Supervision, Coaching*. https://doi.org/10.1007/s11613-025-00947
Graßmann, C., & Schermuly, C. C. (2020). Coaching with artificial intelligence: Concepts and capabilities. *Human Resource Development Review, 20*(1), 106–126. https://doi.org/10.1177/1534484320982891
Harari, Y. N. (2024). *Nexus: A brief history of information networks from the Stone Age to AI*. Random House.
Mai, V., & Rutschmann, R. (2023). Chatbots im Coaching: Potenziale und Einsatzmöglichkeiten von digitalen Coaching-Begleitern und Assistenten. *Organisationsberatung, Supervision, Coaching, 30*, 45–57. https://doi.org/10.1007/s11613-022-00801-3
Passmore, J., Olafsson, B., & Tee, D. (2025). A systematic literature review of artificial intelligence (AI) in coaching: insights for future research and product development. *Journal of Work-Applied Management*. https://doi.org/10.1108/JWAM-11-2024-0164
Schmidt, G. (2004). *Liebesaffären zwischen Problem und Lösung*. Carl-Auer.
Schulz von Thun, F. (1989). *Miteinander reden 2: Stile*. Rowohlt.
Terblanche, N. (2024). Artificial intelligence coaching chatbots. In J. Passmore, S. J. Diller, S. Isaacson, & M. Brantl (Eds.), *The digital and AI coaches' handbook* (pp. 101–109). Routledge.

Chapter 9
AI as a Third Party in Coaching: Balancing Trust, Ethics, and Innovation

Sandra J. Diller and Wendy-Ann Smith

Abstract The integration of artificial intelligence (AI) into a human-to-human coaching relationship presents both fascinating opportunities and significant challenges. This chapter explores AI's evolving role within the coaching relationship, balancing its potential to support both coach and client in their self-development with concerns related to trust, ethics, and process integrity. Much like involving a human third party, AI raises issues of confidentiality, data ownership, informed consent, and potential conflicts of interest. Additionally, a third party such as AI can influence the process—intentionally or unintentionally—by imposing goals, expectations, or assessments that may not align with the client's self-valued goals and needs. Furthermore, AI could shift the dynamic from a 1:1 to a 2:1 setting, outbalancing the relationship and creating pressure on the client's, affecting their openness and engagement. Its involvement further risks introducing bias from training data or becoming overly mechanical, diminishing the human connection central to coaching. The chapter critically examines how AI can be responsibly integrated to complement rather than disrupt the coaching dynamic, ensuring that technological innovation aligns with the core values of coaching.

Keywords Artificial intelligence · Coaching · Ethics · Trust · Autonomy · AI-based coaching · Human–AI–human interaction · Psychological safety and confidentiality · Bias and fairness in AI systems · Third-party interference in coaching processes

---

We would like to make you aware of the Coaching Ethics Forum to discuss these topics together with other practitioners and to engage with thought leadership.

S. J. Diller (✉)
Privatuniversität Schloss Seeburg, Salzburg, Austria
e-mail: sandra.diller@uni-seeburg.at

W.-A. Smith
Ethics Forum International, Orgeval, France
e-mail: wendyann@eclorev.eu

R. Wegener et al. (eds.), *Coaching in the Age of AI*, SpringerBriefs in Psychology, https://doi.org/10.1007/978-3-032-23332-5_9

9.1 Introduction

AI is rapidly transforming many domains, especially social interactions and communication. While people aim to maintain agency in AI-supported exchanges, they often see AI as a separate social actor rather than an extension of themselves, leading to greater reliance on it when they lack experience, suggesting that AI systems not only facilitate but also reshape one-to-one interactions as a third player (Mieczkowski & Hancock, 2022). This additional player can influence people's interactions in prosocial and antisocial ways, therefore not only connecting but also disconnecting human interaction (Hohenstein et al., 2023; Weidinger et al., 2022). Within the human-to-human interaction of coaching, the inclusion of AI could therefore alter the interaction to a human–AI–human interaction—with three parties interacting together (Diller & Passmore, 2023). Yet, with third-party interferences, the complexity of the coaching interaction is heightened and poses several social and ethical risks (Ratlabala & Terblanche, 2022). Drawing on the *Model of Ethical Interdependence in Coaching* by Diller et al. (2026), the AI as a third party could, for instance, positively or negatively interfere with the set goals between coach and client, their relationship, their coaching progress, or their confidentiality (Diller, 2024). Alongside this is Smith's (2025) concept of *intentional ethicality*—a developmental stance that positions ethics as an embodied, relational process grounded in presence, discernment, and responsibility. While Diller et al. (2026) focus on the structural dynamics of ethical interdependence and potential third-party interference, intentional ethicality offers a psychological and developmental scaffolding for engaging with these tensions in practice. The present chapter explores these social dynamics of interdependence, their possibilities and risks, and provides implications for the human–AI–human interaction.

9.1.1 Framing the Coaching Relationship

Coaching can be defined as a relational and reflective process—grounded in trust, confidentiality, and presence—that empowers clients to work toward and attain their self-valued and value-congruent goals (Diller et al., 2020; Smith et al., 2021). Thus, one of the core values of coaching is an autonomy-supportive coach–client relationship in terms of trust, empathy, and the support of self- and value-congruence (Diller et al., 2020; Mühlberger et al., 2024; Schiemann et al., 2019; Smith et al., 2021). Framing the coaching relationship around these values ensures a secure and empowering space for client growth. However, the *Model of Ethical Interdependence in Coaching* (Diller et al., 2026; Fig. 9.1) highlights that this relational dynamic is not sealed off from external influences. According to the model, third-party actors can either support or disrupt the coaching process by affecting the agreed-upon goals, the coach–client relationship, the progression of coaching sessions, or the confidentiality of shared content.

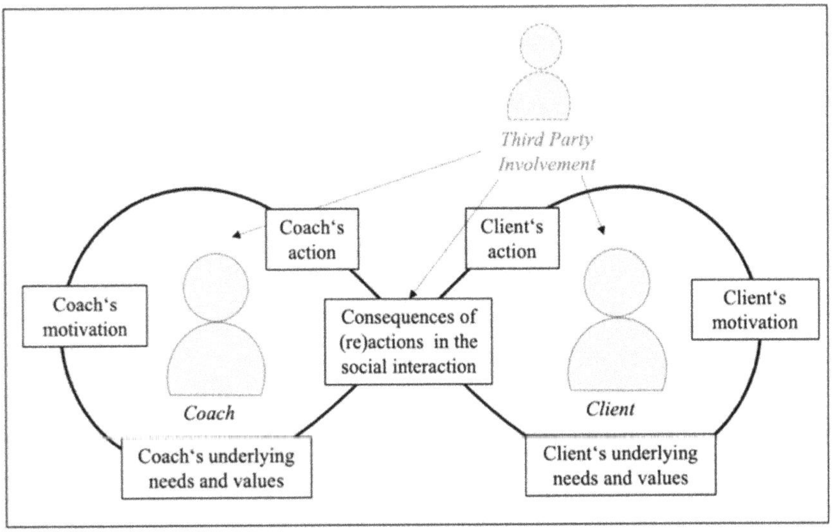

The Coaching Context (e.g., contract, coaching room, organizational aspects of inhouse coaching)

Fig. 9.1 Model of ethical interdependence in coaching (Diller et al., 2026)

When AI enters the coaching space, it functions implicitly or explicitly as a third party—even when AI is not interacting directly with the client, its presence as a listener, analyzer, or recommender carries interactional weight. This could, similarly to a human third party, challenge the co-created social interaction dynamic between coach and client. Hereby, AI could positively interfere, such as by reinforcing the client's goal attainment, or negatively interfere, such as by breaching privacy or redirecting the coaching trajectory away from the client's goals. For a better understanding of positive and negative effects, we will explore them in the following two subchapters.

9.1.2 The Innovativeness of AI as a Third Party in Human-to-Human Coaching

In terms of positive interference, AI has the potential to enhance coaching relationships by supporting clients in achieving their personal and professional goals. For instance, AI-based coaching applications can effectively support clients engaged in human-to-human processes by providing personalized support between sessions, offering reminders, and tracking goal progress (e.g., Kettunen et al., 2022). Thus, rather than replacing the coach, AI can enhance the developmental journey. For instance, some coaching platforms leverage natural language processing to generate session summaries or reflect back key themes from coaching conversations, enabling clients to revisit and deepen their insights, or guide reflective journaling with structured prompts, helping clients sustain momentum and cultivate self-awareness. Adjacent research in mental health interventions has begun to validate the efficacy of these AI features, particularly journaling prompts, in supporting reflection and well-being (e.g., Nepal et al., 2024). In sum, when thoughtfully integrated, AI has the potential to serve as an innovative third party in a human-to-human coaching process.

9.1.3 Challenges and Risks of AI as a Third Party in Human-to-Human Coaching

Despite its potential, integrating AI as a third party in coaching also introduces challenges and ethical risks that need to be carefully considered. For instance, AI's presence in coaching could heighten coaches' anxiety and inhibition, reducing their openness and increasing their resistance and biases toward AI (Diller et al., 2024). Such reactions can potentially undermine the effectiveness of the human-AI-human coaching process. Furthermore, leveraging AI in coaching requires both ethically sound design and responsible application. Core concerns include confidentiality, data ethics, psychological safety, and the impact on trust, empathy, and agency (Diller, 2024). Without thoughtful integration, AI could disrupt rather than enhance the coaching relationship. To explore these challenges, the following sections examine four key risk areas linked to AI's role as a third party, including vignettes to illustrate their relevance and complexity: *(a) Trust, Psychological Safety, and Confidentiality, (b) Client Autonomy and Agency, (c) Bias and Fairness, and (d) Relationship Imbalance and the Emergence of 2:1 Dynamics.*

(a) **Trust, Psychological Safety, and Confidentiality**

Development in coaching relies on a co-created relationship grounded in mutual presence, trust, and psychological safety (Smith & Arnold, 2023). This trust is co-constructed by coach and client, grounded in benevolence, competence, and integrity (Schiemann et al., 2019) and needs to be intentionally built in digital environments (Schilling & Kauffeld, 2024). Introducing AI into this delicate relational field presents unique risks, as even seemingly neutral tools, such as transcriptions, could change the coaching dynamic. Vignette 9.1 illustrates how clients may become more guarded when AI is monitoring the conversation, showing that even minimal AI involvement can influence the dynamic with regard to psychological safety and trust. However, emotional depth needed in coaching relies on a space of safety and trust, which can be compromised without transparent consent, comfort, and clear boundaries around AI use by the coach (Hawley et al., 2024).

Vignette 9.1: Notes in the Room

It was their second session. The coach had noticed the client becoming more open and exploratory in language and relaxed in tone. After greeting, the coach said: *"I'd like to activate an AI note-taker to create a transcript so I can stay focused and review later. It's only for me, and I'll delete it after writing my reflections. Is that okay?"* The client nodded, and the coach activated the tool. A small banner appeared: "This meeting is being recorded and transcribed." As the session progressed, the coach noticed a subtle shift: The client's responses were more measured; their reflections less fluid. The usual rhythm of openness felt disrupted. Something had changed.

***Reflective Questions*:**

- How might the note-taking role have influenced the coachee's psychological safety and/or willingness to express vulnerability (trust)?
- What responsibilities does a coach have (and when) in checking for consent and comfort?

However, there is little to no attention to when the client brings AI to the relationship. Trust and safety require confidentiality and data protection, upheld by ethical guidelines and legal standards, with **both** coaches and clients responsible for safeguarding sensitive information in all forms—verbal, written, and digital. The rise of digital and AI tools raises critical data security questions around ownership, storage, and access, which extends confidentiality concerns into the digital world (Iordanou et al., 2023). For instance, platforms vary in how long coaching data is stored and whether it can truly be deleted. The opaque nature of such systems further complicates informed consent for both parties, making it symbolic rather than substantive as both coaches and clients may not fully understand how their data is collected, processed, or stored. Furthermore, data can be intercepted, altered, or misused, as even the most secure systems can have data breaches (Fouracres, 2024). Due to their responsibility for the coaching process, coaches must therefore be transparent about data practices with their risks, set clear agreements with clients, and adopt robust cybersecurity measures, such as encryption, access controls, and explicit data ownership policies. These are not just ethical imperatives but legal ones: Under regulations like the EU's General Data Protection Regulation (GDPR), coaches using digital tools must adhere to principles such as storage limitation, data minimization, and integrity and confidentiality (Rogers, 2023).

(b) **Client Autonomy and Agency**

The need for autonomy and its support are at the heart of coaching. It's what sets coaching apart as a process that empowers clients to lead their self-valued and value-congruent goal attainment and self-development (Diller et al., 2020; Schiemann et al., 2018). Thus, autonomy-supportive coach behavior, such as empathic listening, can enhance autonomy and self-development (Schiemann et al., 2018), while autonomy-restrictive coach behavior, such as advice, can erode agency and trigger resistance (Klonek et al., 2014). When introducing AI as a generative tool, i.e., generating ideas and therefore advice, it may even with questions steer clients in directions that conflict with their own ideas, values, or goals, possibly shifting the dynamic from client-led growth to externally guided direction, undermining the very self-determination that drives meaningful change (see Vignette 9.2).

Vignette 9.2: Misaligned Goals

The organization used a human-AI-human coaching model supported by an AI-powered platform that suggests key conversation elements after each session, drawing from sentiment analysis, behavioral keywords, and historical coaching data. After one session, the coach reviewed the AI-generated summary and noticed an auto-suggested goal for the client: "*Improve assertiveness in team meetings.*" The coach paused. The client had not raised this concern; in fact, their focus was on how much the client liked to not pushing back" in these situations but stepping back and creating space for others. The AI likely flagged this as a goal instead of a strength. Knowing the client would see the suggestions, the coach debated whether to address them directly and wondered how the client would interpret them. Would this misaligned prompt steer the client away from their values and growth path?

***Reflective Questions*:**

- When AI-generated suggestions contradict the client's stated values or intentions, how should the coach respond and where does accountability lie?
- How might goal-setting algorithms shape the coaching process in ways that subtly undermine co-created meaning or client agency?

(c) **Bias and Fairness**

An additional risk of AI is its source of exclusion and bias, particularly as AI systems are often built by and with assumptions about a white, male, neurotypical, and digitally privileged (Gengler et al., 2024). AI systems have shown discriminatory outcomes across gender, race, sexual identity, age, class, and religion. In a human–AI–human interaction, AI can therefore not only replicate but even amplify societal biases, such as racial disparities in healthcare or recruitment (e.g., Köchling et al., 2021). In coaching, where fairness and inclusivity are paramount, these issues are especially concerning. As Pasha (2024) argues, AI systems often lack the cultural nuance and inclusive language needed to reflect human diversity, risking impersonal or exclusionary coaching experiences. This raises ethical concerns, as inclusion is not just technical but relational (see Vignette 9.3).

Vignette 9.3: The Pattern in the Summaries

The coaching sessions were conducted via a platform that included built-in AI-generated summaries, which are promoted as helpful for continuity and progress tracking. After each session, a polished paragraph appeared automatically in the shared workspace. At first, the summaries seemed tidy, efficient, and accurate. However, over time, the coach began to notice a pattern: The summaries often emphasized agentic language, such as "determined," confident," "independent," or "driven" even though these words were not used by the client. One afternoon, after reading a summary focused on "self-advocacy in high-stakes decision-making," the coach asked the client: "*Does this summary reflect what felt important to you today?*" The client laughed gently, seemingly relieved that the coach addressed it: "*Not really —the content is right but I would never use these words.*" The coach wondered: If AI filtered out language and nuance, whose voice was it amplifying—and whose was it quietly erasing?

***Reflective Questions*:**

- How might AI tools reinforce dominant norms, and what is the coach's responsibility in noticing and addressing this?
- What might it look like to collaboratively renegotiate the role of AI in the coaching relationship when its output does not reflect the client's experience?

(d) **Relationship Imbalance and 2:1 Dynamics**

As perceived in the previous vignettes, integrating AI into coaching subtly alters the relational dynamic. Depending on who introduced and manages the AI tool, this can create a perceived 2:1 interaction, where the one partner is additionally supported by AI. This shift can disrupt co-creation, introduce power imbalances, and compromise the human integrity of the coaching space. In other words, AI may influence what the coach notices, what the client explores, and which topics gain emphasis, possibly making the process less relational and more machine-guided. What if their own experiences, insights, or intuitions are influenced by AI-generated information? Even when silent, AI mediates the process by highlighting certain themes or generating summaries, subtly steering attention and shaping the narrative (Blease et al., 2019). The complexity deepens when AI tools are provided by a sponsoring organization. In such cases, clients may be embedded in a multi-party system with unclear agendas and data flows (Lai & Turner, 2023). Coaches, too, may be unconsciously influenced by platform language or metrics, further shifting the dynamic. Unlike human participants, AI tools are not relationally accountable.

Vignette 9.4: Quiet Shifts

At the outset of the coaching process, the coach and client agreed to integrate an AI tool to support self-reflection and track progress between sessions. After setting initial coaching goals during their first meeting, the coach designed the second session to focus on a resource-oriented approach. However, as the session began, the client opened with an unexpected comment: "*Before we start, there is something I need to share. I have reflected with the AI tool on my goals and want to change them.*" While shifting goals is not unusual in coaching, the coach was struck by the quiet nature of this change. Typically, such developments emerge within the coaching conversation itself or through self-reflection in between sessions—not with the help of AI. The coach, now sensing a gap in understanding what had transpired between sessions with the AI, decided to explore the revised goals together, unpacking the client's reflections and reasoning. After further reflection, the client decided to revert to their original goals, seemingly confused why he questioned his goals in the first place and a bit unhappy about this additional loop. This has the coach reflecting on the use of AI and whether this loop was a natural part of AI-enhanced reflection, a signal that the goals needed more attention, or an interference in the coaching process.

***Reflective Questions*:**

- When using AI tools, how can a coach stay attuned to shifts and who is responsible for these shifts?
- What strategies might help coaches to have meaningful instead of interfering coach-AI-client processes and how can meaningful loops versus interfering loops be differentiated?

9.1.4 A.C.T.I.V.E.: A Framework for Ethical AI Integration

How AI is integrated into coaching processes is of critical importance, as it can significantly influence the quality of the working alliance between coach and client (Mai et al., 2022). A thoughtful integration enhances collaboration and trust, while poorly implemented AI risks undermining the relational foundation essential to effective coaching. Recognizing both the potential and the risks, the European Union has taken proactive steps through the Artificial Intelligence Act (European Parliament, 2023), which aims to establish comprehensive, trustworthy regulations around AI technologies. These rules help ensure that AI systems act as supportive third-party tools—enhancing, rather than disrupting, human-led processes—by promoting transparency, accountability, and user safety. Complementing these regulatory advances, Diller et al. (2026) identified key practices that foster a more ethical coaching approach. Their findings emphasize the value of legal safeguards, ongoing supervision, structured methods for self-awareness, guidance by ethical codes (whether institutional or personal), role and expectation clarity, transparency, and collaboratively set ethical frameworks.

While such structural practices offer valuable scaffolding for ethical coaching, they benefit from being held within a deeper relational and developmental grounding. Smith (2025) advances this conversation through the lens of *intentional ethicality*—a developmental stance that moves beyond procedural compliance toward an embodied way of being in practice. This approach is grounded in a **three-part reflective stance**: *intentional presence*, *relational responsibility*, and *attunement to ethical tensions*. It invites coaches to inhabit ethics as a lived process, not a checklist—to navigate uncertainty through conscious discernment and to stay reflexively engaged with the evolving needs of the relationship. Rather than treating ethics as a static framework, intentional ethicality positions it as *relationally enacted and dynamically co-constructed*. In this view, ethical maturity is not measured by rule adherence but by a coach's capacity to stay present, value-conscious, and developmentally responsive, even in complexity. This inner orientation becomes all the more essential when AI enters the coaching space, amplifying the need for conscious ethical discernment in real time. It is within this more refined ethical grounding that we situate the A.C.T.I.V.E. tool—a practice-oriented framework designed to support relationally aware, ethically intentional use of AI across all stages of the coaching journey.

A.C.T.I.V.E.

Before AI Use

A—Alignment of Purpose

Clarify the *purpose* of AI in the coaching process:

- Is it aligned with the client's growth and goals?
- Who benefits from its use (client, coach, organization, platform)?
- Would coaching be similarly effective without it?

C—Clear Consent

Ensure a transparent and pressure-free *consent process*:

- Be transparent about what the AI does, how it works, and what data it handles—in plain language
- Make sure consent is actively and freely given, with room to withdraw or revise it at any point

During AI Use

T—Trust & Transformation in Process

Stay attuned to how AI *influences the coaching space*:

- Does it affect openness, emotional tone, or client engagement?
- Are trust or the relationship enhanced or disrupted by its presence?

I—Inner Reflection (Coach Awareness)

Stay reflective on AI's impact:

- Are any ethical tensions arising?
- Are you seeing personal biases or discomforts around AI use?
- Do you use supervision or peer dialogue to support this reflection?

V—Value-Centered Boundaries

Ensure AI supports—not replaces—core coaching principles:

- Is the client's autonomy still uphold?
- Are the relational depth and co-created direction or other aspects of the human-to-human essence of coaching still protected?
- Is data privacy still ensured (not a one-time checkbox but an ongoing check)?

After AI Use

E—Evaluation and Ethics Review

Reflect on outcomes and process integrity:

- Was the client's autonomy preserved?
- Were data securely managed and appropriately deleted?
- What learnings or policy adjustments emerged?

9.2 Conclusion

This chapter has explored the opportunities and challenges of integrating AI as a third party within the one-to-one coaching relationship, highlighting how its presence can both support and disrupt the coaching process. Beyond immediate interactions, AI also introduces deeper ethical considerations that may extend beyond what is typically anticipated. To navigate these complexities, the *A.C.T.I.V.E. tool* offers a practical framework for fostering thoughtful, ethically engaged, relationally aware, and intentionally grounded use of AI in coaching—ensuring that technology serves the coaching relationship rather than undermining it.

References

Blease, C., Kaptchuk, T. J., Bernstein, M. H., Mandl, K. D., Halamka, J. D., & DesRoches, C. M. (2019). Artificial intelligence and the future of primary care: Exploratory qualitative study of UK general practitioners' views. *Journal of Medical Internet Research, 21*(3), e12802. https://doi.org/10.2196/12802

Diller, S. J. (2024). Ethics in digital and AI coaching. *Human Resource Development International*, 1–13. https://doi.org/10.1080/13678868.2024.2315928

Diller, S. J., & Passmore, J. (2023). Defining digital coaching: A qualitative inductive approach. *Frontiers in Psychology, 14*. https://doi.org/10.3389/fpsyg.2023.1148243

Diller, S. J., Muehlberger, C., Braumandl, I., & Jonas, E. (2020). Supporting students with coaching or training depending on their basic psychological needs. *International Journal of Mentoring & Coaching in Education, 10*(1), 84–100. https://doi.org/10.1108/IJMCE-08-2020-0050

Diller, S. J., Stenzel, L. C., & Passmore, J. (2024). The coach bots are coming: Exploring global coaches' attitudes and responses to the threat of AI coaching. *Human Resource Development International, 27*(4), 597–621. https://doi.org/10.1080/13678868.2024.2375934

Diller, S. J., Passmore, J., & Frey, D. (2026). *A multi-site qualitative inductive approach towards a collection of ethical issues and strategies in coaching.* Manuscript under review.

European Parliament. (2023). *Artificial intelligence act: Deal on comprehensive rules for trustworthy AI.* European Parliament. Retrieved March 24, 2024, from https://www.europarl.europa.eu/news/en/press-room/20231206IPR15699/artificial-intelligence-act-deal-on-comprehensive-rules-for-trustworthy-ai

Fouracres, A. J. S. (2024). Managing cybersecurity. In J. Passmore, S. J. Diller, S. Isaacson, & M. Brantl (Eds.), *The digital and AI coaches handbook: The complete guide to the use of online AI and technology in coaching* (pp. 203–211). Routledge.

Gengler, E., Hagerer, I., & Gales, A. (2024). Diversity bias in artificial intelligence. In J. Passmore, S. J. Diller, S. Isaacson, & M. Brantl (Eds.), *The digital and AI coaches handbook: The complete guide to the use of online AI and technology in coaching* (pp. 229–240). Routledge.

Hawley, R., Turner, E., & Iordanou, I. (2024). Managing ethics online. In J. Passmore, S. J. Diller, S. Isaacson, & M. Brantl (Eds.), *The digital and AI coaches handbook: The complete guide to the use of online AI and technology in coaching* (pp. 212–221). Routledge.

Hohenstein, J., Kizilcec, R. F., DiFranzo, D., Aghajari, Z., Mieczkowski, H., Levy, K., Naaman, M., Hancock, J., & Jung, M. F. (2023). Artificial intelligence in communication impacts language and social relationships. *Scientific Reports, 13*, 5375. https://doi.org/10.1038/s41598-023-30938-9

Iordanou, C., Hawley, R., & Iordanou, I. (2023). Ethical issues in note-taking and record-keeping in coaching. In W. A. Smith, J. Passmore, E. Turner, Y.-L. Lai, & D. Clutterbuck (Eds.), *The ethical coach's handbook: A guide to developing ethical maturity in practice* (pp. 167–181). Routledge.

Kettunen, E., Kari, T., & Frank, L. (2022). Digital coaching motivating young elderly people towards physical activity. *Sustainability, 14*(13), 7718. https://doi.org/10.3390/su14137718

Klonek, F. E., Lehmann-Willenbrock, N., & Kauffeld, S. (2014). Dynamics of resistance to change: A sequential analysis of change agents in action. *Journal of Change Management, 14*(3), 334–360. https://doi.org/10.1080/14697017.2014.896392

Köchling, A., Wehner, M., & Ruhle, S. A. (2021). Feeling treated fairly? Employee reactions toward AI in career development systems. *Academy of Management Proceedings, 2021*(1), 13802. https://doi.org/10.5465/AMBPP.2021.13802abstract

Lai, Y.-L., & Turner, E. (2023). Ethics of multiparty contracting and coaching. In W.-A. Smith, J. Passmore, E. Turner, Y.-L. Lai, & D. Clutterbuck (Eds.), *The ethical coach's handbook: A guide to developing ethical maturity in practice* (pp. 215–230). Routledge.

Mai, V., Neef, C., & Richert, A. (2022). 'Clicking vs. Writing': The impact of a chatbot's interaction method on the working alliance in AI-based coaching. *Coaching Theorie & Praxis, 8*(1), 15–31. https://doi.org/10.1365/s40896-021-00063-3

Mieczkowski, H., & Hancock, J. (2022). *Examining agency, expertise, and roles of AI systems in AI-mediated communication*. OSF Preprints. https://doi.org/10.31219/osf.io/asnv4

Mühlberger, C., Zerle, G., Möller, J., Diller, S. J., Greif, S., Kinder, N., & Jonas, E. (2024). Zooming in on the self in workplace coaching: Self-regulation and its connection to coaching success. *Journal of Occupational and Organizational Psychology, 98*(1). https://doi.org/10.1111/joop.12543

Nepal, S., Pillai, A., Campbell, W., Massachi, T., Heinz, M. V., Kunwar, A., Choi, E. S., Xu, O., Kuc, J., Huckins, J., Holden, J., Preum, S. M., Depp, C., Jacobson, N., Czerwinski, M., Granholm, E., & Campbell, A. T. (2024). MindScape study: Integrating LLM and behavioral sensing for personalized AI-driven journaling experiences. *Proceedings of the ACM on interactive, mobile, wearable and ubiquitous technologies, 8*(4), 1–44.

Pasha, N. (2024). Diversity, inclusion and belonging in digital coaching. In J. Passmore, S. J. Diller, S. Isaacson, & M. Brantl (Eds.), *The digital and AI coaches handbook: The complete guide to the use of online AI and technology in coaching* (pp. 241–253). Routledge.

Ratlabala, P., & Terblanche, N. (2022). Supervisors' perspectives on the contribution of coaching supervision to the development of ethical organisational coaching practice. *SA Journal of Human Resource Management, 20*, a1930. https://doi.org/10.4102/sajhrm.v20i0.1930

Rogers, K. M. (2023). Legal considerations of ethical decision making and coaching. In W. A. Smith, J. Passmore, E. Turner, Y.-L. Lai, & D. Clutterbuck (Eds.), *The ethical coach's handbook: A guide to developing ethical maturity in practice* (pp. 102–113). Routledge.

Schiemann, S. J., Mühlberger, C., & Jonas, E. (2018). Striving for autonomy: The importance of the autonomy need and its support within coaching. *International Journal of Evidence Based Coaching and Mentoring, S12*, 98–110. https://doi.org/10.24384/000543

Schiemann, S. J., Mühlberger, C., Schoorman, F. D., & Jonas, E. (2019). Trust me, I am a caring coach: The benefits of establishing trustworthiness during coaching by communicating benevolence. *Journal of Trust Research, 9*(2), 164–184. https://doi.org/10.1080/21515581.2019.1650751

Schilling, H., & Kauffeld, S. (2024). Building empathy and trust in online environments. In J. Passmore, S. J. Diller, S. Isaacson, & M. Brantl (Eds.), *The digital and AI coaches' handbook: The complete guide to the use of online, AI, and technology in coaching* (pp. 154–165). Routledge. https://doi.org/10.4324/9781003383741-17

Smith, W. A. (2025). The intentional coach: Bridging intentionality and ethicality. *Journal of Coaching Ethics, 2*(1), 1–31. https://doi.org/10.62882/m8cjnh07

Smith, W. A., & Arnold, C. (2023). Ethical coaching and its relationships. In W. A. Smith, J. Passmore, E. Turner, Y.-L. Lai, & D. Clutterbuck (Eds.), *The ethical coaches' handbook: A guide to developing ethical maturity in practice*. Routledge. https://doi.org/10.4324/9781003277729

Smith, W. A., King, S., & Lai, Y. L. (2021). Coaching with emotions and creating high quality connections in the workplace. In W. A. Smith, I. Boniwell, & S. Green (Eds.), *Positive psychology coaching in the workplace* (pp. 123–139). Springer. https://doi.org/10.1007/978-3-030-79952-6_10

Weidinger, L., Mellor, J., Rauh, M., Griffin, C., Uesato, J., Huang, P. S., et al. (2022). *Ethical and social risks of harm from language models* (arXiv No. 2112.04359). arXiv. https://arxiv.org/abs/2112.04359

Chapter 10
Social Constructionist Counselling and Coaching: Paradigms, Digitisation Potentials, and the Role of Artificial Intelligence

Marc Schreiber and Gregor J. Jenny

Abstract In this chapter, we present the development of a digital, social constructionist counselling intervention: the platform 'Meaning@Work'. To situate this innovation within the broader landscape of digital counselling and coaching, we propose a framework that distinguishes three paradigms: matching, managing/coaching, and meaning-making. These paradigms differ in their epistemological assumptions and in the role assigned to the counsellor, ranging from expert, to process-oriented, to identity-construction counsellor. We outline how digital solutions—such as self-management interventions—and Generative Artificial Intelligence (GenAI) are being integrated within each paradigm and how we ourselves intend to build our platform within the third paradigm of meaning-making and enhance it with AI.

Keywords Coaching · Counselling · Chatbots · Digitization · Artificial intelligence · Social constructionist counselling · Digital coaching interventions · Meaning-making · Generative AI in counselling · Narrative identity

10.1 Introduction

Social Constructionist Counselling and Coaching (SCC) is rooted in postmodern critiques of modern psychology. It encompasses a broad range of methods applied across various counselling and coaching settings. In this chapter, we position SCC within the evolution of counselling paradigms over the last century. We parallel this

M. Schreiber (✉)
Institute of Applied Psychology, ZHAW Zurich University of Applied Sciences, Zürich, Switzerland
e-mail: marc.schreiber@zhaw.ch

G. J. Jenny
FHNW School of Applied Psychology, School of Applied Psychology, Olten, Switzerland
e-mail: gregor.jenny@fhnw.ch

R. Wegener et al. (eds.), *Coaching in the Age of AI*, SpringerBriefs in Psychology, https://doi.org/10.1007/978-3-032-23332-5_10

evolution with developments in digitisation and present a research project grounded in SCC and integrating Generative Artificial Intelligence (GenAI). First, we outline three distinct counselling paradigms and corresponding methods: the *matching* paradigm, the *managing/coaching* paradigm, and the *meaning-making* paradigm. Second, we elaborate on digitisation potentials and the role of AI within these three paradigms and their methods. And third, we present a research project, which develops a comprehensive counselling process grounded in social constructionist principles and oriented towards co-constructing a person's life portrait. The project digitises the counselling process and integrates GenAI into it.

10.2 Counselling Paradigms and Corresponding Methods

With reference to career counselling, Savickas (2012, 2015, 2020; see also Schreiber 2022) identifies three counselling paradigms: (1) *matching* (also referred to as vocational guidance), (2) *managing/coaching* (also referred to as career education), and (3) *meaning-making* (also referred to as life design). Each paradigm is associated with particular professional attitudes, concrete methods, and roles adopted by counsellors (Table 10.1). These paradigms, deriving from career counselling, reflect the changing nature of work and the demands placed on employees.

(1) During the period of industrialisation and urbanisation (around 1900), **matching** emerged as a dominant counselling paradigm. This approach is grounded in a positivist worldview and emphasises the counsellor's role in applying objective scientific knowledge to clients' challenges—such as choosing between career options. Clients are conceptualised as social actors who engage with the guidance offered by the counsellor, who functions as an expert counsellor. Such guidance is based on meta-narratives that evolved from quantitative-oriented scientific practices, which

Table 10.1 Counselling paradigms and corresponding methods

Counselling paradigms	Corresponding methods
Matching (vocational guidance; expert counsellor)	
Social actors engage in performing vocational tasks Work environment characterised by *stability*	Questionnaires, ability tests Matching approaches
Managing/coaching (career education; process-oriented counsellor)	
Motivated agents aim to achieve successful occupational transitions Work environment characterised by a high degree of *predictability*	Process-oriented counselling (e.g. cognitive-behavioural, solution-focused, systemic) Lifelong learning (e.g. psychoeducation, competencies development)
Meaning-making (life design; identity construction counsellor/co-constructor)	
Autobiographical authors interpret and find meaning in work-related challenges Work environment characterised by unforeseeable *transformation*	Self and identity development Narrative methods

assume a stable world. Common counselling methods in this paradigm include questionnaires, cognitive ability tests, and techniques derived from quantitative empirical traditions, such as various matching approaches (e.g. partner or job matching).

(2) As specialisation increased and hierarchical, multinational organisations expanded after World War II, **managing/coaching** emerged as a complementary counselling paradigm. Instead of aligning scientific facts with clients' challenges, this paradigm focuses on guiding clients—viewed as motivated agents striving for successful solutions to their challenges—through processes of self-management and self-actualisation, as rooted in humanistic and existential perspectives. The primary objective is to assist clients in identifying their personal motives and goals, and in translating these into actionable steps aimed at goal attainment and the navigation of potential obstacles. Personal development is frequently framed within an economic world that prioritises continuous growth and predictability. Given the ever-evolving nature of the world, counsellors act as process-oriented counsellors, emphasising lifelong learning and the cultivation of competencies relevant to goal achievement (e.g. solution-focused coaching, systemic coaching, psychoeducation, reframing, etc.).

(3) In response to the evolving challenges of the postmodern world of work—characterised by continuous and unpredictable transformation—**meaning-making** has emerged as a vital counselling paradigm for the twenty-first century. Whereas the matching paradigm is grounded in the assumption of a stable world of work, and the managing/coaching paradigm relies on predictability, the meaning-making paradigm centres on navigating constant change. Rooted in postmodern psychology (e.g. Gergen, 1985; Kvale, 1992), the meaning-making paradigm shifts the focus from isolated individual agency to the socially and linguistically constructed nature of reality. Gergen (1985) posits that truth claims are contingent upon social consensus and are inherently situated within relational and cultural narratives. Consequently, language is seen as constitutive of reality, shaping it through individual expression. Counselling methods informed by this approach are person-centred, emphasising the co-construction of narratives within specific sociocultural contexts. Grounded in the assumption of the complex and dynamic nature of human experience and behaviour, these methods aim to support self and identity development through coherent identity narratives (Savickas, 2012, 2015). Identity construction counsellors assist clients—seen as autobiographical authors—in identifying a central narrative thread and making meaning of personal challenges and dissonances through the use of narrative methods. Depending on the counsellor's orientation, they may also contribute new perspectives within the narrative process or function as idea-generators. Importantly, a comprehensive understanding of individuals in a complex world must incorporate all three perspectives, that is, matching, managing/coaching, and meaning-making.

10.3 Digitisation Potentials and the Role of Artificial Intelligence

The digitisation of work processes has advanced in parallel with increasing specialisation and globalisation. In recent years, its potential has been thoroughly explored in the fields of counselling and coaching (Allemand & Flückiger, 2022; Klein et al., 2025; Passmore et al., 2024). Klein et al. (2025) distinguish between video counselling and Internet-based self-management interventions (SMIs). SMIs, whether applied in counselling, coaching, or psychotherapy, draw on a variety of psychological or therapeutic approaches, including cognitive-behavioural, solution-focused, and systemic. These interventions are typically low-threshold and highly scalable, making them a valuable complement to traditional face-to-face services. Most SMIs follow standardised, predefined protocols. When user interaction is included, the responses are generally scripted by professionals and embedded into the system, activated through rule-based algorithms. The effectiveness of such interventions is significantly influenced by users' expectations and beliefs regarding their efficacy, as well as by the perceived quality of the working alliance with the counsellor. This alliance may be fostered through initial contact or asynchronous communication (Klein et al., 2025; Probst et al., 2022). However, these findings should be interpreted with caution, as they are based on self-selected individuals who voluntarily engaged with SMIs (Klein et al., 2025).

In theory, GenAI tools such as ChatGPT could be used to deliver personalised counselling and coaching interventions via chat-based interfaces (see also Terblanche, 2024). However, GenAI remains inherently opaque, as it simulates human interaction based on Large Language Models (LLMs) trained on extensive text data (e.g. Internet-based datasets). Rather than relying on explicitly human-encoded content—as is typical of current SMIs—LLMs generate language by probabilistically predicting the next word based on statistical patterns of word co-occurrence. As Klein et al. (2025) note, it is likely to take a significant amount of time before AI—particularly GenAI—is fully integrated into counselling and coaching SMIs.

In light of this, we align recent technological developments with the three counselling paradigms (Table 10.2). The *matching paradigm* has historically driven digitisation efforts, particularly through online questionnaires and ability tests administered via digital platforms, sometimes with matching included (e.g. person–environment matching in career counselling using tools such as the Explorix (Joerin Fux et al., 2013)). Sentiment analysis and personality computing (i.e. the extraction of personality characteristics through AI) also align with the matching paradigm. For example, in the context of sentiment analysis, Steppan et al. (2024) explored the use of Machine Learning (ML) to track facial emotional expressions. The application of ML consists of a variable of interest (e.g. expert classifications of emotional expressions such as neutral, happy, or sad) that is predicted by predictor variables (e.g. facial emotion recognition based on video recordings during therapy sessions). Their findings showed that both ML-detected neutral expressions and reduced

Table 10.2 Counselling paradigms, digitisation potentials, and the role of AI

Counselling paradigm	Digitisation potential	Role of AI
Matching	Online testing platforms Person–Environment matching tools: e.g. Explorix	ML algorithms providing expert information (e.g. for sentiment analysis, personality computing, or matching)
Managing/ coaching	Rule-based, scripted by professionals: e.g. SMIs	GenAI chatbot (e.g. ChatGPT) as process-oriented facilitator (*future scenario?*) [potentially including ML analyses of speech and emotion patterns, referring to the matching paradigm]
Meaning-making	Rule-based, scripted by professionals: e.g. My Career Story (MCS)	GenAI chatbot (e.g. ChatGPT) as process-oriented facilitator for narrative methods (*future scenario?*) GenAI chatbot as a co-constructor (*future scenario?*)

social smiling were linked to a higher likelihood of psychotherapy dropout. Earlier work by IBM (Biondi et al., 2017) had already introduced algorithms designed to detect emotions from facial expressions. Similarly, as an example of personality computing, the *myPersonality* application (Kern et al., 2014; Stillwell & Kosinski, 2012) analysed written texts by extracting semantic and syntactic language features to predict self-reported Big Five personality traits. Although such tools often yield statistically significant results, their practical utility in counselling and coaching contexts remains insufficiently demonstrated (see Schreiber et al., 2025). Excessive integration of additional data sources into counselling or coaching sessions risks distracting both counsellors and clients, potentially undermining the counselling process.

Most SMIs, as described above, fall within the *managing/coaching paradigm*, as they support clients in specifying their goals and transforming them into concrete, actionable steps within a predictable work environment. The coaching sector has already begun integrating AI in various forms (Passmore et al., 2024; Terblanche, 2024). For example, platforms such as BetterUp (www.betterup.com), CoachHub (www.coachhub.com), or Woebot (https://woebothealth.com; Prochaska et al., 2021; Qi, 2025) utilise AI to deliver real-time feedback during coaching sessions, analyse speech patterns and emotional tone, and recommend personalised development activities. These AI-supported tools assist coaches by generating session summaries, identifying emotional cues, and proposing follow-up actions aligned with the client's goals. They are grounded in the matching paradigm, where ML algorithms (or GenAI chatbots) analyse audio and/or video data to capture ostensibly objective information. This 'objectivity' typically relies on the so-called ground truth—standardised data sets often derived from human assessments, such as the labelling of emotional expressions in images or videos. However, these ground truths are inherently limited by subjective interpretations and considerable variability across individuals and cultures in emotional display. Within the *managing/coaching* paradigm, we could also think of a future scenario in which a GenAI chatbot (e.g. ChatGPT, …) serves as a process-oriented facilitator, systematically supporting process-guidance, psychoeducation, reframing, and competency development to help clients achieve their goals.

Within the *meaning-making* paradigm, where the work environment is characterised by unpredictable transformation, digitisation—and particularly the application of AI—has not yet been widely adopted. However, co-construction processes may also be supported through SMIs designed to foster self and identity development through coherent identity narratives. For example, the platform Laufbahndiagnostik (www.laufbahndiagnostik.zhaw.ch) delivers a digital version of the My Career Story (MCS) (Savickas & Hartung, 2021). A central question is whether co-construction processes between counsellor and client can be effectively supported through a digital system. The following section introduces a research project focused on the development of a digital counselling and coaching platform, *Meaning@Work*, which integrates social constructionist principles and GenAI to support self and identity development in the job context.

10.4 Digital Counselling Platform 'Meaning@Work'

The platform 'Meaning@Work' is grounded in theories of personality and identity construction (Schreiber, 2022) and organisational health development (Jenny & Bauer, 2013), aiming to deliver digital SCC. Users are guided to narratively reconstruct their self and identity narratives through a structured three-phase process (Fig. 10.1): (I) rise of tension, (II) supported meaning-making, and (III) dual crafting. This process aligns with the meaning-making paradigm described earlier, emphasising self-reflection, meaning-making, and adaptability in navigating work and life transitions. According to Savickas (2020), SCC follows a four-step procedure integrated into Phases II and III: *construction*, where individuals create 'micro-narratives' based on personal experiences; *deconstruction*, where they critically examine these 'micro-narratives' to identify recurring themes, dispositions, and motives; *reconstruction*, where these insights are synthesised into a coherent new identity narrative ('macro-narrative'); and *co-construction*, where identity narratives are translated into everyday life through self- and system-oriented crafting (e.g. attempting to modify personal behavioural patterns and/or adapting the work environment to better align with one's identity narrative). The platform supports users in developing a Meaning@Work Card (MWC) (Schreiber et al., 2020), which brings together self-relevant themes, dispositions, motives, and self-advice. The MWC acts as a reflective tool for exploring potential career directions and planning next steps towards a more meaningful and fulfilling life.

A key innovation of this intervention is the integration of GenAI not only as a process-oriented facilitator for narrative methods but also as a co-constructor, providing non-directive inspirations based on participant-generated data (texts, images,

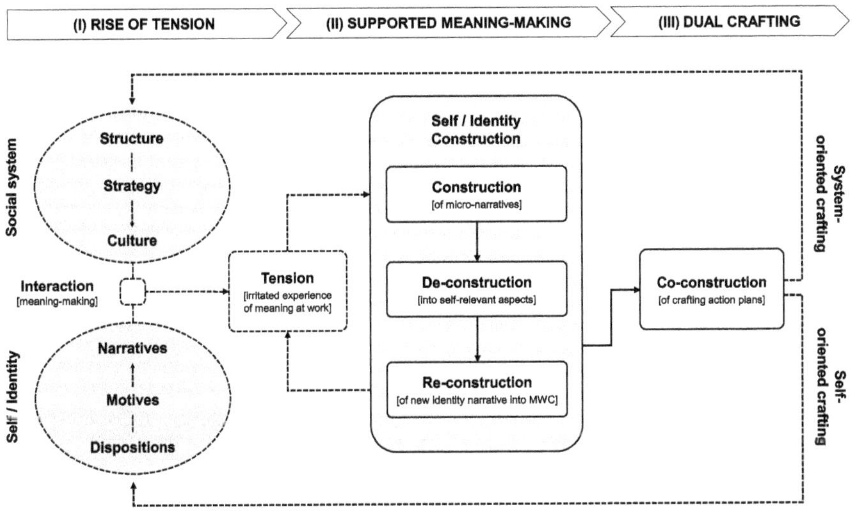

Fig. 10.1 Basic logic model (straight lines = actions within the digital platform 'Meaning@ Work'; dotted lines = experiences and behaviours at work; MWC = Meaning@Work Card)

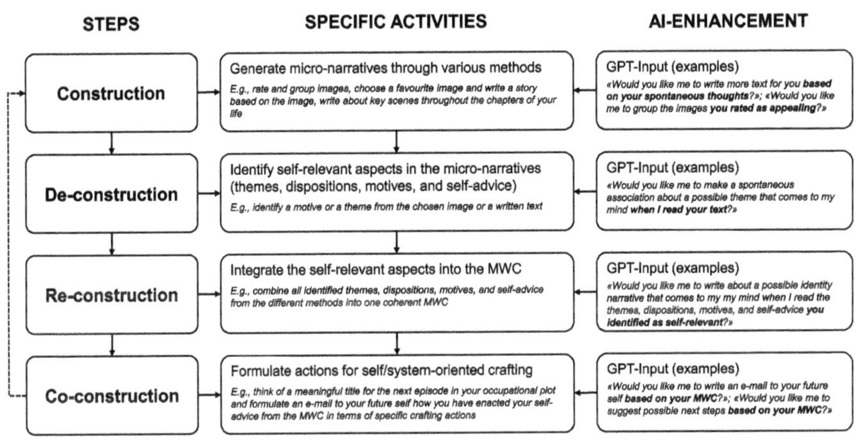

Fig. 10.2 Components of the generative AI-enhanced procedure

and dispositional information). Rather than offering prescriptive advice, the AI generates reflective prompts to enrich self-exploration, supporting users in deconstructing and reconstructing their identity narratives. This AI facilitates the application of narrative methods, thereby preserving the participants' authorship of their identity narratives, while also making the process more engaging and effective in fostering self and identity development (Fig. 10.2).

10.5 Research Design

The platform will be tested through a three-phase research design: (1) conceptual development of the Meaning@Work procedure, (2) application of AI-enhanced techniques, and (3) process and outcome evaluation. In balancing technological innovation with an ethical, client-centred approach, the platform Meaning@Work aims to contribute to the evolving field of digital counselling and coaching practice and research. Thus, our evaluation of the counselling process will focus on measures that assess both client satisfaction (i.e. clients' perceptions of the counselling experience) and changes in narrative identity (i.e. content-related shifts in clients' personal narratives). To this end, we will employ a pre-post measurement design incorporating both quantitative and qualitative methods. In doing so, we aim to highlight the potential of digital tools to support self and identity development, while reaffirming the importance of narrative co-construction as a fundamentally human endeavour.

10.6 Conclusion

While GenAI chatbots potentially offer promising opportunities for enhancing reflective depth, self-exploration, and making the process more engaging by serving as process-oriented facilitators and co-constructors for narrative methods, their integration into self and identity development according to the meaning-making paradigm also raises significant limitations and risks.

GenAI operates on an epistemology rooted in positivism, generating responses through statistical predictions based on LLMs. In contrast, the meaning-making paradigm is grounded in social constructionism, which emphasises the contextual and co-constructed nature of knowledge. Within this framework, a counsellor's unique experience, emotions, and intuition are essential. Unlike human counsellors, who draw on implicit knowledge and embodied experience, GenAI is limited to processing explicit datasets (e.g. text, video). While this reliance on explicit data can offer certain advantages such as complex pattern recognition, it also introduces interpretative constraints due to a lack of contextual and interpersonal sensitivity. These limitations become particularly significant given the potential risk of clients over-relying on AI-generated insights—a concern that, admittedly, is not exclusive to AI but also applies to human counselling.

We conclude that GenAI should be held to standards comparable to those of human counsellors. Crucially, the underlying counselling paradigm must be taken into account. In expertise-driven counselling (aligned with the matching paradigm), the focus lies in providing guidance based on scientifically validated, 'objective' facts. In this context, ML algorithms—despite the difficulty in establishing definitive ground truths for training and the risk that overloading sessions with additional data sources could divert attention from the core counselling process—can offer valuable contributions to counselling and coaching.

In contrast, process-oriented counselling (aligned with the managing/coaching paradigm) prioritises the client's subjective reality, including facilitating progress towards personal goals and navigating one's life trajectory. Effective process facilitation in this context depends not only on following established procedures but also on the counsellor's capacity to engage intuitively, draw upon lived experience, and commit to ongoing reflection and professional supervision. The same applies to co-construction within the meaning-making paradigm, which explicitly aims to support self and identity development within a work environment that is unforeseeable. As written above, we believe that this is a deeply human undertaking.

References

Allemand, M., & Flückiger, C. (2022). Personality change through digital-coaching interventions. *Current Directions in Psychological Science, 31*(1), 41–48. https://doi.org/10.1177/09637214211067782

Biondi, G., Franzoni, V., & Poggioni, V. (2017). A deep learning semantic approach to emotion recognition using the IBM Watson Bluemix Alchemy Language. In *Lecture notes in computer science (including subseries lecture notes in artificial intelligence and lecture notes in bioinformatics), 10406 LNCS* (pp. 719–729). https://doi.org/10.1007/978-3-319-62398-6_51

Gergen, K. J. (1985). The social constructionist movement in modern psychology. *American Psychologist, 40*(3), 266–275. https://doi.org/10.1037/0003-066X.40.3.266

Jenny, G. J., & Bauer, G. F. (2013). The limits of control: A systemic, model-based approach to changing organisations towards better health. In G. F. Bauer & G. J. Jenny (Eds.), *Salutogenic organizations and change: The concepts behind organizational health intervention research* (pp. 167–187). Springer. https://doi.org/10.1007/978-94-007-6470-5_10

Joerin Fux, S., Stoll, F., Bergmann, C., & Eder, F. (2013). *Explorix—Das Werkzeug zur Berufswahl und Laufbahnplanung*. Huber.

Kern, M. L., Eichstaedt, J. C., Schwartz, H. A., Dziurzynski, L., Ungar, L. H., Stillwell, D. J., Kosinski, M., Ramones, S. M., & Seligman, M. E. P. (2014). The online social self: An open vocabulary approach to personality. *Assessment, 21*(2), 158–169. https://doi.org/10.1177/1073191113514104

Klein, J. P., Knaevelsrud, C., Berger, T., & Voderholzer, U. (2025). Internetbasierte Interventionen bei psychischen Erkrankungen. In U. Voderholzer (Ed.), *Therapie psychischer Erkrankungen* (20th ed., pp. 675–682). Urban & Fischer. https://doi.org/10.1016/B978-3-437-21224-6.00037-2

Kvale, S. (1992). Postmodern psychology: A contradiction in terms? In S. Kvale (Ed.), *Psychology and postmodernism* (pp. 31–57). Sage Publications.

Passmore, J., Diller, S. J., Isaacson, S., & Brantl, M. (Eds.). (2024). *The digital and AI coaches' handbook: The complete guide to the use of online, AI, and technology in coaching*. Routledge.

Probst, G. H., Berger, T., & Flückiger, C. (2022). The alliance–outcome relation in internet-based interventions for psychological disorders: A correlational meta-analysis. *Verhaltenstherapie, 32*(Suppl. 1), 135–146. https://doi.org/10.1159/000503432

Prochaska, J. J., Vogel, E. A., Chieng, A., Kendra, M., Baiocchi, M., Pajarito, S., & Robinson, A. (2021). A therapeutic relational agent for reducing problematic substance use (Woebot): Development and usability study. *Journal of Medical Internet Research, 23*(3), e24850. https://doi.org/10.2196/24850

Qi, Y. (2025). Pilot quasi-experimental research on the effectiveness of the Woebot AI chatbot for reducing mild depression symptoms among athletes. *International Journal of Human–Computer Interaction, 41*(1), 452–459. https://doi.org/10.1080/10447318.2023.2301256

Savickas, M. L. (2012). The 2012 Leona Tyler Award address: Constructing careers—Actors, agents, and authors. *The Counseling Psychologist, 41*, 648–662. https://doi.org/10.1177/0011000012468339

Savickas, M. L. (2015). Career counseling paradigms: Guiding, developing, and designing. In P. J. Hartung, M. L. Savickas, & W. B. Walsh (Eds.), *APA handbook of career intervention: Foundations* (Vol. 1, pp. 129–143). American Psychological Association. https://doi.org/10.1037/14438-000

Savickas, M. L. (2020). Career construction theory and counseling model. In S. D. Brown & R. W. Lent (Eds.), *Career development and counseling: Putting theory and research to work* (pp. 165–200). Wiley & Sons.

Savickas, M. L., & Hartung, P. J. (2021). *My career story*. www.vocopher.com

Schreiber, M. (Ed.). (2022). *Narrative Ansätze in Beratung und Coaching: Das Modell der Persönlichkeits- und Identitätskonstruktion (MPI) in der Praxis*. Springer. https://doi.org/10.1007/978-3-658-37951-3

Schreiber, M., Gschwend, A., & Iller, M. L. S. (2020). The vocational ID–Connecting life design counselling and personality systems interaction theory. *British Journal of Guidance and Counselling, 48*(1), 52–65. https://doi.org/10.1080/03069885.2018.1538495

Schreiber, M., Jenny, G. J., Hürlimann, M., Parfenova, Y., von Däniken, P., & Cieliebak, M. (2025). A discourse on the use of machine learning (ML) in personality psychology: Can we expect ML to predict questionnaire scores from idiographic text-based data? *Journal of Research in Personality, 107*, 104666. https://doi.org/10.1016/j.jrp.2025.104666

Steppan, M., Zimmermann, R., Fürer, L., Southward, M., Koenig, J., Kaess, M., Kleinbub, J. R., Roth, V., & Schmeck, K. (2024). Machine learning facial emotion classifiers in psychotherapy research: A proof-of-concept study. *Psychopathology, 57*(3), 159–168. https://doi.org/10.1159/000534811

Stillwell, D. J., & Kosinski, M. (2012). *myPersonality project: Example of successful utilization of online social networks for large-scale social research*. The Psychometrics Centre, University of Cambridge. https://drive.google.com/file/d/1KzTSyd2coi0oTprgHRRYwWScQ7-TaWIs/view

Terblanche, N. H. D. (2024). Artificial intelligence (AI) coaching: Redefining people development and organizational performance. *The Journal of Applied Behavioral Science, 60*(4), 631–638. https://doi.org/10.1177/00218863241283919

Part IV
AI Used for Training and Supervisory Purposes

Chapter 11
Artificial Intelligence Coaching for Leader Development and Supervision

Olivier Malafronte

Abstract This chapter explores Artificial Intelligence Coaching (AIC) as a tool for training and supervising leaders within organizations. Drawing on empirical research comparing human-based and AI-based coaching conversations, and studies investigating leaders' schema changes in AIC conversations, the chapter synthesizes findings related to reflectivity, schema regulation, and competencies augmentation. It proposes a framework illustrating how AIC facilitates reflective practice, leading to cognitive and affective schema changes, thereby augmenting essential leadership competencies and enabling leaders to self-supervise in the flow of work. The chapter discusses theoretical and practical implications, highlighting opportunities for scaling development initiatives while considering current limitations and outlining a future research agenda.

Keywords Artificial intelligence · Coaching · Leadership development · Reflective practice · Schema regulation · Competencies · Human augmentation · Coaching conversations · Human–AI interaction

11.1 Introduction

The rapidly evolving organizational landscape requires managers and leaders to act as facilitators and coaches (Ellinger et al., 2018; Ibarra & Scoular, 2019). While online coaching is disrupting leadership development (Bersin, 2022; Graßmann & Schermuly, 2020) and recent research indicates that AI Coaching (AIC) can develop leadership competencies (Malafronte, 2024), the integration of AI into coaching practice presents both opportunities and challenges, as well as questions remain about its effectiveness compared to human coaching challenges (Bachkirova & Kemp, 2024; Passmore & Tee, 2024).

O. Malafronte (✉)
Université Côte d'Azur, Institut d'Administration des Entreprises (IAE), IAE Nice Graduate School of Management, Nice, France

R. Wegener et al. (eds.), *Coaching in the Age of AI*, SpringerBriefs in Psychology, https://doi.org/10.1007/978-3-032-23332-5_11

Additionally, the literature on training and supervising leaders' coaching skills represents an emerging but understudied area. Traditional approaches to coaching supervision (de Haan, 2025; Laske, 2006) rarely address the challenges leaders face when serving dual roles as both coach and authority figure. This leads to our central research question: How can AI coaching train and supervise leaders to develop good leadership in organizations?

11.2 An Overview of Four Different Studies

This chapter draws from four studies by Malafronte (2025, PhD thesis under publication) employing qualitative, exploratory, and comparative methodologies to investigate AIC in leadership development.

Study 1 used a comparative design to explore user feedback from two AIC tools: *PocketConfidant* (an early AIC chatbot) and *AI Coach* (based on ChatGPT4 and an avatar interface). Data was collected from company leaders, managers, a freelance agent, and Master's level business students using the tools between 2018 and 2023.

Study 2 used multiple cases of AIC conversations with mid-level leaders. Data collection occurred in two stages (2020–2024), utilizing two different AI coaches, one including a scripted-AI approach and one including ChatGPT-4. The AI coaches were designed with a common general coaching process guiding leaders through steps like reflecting on feelings, situation, desired change, resources, strengths, goals, action plans, awareness, and satisfaction, so that the coaching process was maintained under control and similar with both AI coaches.

Study 3 followed the same approach to Study 2 but focused only on exploring the types of reflectivity emerging in AIC conversations.

Study 4 compared AI-Based Coaching Conversations (AIBCC) and Human-Based Coaching Conversations (HBCC) using 20 executive coaching conversations from four countries and ten organizations. Participants volunteered and engaged with the AI Coach over a maximum of 2 months or enrolled in a human coaching program.

11.3 What Can We Learn?

11.3.1 Competencies Augmentation (Study 1)

The concept of competencies augmentation illustrates the potential contributions of coaching and AI to managerial competencies. This concept highlights the ability of AIC tools to engage users in reflective experiences that lead to taking a step back and adjusting cognitive and affective representations. The augmentation of human capabilities through the automation and adaptation features of machines adds value in work and learning activities. This value appears contingent on users having a prior goal for using the innovative tool.

11.3.2 The Role of Reflectivity and Schema Change (Studies 2 and 3)

AIC is capable of engaging leaders in reflection on their situations, helping them mobilize and regulate their capacities for reasoning, learning, adapting to change, and managing relationships by reproducing human behaviors like questioning and reasoning. The coaching reflective conversation process favors changes in leaders' cognitive and affective schemas. It helps users engage in reflective experiences that allow for taking a step back, adjusting cognitive and affective representations in complex situations, and mobilizing resources using reflective questioning. For instance, a leader starts an AI Coaching conversation feeling "anxious" about "sharing a decision that could shake up the team." Through open and reflective questioning, the leader navigates desired states, resources and ends the conversation with the goal of "meeting as a team to find solutions" and feeling "more reassured," perceiving that "it is possible."

AIC can facilitate leadership competency development, particularly reflectivity, through the analysis of schemas in conversations. Reframing issues through conversation with an AI Coach can lead to the "socialization" of these issues, fostering the development of important leadership competencies like communication and collaboration. AI Coaching can encourage trust, help in taking a step back, managing stress, goal development, work organization, priority management, and activating empathic mechanisms, fostering relational competencies important for leaders.

Finally, leaders' expectations, particularly for receiving advice, can mediate schema regulation and influence affective schema change. While automated open questioning may facilitate reflective mediation, AI coaching users must have a clear purpose and understanding of AIC tools to generate positive outcomes.

11.3.3 Similarities and Differences with Human Coaching (Study 4)

A comparison between AI and Human coaching conversations reveals that AIBCC can achieve similar surface outcomes (shifting negative affect to positive affect and supporting positive reflection to clarify and frame a goal) as HBCC, often in a shorter time (15 vs. 60 min on average). Both types of coaching utilized open reflective questioning as a main active ingredient. Differences between AIBCC and HBCC include AIBCC not talking over coachees, hence giving more space to coachees; however, HBCC offer human warmth, deeper emotional connection, and identity exploration.

11.4 Proposed Framework: The AIC Augmentation Loop for Leadership Development and Supervision

The synthesis of empirical findings across multiple studies revealed consistent patterns in how AIC influences leader development, conceptualized as the "AIC Augmentation Loop." This framework is theoretically grounded in three interconnected dimensions:

1. Reflective practice theory (Schön, 1983), emphasizing the importance of cognitive processing of experience.
2. Schema regulation (Gottfredson & Reina, 2020), explaining how mental structures are adjusted through new information.
3. Competency development theory (Coulet, 2014), addressing how new capabilities are formed and sustained.

Unlike previous models that treat coaching as a linear intervention, this framework captures the cyclical and iterative nature of leadership development through AI-facilitated reflection. The seven components represent distinct but interconnected processes:

1. **Initiation and Goal Setting**: The leader initiates a conversation with the AI Coach, bringing a specific work situation, problem, or development goal. The AI Coach guides the leader in defining their present situation, desired outcome, and setting clear objectives. *Example: I'm feeling anxious about sharing a decision that can shake up the team. We need to transform the team's organization to externalize developments.*
2. **Reflective Dialogue**: The AI Coach employs open, reflective questioning as its primary function. This emulates a core human coaching behavior. The questioning sequence guides the leader to analyze the situation, identify resources, reflect on past experiences, and explore potential solutions. *Example: The leader remembers] the delivery of a project that is beneficial for the company, both in terms of revenue and internal efficiency.*
3. **Schema Activation and Regulation**: The reflective questioning prompts the leader's cognitive and affective schemas related to the situation. The dialogue facilitates taking a step back and adjusting these representations. *Example: I'm a little more reassured; I think that all of this is possible.*
4. **Insight Generation and Awareness**: Through reflection and schema regulation, the leader gains new insights and increases self-awareness at different levels. This includes identifying strengths and potential actions. *Example: Putting my strengths into perspective, to reassure myself and to know that we are capable of rising to the challenge.*

5. **Action Planning and Commitment**: The AI Coach supports the leader in formulating solutions, defining specific actions, and planning for follow-through. This step emphasizes commitment to change. *Example: Meeting as a team to design a technological solution.*
6. **Competency Augmentation**: The repeated engagement in this reflective process and the resulting schema changes augment specific leadership competencies. These include:
   - Reflexivity: The ability to analyze situations and one's role
   - Self-Regulation: Managing thoughts, feelings, and actions
   - Problem-Solving: Generating and evaluating solutions
   - Goal Setting and Organization: Defining objectives and planning tasks
   - Communication and Collaboration: Potentially fostered by practicing articulating issues and engaging empathic mechanisms
7. **Application in Practice (Training and Supervision)**: The augmented competencies are applied in real-world leadership situations.

What distinguishes this framework is its focus on the augmentation relationship between human and AI, rather than replacement or competition. The data consistently revealed that AIC's primary contribution is in amplifying leaders' inherent capabilities through structured reflection, rather than providing external expertise.

11.5 Leadership Competencies Augmented Through AIC

Competency category	Specific skills	AIC mechanism	Evidence from research
Cognitive competencies	• Reflexivity • Critical thinking • Problem-solving • Analytical reasoning	Structured reflective questioning prompts cognitive schema activation	Leaders reported enhanced ability to "take a step back" and reframe complex situations
Self-management competencies	• Self-regulation • Stress management • Goal setting • Work organization	Regular reflective practice develops metacognitive abilities	AIC users demonstrated improved organization and priority management
Relational competencies	• Communication • Empathy • Collaboration • Trust-building	"Socialization" of issues through dialogue activates empathic mechanisms	Practicing articulation of challenges in AIC conversations transferred to human interactions

Competency category	Specific skills	AIC mechanism	Evidence from research
Leadership-specific competencies	• Decision-making • Change management •Vision development • Coaching others	Iterative reflection on leadership challenges builds capacity	Leaders reported applying insights from AIC conversations to their own coaching of team members
Developmental meta-competencies	• Learning agility • Adaptability •Self-directed development	AIC as a self-supervision tool empowers continuous learning	Studies showed evidence of leaders initiating their own development activities following AIC

11.6 Theoretical Contribution

The introduction of "competencies augmentation" as a theoretical construct bridges human resource management and AI literature by explaining how technological tools can enhance rather than replace human capabilities. By demonstrating how AIC tools engage leaders in reflective experiences that facilitate cognitive distancing and schema adjustment, we provide a mechanism-based explanation for how leadership competencies develop through AI-mediated interactions.

11.7 Practical Contributions

Our findings offer several actionable insights for HR professionals, leadership developers, and organizational leaders. First, managing expectations is crucial for AIC implementation success. Organizations must clearly communicate how AI Coaching works and the nature of content it provides, as user expectations significantly influence perceived quality and outcomes. Particularly important is clarifying that AIC primarily facilitates reflection rather than providing directive advice, despite many leaders' initial expectations.

Second, our research demonstrates that AI-automated coaching can effectively develop several critical leadership competencies, including reflexivity, self-regulation, problem-solving, and interpersonal skills. Organizations can strategically deploy AIC to help leaders build confidence, manage stress, develop goals, organize work, manage priorities, and activate empathic mechanisms.

Third, our findings support a complementary rather than replacement approach to coaching implementation. AIC can serve as an accessible entry point to coaching culture, a supplement to human coaching programs, or a follow-up mechanism to extend coaching impact. The AIC augmentation loop framework provides organizations with a model for integrating AI tools into comprehensive leadership development strategies that leverage both technological and human coaching approaches according to specific development needs.

Fourth, the concept of competencies augmentation can serve as a pedagogical element to facilitate understanding and adoption of AI tools among leaders and learners. By framing AI as an augmentation tool rather than a replacement technology, organizations can reduce resistance and foster productive engagement with these emerging coaching approaches.

11.8 Limitations and Future Research Agenda

Several avenues for future research emerge from our research. Comparative studies of different AIC tools and algorithms could identify the specific design features that maximize effectiveness for different development goals. Longitudinal studies tracking specific competency development would provide more definitive evidence of AIC's developmental impact. The integration of AIC into formal training programs merits investigation to assess its pedagogical effectiveness alongside traditional content.

Future research should also address the intersection of human and artificial coaching by examining blended approaches that leverage the strengths of each modality. Studies exploring potential risks—such as algorithmic bias, privacy concerns, and perceived dehumanization—are essential, though our findings suggest that well-designed AIC might actually strengthen human capacities like empathy rather than diminish them.

11.9 Conclusion

AIC represents an emerging practice with significant potential to transform how organizations train and supervise leaders. Drawing on empirical evidence from multiple studies, this chapter has illustrated how AI coaching, primarily through facilitated reflective dialogue and the AIC augmentation loop framework, can drive changes in leaders' cognitive and affective schemas, thereby augmenting key leadership competencies. Our research demonstrates that AIC offers scalable and efficient developmental opportunities, particularly for foundational reflective practice, while also clarifying its limitations for deeper emotional and identity work where human coaching maintains distinct advantages.

The concept of competencies augmentation provides both a theoretical framework for understanding AI's role in leadership development and a practical approach for implementation that emphasizes enhancement rather than replacement of human capabilities. As organizations navigate the integration of AI into leadership development initiatives, this research offers evidence-based guidance for leveraging these technologies to foster effective leadership while maintaining the essential human dimensions of development and growth.

References

Bachkirova, T., & Kemp, R. (2024). 'AI coaching': Democratising coaching service or offering an ersatz? *Coaching: An International Journal of Theory, Research and Practice, 18*(1), 27–45. https://doi.org/10.1080/17521882.2024.2368598

Bersin, J. (2022, January). *Online coaching is so hot it's now disrupting leadership development*. Josh Bersin. https://joshbersin.com/2022/01/online-coaching-is-so-hot-its-now-disrupting-leadership-development/

Coulet, J.-C. (2014). Des caractéristiques de l'expertise au management des compétences individuelles et collectives. *Management & Avenir, 67*(1), 122–135. https://doi.org/10.3917/mav.067.0122

de Haan, E. (2025). How can coaches choose their approach and their interventions based on the evidence we now have? *Consulting Psychology Journal, 77*(1), 84–98. https://doi.org/10.1037/cpb0000276

Ellinger, A., Beattie, R., & Hamlin, R. (2018). The manager as coach. In C. Elaine, T. Bachkirova, & D. A. Clutterbuck (Eds.), *The complete handbook of coaching* (pp. 262–278). SAGE Publications.

Gottfredson, R. K., & Reina, C. S. (2020). Exploring why leaders do what they do: An integrative review of the situation–trait approach and situation–encoding schemas. *The Leadership Quarterly, 31*(1), 101373. https://doi.org/10.1016/j.leaqua.2019.101373

Graßmann, C., & Schermuly, C. C. (2020). Coaching with artificial intelligence: Concepts and capabilities. *Human Resource Development Review, 20*(1), 106–126. https://doi.org/10.1177/1534484320982891

Ibarra, H., & Scoular, A. (2019). The leader as coach. *Harvard Business Review, 97*(6), 110–119.

Laske, O. E. (2006). From coach training to coach education: Teaching coaching within a comprehensively evidence based framework. *International Journal of Evidence Based Coaching and Mentoring, 4*(1), 45–57.

Malafronte, O. (2024). Développement des leaders avec coaching et intelligence artificielle: Augmentation des compétences. *Management & Avenir, 142*(4), 39–59. https://doi.org/10.3917/mav.142.0039

Malafronte, O. (2025). *Developing leader competence in situation through Artificial Intelligence and coaching*. Doctoral dissertation. Université Côte d'Azur. Theses.fr. https://theses.fr/s316441

Passmore, J., & Tee, D. (2024). The library of Babel: Assessing the powers of artificial intelligence in knowledge synthesis, learning and development and coaching. *Journal of Work-Applied Management, 16*(1), 4–18. https://doi.org/10.1108/JWAM-06-2023-0057

Schön, D. A. (1983). *The reflective practitioner: How professionals think in action* (1st ed.). Basic Books.

Chapter 12
When AI, Video, and Coach Development Collide

James Bridgeman and Andrea Giraldez-Hayes

Abstract This chapter examines the intersection of artificial intelligence, video feedback (VF), and coach development, inquiring whether AI can assist coaches in becoming more human-centred in their practice. While VF and performance data are well-established in sports and other helping professions, their integration into coaching education has lagged. Post-pandemic shifts to virtual coaching and advances in AI now make it feasible for coaches to record, analyse, and reflect on their sessions in powerful new ways. Here we refer to a study that examines the use of Ovida, an AI-driven video analysis tool, by novice coaches over a period of several weeks. Through a thematic analysis of interviews, the findings reveal how AI-enhanced VF supports deeper reflection, raises self-awareness, and helps fine-tune core coaching competencies, such as questioning, listening, and presence. Coaches valued the objectivity of the data and reported measurable skill development, greater confidence, and a stronger sense of accountability. However, challenges included initial discomfort with self-observation, data misinterpretation without human context, and technology-related anxieties. The study concludes that AI-enhanced VF, when paired with expert supervision and a growth mindset, can accelerate coach development by highlighting 'moments that matter' and supporting intentional skill refinement. Future research should explore its long-term impact and applications across experience levels and cultural contexts.

Keywords Artificial intelligence · Video feedback · Ethics in coach training · Coaching supervision · Reflective practice · Self-awareness development · Coaching competencies · AI-supported video analysis · Digital coach development · Human–AI interaction

---

J. Bridgeman
Bridgford Consultancy, Altrincham, UK

A. Giraldez-Hayes (✉)
University of Cambridge, London, UK

R. Wegener et al. (eds.), *Coaching in the Age of AI*, SpringerBriefs in Psychology, https://doi.org/10.1007/978-3-032-23332-5_12

12.1 Setting the Scene

Given the widespread use of video feedback (VF) and data analysis across sports coaching and in training professionals across many disciplines, it is surprising that the coaching profession has generally been slow to adopt this tool for raising self-awareness and developing core skills such as generating rapport, active/empathic listening, using certain questioning techniques. Post-Covid, with the majority of coaching sessions now taking place virtually, there is a clear opportunity for coaches to record and review regularly their coaching sessions to determine how they might develop their skills further. Pairing video recordings with AI-crunched data enables not just transcription and a summary of core themes, but also detailed data analysis highlighting areas of specific interest in the coach–client conversation. Coaches can now understand through data how many open questions they are using (open questions will produce broader thinking, and give the client agency) (Clutterbuck, 2020); see when they are 'stacking' questions ('stacked' questions can confuse the client); and analyse how much they are talking in a session compared to their client (more experienced coaches will generally talk much less than their client, relying on a well-placed question to prompt further thinking) (Stanier, 2016). Given these are fundamental skills in forging human connection, this chapter investigates a question that we asked in scoping our research (Bridgeman & Giraldez-Hayes, 2024): Could we use AI to enable us to become *even more* human?

12.2 Video, Data, Sports, and Coaching: Developments over Time

From a spectacular running forehand down the line from Carlos Alcaraz to a stunning curled free kick into the top corner from Lionel Messi, twenty-first century sports fans are familiar with the slow-motion replay, overlaid with visual data that tracks the trajectory of the ball, its spin speed and bounce. Video replays enhance the viewing experience in all sports, often now complemented by ever-more complex data to observe the subtle nuances of the highly skilled professional. We can see just how the pros manage to pull off incredible feats of physical skill.

Of course, it's not just the viewers and fans who benefit from this technology. Sports coaches have long used VF to enhance skills and reflective capability (Wilson, 2008), raising awareness levels in athletes from rock-climbers (Walker et al., 2020) to badminton players (Mekruksavanich et al., 2022), enabling a golf swing's trajectory to be tweaked by a degree or two, or helping rowing crews ensure their rhythm and stroke timing is optimised. It raises self-awareness in athletes as well as amateurs, and enables sports coaches to fine-tune an athlete's technique, developing motor skills—with the athlete observing their own performance, after the fact. It enables highly specific and evidenced reflection-on-action, as coined by Donald Schön (1983). Studies indicate that video feedback in physical education classes 'allows learners to monitor, evaluate and adjust their performance' (Souissi et al., 2022, p. 1408). Beyond raising athletes' self-awareness, VF has been shown to be effective in doing so for the sports coach too, reminding them of lost moments—'reducing incorrect analysis caused by poor recall' (Carson, 2008, p. 386) and enabling a more objective view of verbal and non-verbal signals they send to their coachees (Meade et al., 2014; Partington et al., 2015).

Termed the 'gold standard of communication teaching' (Kurtz et al., 2005, cited in Hammoud et al., 2012, p. 20), VF has long been used in the helping professions as a tool for reflective practice in the training of, e.g., psychotherapists, doctors (Freytag et al., 2022), and teachers. Fukkink et al. (2011) in their meta-analysis of VF studies argue that reflective practice using video helps reinforce and encourage positive behaviours while also enabling the 'weeding out' of less desirable actions. As with many helping professions (Tarrant, 2013), coaches are encouraged to use regular reflective practice to develop their own self-awareness (Carden et al., 2021), which is a key component of the competency frameworks of the major coaching bodies (Association for Coaching, 2021; European Mentoring and Coaching Council, 2015; International Coaching Federation (ICF), 2019).

From Gallwey's Inner Game (Gallwey, 1974) to Sir John Whitmore (Whitmore, 2009), the profession of executive coaching has borrowed techniques and principles from the world of sport. Furthermore, incorporating artificial intelligence and video feedback into the training of sports coaches draws upon a well-established tradition in psychotherapy, where recorded sessions have long been used to enhance professional development. A systematic review by Aafjes-van Doorn et al. (2022) provides compelling empirical support for the practice, analysing 27 studies that examine the impact of video-recorded counselling sessions on practitioner growth. Despite initial anxiety reported by both counsellors and clients, the findings suggest that video recordings are not only non-harmful but also offer significant benefits. These include improved self-assessment, skill acquisition, and greater insight into in-session dynamics. Counselling supervisors, too, benefit from enhanced diagnostic accuracy (i.e. how well a therapist's assessment aligns with a client's actual condition, which is crucial for effective treatment) and a clearer view of trainee competency. Crucially, recordings provide an unfiltered, objective account of the session, countering the limitations of memory and subjective reporting. This model can and should be extended to coaching, where AI-enhanced video analysis offers the potential for real-time, granular feedback and the opportunity to systematically identify subtle behavioural patterns, blind spots, and relational dynamics. Like in psychotherapy, the thoughtful integration of video feedback can deepen reflective practice and accelerate skill development in coaching professionals.

This begs the question: Why is the use of VF not widespread throughout coach training and continuous professional development? Historically, a crucial limiting factor in the use of VF is that reviewing sessions takes time, for the coach and a supervisor. Vital to speeding up this process is the addition of data (Tuyls et al., 2021): now, computers can generate cues within videos that enable learners to jump to relevant moments, which coupled with expert discussion (e.g. a supervisor) can speed up the reflective process and lead to deeper discussions (Arakawa & Yakura, 2020).

12.3 What is Ovida? Combining VF with AI Data

Ovida (2024) is a web-based software employing AI for data analysis of recorded online coaching conversations. This helps coaches analyse, reflect on, and improve their skills. Ovida is likely the first software tailored specifically for coaches, based on the skills frameworks from the major coaching bodies. Both the researchers and participants had free access to Ovida for the purpose of the study.

In addition to an accurate transcript of the conversation, Ovida's AI provided data insights around core coaching competencies, such as share of voice percentage, coach question rate, the ratio of open-to-closed questions, percentage comparing number of questions to statements, and the number of times the coach interrupted their client. Coaches were able to track their progress over time via a stats dashboard. A 'key moments' feature, similar to features trialled by Arakawa and Yakura (2020), highlighted significant sections of conversations.

12.4 Using Ovida in Coach Development: A Qualitative Study

Our 2023 study (Bridgeman & Giraldez-Hayes, 2024) sought to understand the experience of coaches using VF coupled with AI-generated data to review and reflect on past coaching sessions with their clients. We spoke to 15 coaches, most with fewer than 200 h of coaching experience, who were students at the MSc in Applied Positive Psychology and Coaching Psychology at the University of East London. Each used Ovida to record a minimum of four coaching sessions with clients and review and reflect on those sessions over a period of several weeks.

Following semi-structured interviews and a reflexive thematic analysis (Braun & Clarke, 2021) of the transcripts, three clear themes, each with three sub-themes, emerged. We'll summarise them here, and more detail can be found in our journal article (Bridgeman & Giraldez-Hayes, 2024).

12.4.1 Deeper Reflection Through AI-Driven Data Insights and Video

All coaches said that through viewing the video, they derived insights into their coaching style and how they build rapport with their clients. Some were enthusiastic from the start of using the reflective tool, while others took longer to be won over. Coaches appreciated the chance to play the role of observer in one of their own sessions, enabling them to rediscover what Carson (2008) refers to as 'lost moments'.

Coaches found reviewing the videos gave them new knowledge about their coaching style and practice.

12.4.1.1 Raised Self-Awareness

Initial self-consciousness viewing the sessions ('I can't bear to look at myself') tended to wear off once coaches appreciated the opportunity to review and reflect, catching things they 'didn't necessarily see the first time'.

12.4.1.2 Objective View from Video Evidence

The observer's viewpoint helped coaches to gain new insights into how they were coming across as a coach to their clients. The video evidence provided a more precise form of reflection-on-action. Some focused on themselves, their body language and facial expressions, while others were interested to note the reactions of their client, seeing again the effect that specific questions had.

12.4.1.3 Charting Performance with Data

Coaches found value in seeing their performance metrics on coaching skills, displayed alongside the video evidence, relating the one to the other. Visualised data such as pie charts helped deepen their reflection, enabling more evidence-based decision-making, learning to 'love data'.

12.4.2 Growth Mindset and Skills Development

Coaches were quick to see how they could use the platform to develop their coaching skills. Participants all reported making specific changes to their coaching skills in sessions following reflective review. Over just a few weeks using the platform, for four coaching sessions, participants all reported a rise in their confidence, with some more emphatic than others. Reports of increased confidence came from several areas. Some felt satisfaction at having trialled and learned to use a new technology, while many took personal pride in seeing evidenced improvement in their coaching skills, also noting how this improvement had impacted clients in subsequent sessions.

12.4.2.1 Fine-Tuning Coaching Skills

Coaches appreciated the ability to analyse their data and make decisions based on what it was telling them: some resolved to be silent for longer, to focus on their share of voice; others considered how they might use more open questions to aid discovery and new thinking. Lots of our coaches specifically noticed they were 'stacking' questions and made deliberate moves to stop this. Participants all reported making specific changes to their coaching skills in sessions following reflective review. From one session to the next, coaches would plan a new strategy and execute it intentionally the next time. Crucial to encouraging deeper reflective practice was the tendency for the video and data insights to elicit further questions, as coaches searched for the 'so what?' behind what they saw, followed often by a 'now what?' leading to development opportunities.

12.4.2.2 A Tool to Stay On-Track

The theme of accountability and personal development ran throughout many of the coaches' attitudes to the data. One coach noticed they needed to focus on doing more rigorous contracting at the beginning of sessions. As coaches used the software over time, they could chart their progress using the data and see how the changes they were implementing played out in coaching sessions. This data over time, displayed on a coach dashboard, gave a sense of progression and growth, with some coaches personifying the software as a guide to their practice. A longer duration of study (perhaps over several months or more) would be useful to understand the long-term effects of using this data over time.

12.4.2.3 Feeling more Confident in Coaching

Every coach we spoke to reported a rise in confidence in their practice. They felt more self-efficacy in that they could see the effects of their coaching through the observer's view; decisions to ask certain questions at certain times were validated by a review of the interaction; others were proud of the evidence of development provided by the data. Some were emphatic: 'My coaching has got exponentially better'.

12.4.3 Drawbacks and Risks from Use

It is of course very common for us all to feel discomfort at seeing ourselves on video, though that may be shifting with younger generations. Perhaps unsurprisingly then, for our participants, one of the strongest sub-themes to come through was around a sense of judgement.

12.4.3.1 Judgement, from Machine and Inner Critic

A feeling of being judged arose in several participants, especially at the start of using the software. Some felt the widely accepted human discomfort at seeing themselves recorded; others were conscious of being 'judged' by the objective data—their inner-critic voice coming through during reflection, risking a perfectionist mindset: 'I wanted to ask the best questions in the world'. The inner critic led to participants focusing on negative aspects of their coaching sessions, in the video or considering the data, leading to feelings of shame or striving for perfection. The majority reported this waning over time. Coaches, on reflection, noted that much of this risk was down to the coach's own mindset going into the reflection: 'in the wrong frame of mind…I could go into being too critical'.

12.4.3.2 Technology Anxiety

It's no secret that many of us can feel nervous when using a new tool or technology for the first time. Coaches reported feeling uneasy about the recording of the sessions, with concerns around confidentiality and data protection despite clear assurances from Ovida around compliance. Others wondered whether the experience of being recorded, knowing that the data would be presented afterwards, may have led to their being less present in the coaching conversations—distracted by these thoughts.

12.4.3.3 Important Nuance and Context Can Be Missed

Some felt that there were occasions where the software didn't understand or appreciate the deeper context within a conversation moment. One coach pointed out that too great a focus on asking questions risks lessening another key coaching skill of summarising and paraphrasing back the client's own words. Many noted the opportunity the software provides of pairing the analysis with a human supervisor, who through emotional intelligence would be able to interpret the sessions with an expert eye. In general, coaches felt that when using a data-driven tool such as Ovida, the responsibility still lies with the human users of coach and supervisor, to reflect on the data and what it's telling them, working towards what this means for their development.

12.5 Discussion

The findings from this study give further evidence to the widely accepted efficacy of using VF in developing skills in learners through raising self-awareness and enabling action-planning based on objective visual evidence. We found that VF can be applied to coaching skills just as it can be applied to sports performance and that the observer's view of one's own performance can lead to deeper and more informed reflective practice, even over a short time period. A watch-out is the risk of negativity bias, which could lead to a reduction in confidence; what our participants told us (Judgement, from machine or inner critic) is that viewing one's performance with a growth mindset is key to focusing on what could be improved, and how it can be improved in future sessions. Over time, reviewing VF led to more confident coaches who were improving their coaching skills intentionally through reflective practice.

So far, so good, and of course there are already coach training providers that will require trainees to submit recordings of coaching sessions to assess their performance—indeed the (ICF) requires an expert-assessed recording as part of its credentialling process.

We believe our study shows the value of combining the VF with objective, AI-processed data on coach performance, to inform reflection and chart progress over time. This can speed up the reflective process—viewing video recordings of sessions can be time-consuming—by having 'key moments' identified by the software which can assist coaches in reflecting on 'moments that matter'. Empirical data around share of talk time, use of open questions, and other key performance indicators, enabled coaches to review their data, seek confirmation and evidence in the video, and make conscious efforts to refine their approach in future sessions. Although these initial results were promising, the sample size was small and the time available was limited. Further diverse, longitudinal, qualitative, and quantitative studies are required to examine the long-term developmental effects of using AI-enabled video reflection in coaching.

12.6 Conclusion and Moving Forward

This study raises several pertinent questions: Which level of coaches—beginner, intermediate, or master-level—would benefit the most from this approach? Or will it provide distinct advantages to each experience level, but in different ways? What elements of data analytics prove to be most beneficial for coaches? What cultural considerations underlie the use of video review? Additionally, what perspective does the client hold? How can the software be integrated with expert human supervision, both asynchronously and synchronously?

The field of AI is moving exponentially quickly, such that by the time you read this chapter, even a few months after publication, the landscape will have shifted significantly. New tools are being developed constantly, offering further opportunities for coach development. An increasing number of coaching chatbots offer 24/7 access to coaching conversations through text. Internal leader-coaches seeking practice coaching conversations (before trying out their skills on a 'real' human) can now do so with an AI-powered avatar coachee, who responds accordingly based on the coaching approach used, testing your coaching skills in the moment, and offering data-driven insights into your performance (see, for example, ELECTRIC Conversations, from The OCM in the UK (https://www.theocm.co.uk/ocm-enable/services/building-coach-mentoring-skills-in-leaders). This field will continue to move at pace, disrupting and changing the coaching industry as much as it will any other industry. The question for us as coaches is: Can we use AI to make us even better at the skills of human connection?

12.7 So, What Is Next? Implications for Coaching and Coaches

Coach training programmes could seek to integrate AI-enhanced video reflection with expert supervision to boost coach development. Tools like ELECTRIC Conversations allow trainee coaches to role-play coaching conversations, developing skills through interaction with an AI coachee.

Independent coaches and coaching organisations could make use of AI-enhanced video reflection for some online sessions and regularly review their coaching style with a coach supervisor.

Coach supervisors could offer AI-enhanced video reflection to help coaches build core skills of rapport, increase their self-awareness, and develop towards mastery.

References

Aafjes-van Doorn, K., Liu, A., & Kamsteeg, C. (2022). Videorecorded treatment sessions for professional development. *Counselling Psychology Review, 37*(1), 4–20.

Arakawa, R., & Yakura, H. (2020). INWARD: A computer-supported tool for video-reflection improves efficiency and effectiveness in executive coaching. In *Proceedings of the 2020 CHI conference on human factors in computing systems* (pp. 1–13). ACM. https://doi.org/10.1145/3313831.3376703

Association for Coaching. (2021). *Coaching competency framework*. Retrieved October 12, 2022, from https://www.associationforcoaching.com/page/CADetails

Braun, V., & Clarke, V. (2021). *Thematic analysis: A practical guide*. SAGE.

Bridgeman, J., & Giraldez-Hayes, A. (2024). Using artificial intelligence-enhanced video feedback for reflective practice in coach development: Benefits and potential drawbacks. *Coaching: An International Journal of Theory, Research and Practice, 17*(1), 32–49.

Carden, J., Jones, R. J., & Passmore, J. (2021). An exploration of the role of coach training in developing self-awareness: A mixed methods study. *Current Psychology*. https://doi.org/10.1007/s12144-021-01929-8

Carson, F. (2008). Utilizing video to facilitate reflective practice: Developing sports coaches. *International Journal of Sports Science & Coaching, 3*(3), 381–390. https://doi.org/10.1260/174795408786238515

Clutterbuck, D. (2020). Questions in coaching. In J. Passmore (Ed.), *The coaches' handbook* (pp. 92–103). Routledge.

European Mentoring and Coaching Council. (2015). *EMCC global competence framework V2*. Retrieved October 12, 2022, from https://www.emccglobal.org/wp-content/uploads/2018/10/EMCC-competences-framework-v2-EN.pdf

Freytag, J., Chu, J., Hysong, S. J., Street, R. L., Markham, C. M., Giordano, T. P., Westbrook, R. A., Njue-Marendes, S., Johnson, S. R., & Dang, B. N. (2022). Acceptability and feasibility of video-based coaching to enhance clinicians' communication skills with patients. *BMC Medical Education, 22*(1), 85. https://doi.org/10.1186/s12909-021-02976-2

Fukkink, R. G., Trienekens, N., & Kramer, L. J. C. (2011). Video feedback in education and training: Putting learning in the picture. *Educational Psychology Review, 23*(1), 45–63. https://doi.org/10.1007/s10648-010-9144-5

Gallwey, W. T. (1974). *The inner game of tennis*. Random House.

Hammoud, M., Morgan, H., Lyon, J. A., & White, C. (2012). Is video review of patient encounters an effective tool for medical student learning? A review of the literature. *Advances in Medical Education and Practice, 3*, 19–30. https://doi.org/10.2147/AMEP.S20219

International Coaching Federation. (2019). *Updated ICF core competencies*. Retrieved October 12, 2022, from https://coachingfederation.org/credentials-and-standards/core-competencies

Meade, E., Dozier, M., & Bernard, K. (2014). Using video feedback as a tool in training parent coaches: Promising results from a single-subject design. *Attachment & Human Development, 16*(4), 356–370. https://doi.org/10.1080/14616734.2014.912488

Mekruksavanich, S., Jantawong, P., Hnoohom, N., & Jitpattanakul, A. (2022). Badminton activity recognition and player assessment based on motion signals using deep residual network. In *2022 IEEE 13th international conference on software engineering and service science (ICSESS)* (pp. 80–83). https://doi.org/10.1109/ICSESS54813.2022.9930147

Ovida. (2024). *Ovida*. https://ovida.io/

Partington, M., Cushion, C. J., Cope, E., & Harvey, S. (2015). The impact of video feedback on professional youth football coaches' reflection and practice behaviour: A longitudinal investigation of behaviour change. *Reflective Practice, 16*(5), 700–716. https://doi.org/10.1080/14623943.2015.1071707

Schön, D. A. (1983). *The reflective practitioner: How professionals think in action*. Basic Books.

Souissi, M. A., Trabelsi, O., Souissi, H., Elghoul, Y., Ammar, A., Chamari, K., & Souissi, N. (2022). The video feedback viewing in novice weightlifters: Total control strategy improves snatch technique during learning. *International Journal of Sports Science & Coaching, 17*(6), 1408–1417. https://doi.org/10.1177/17479541211062596

Stanier, M. B. (2016). *The coaching habit: Say less, ask more & change the way you lead forever*. Box of Crayons Press.

Tarrant, P. (2013). *Reflective practice and professional development*. SAGE. https://doi.org/10.4135/9781526402318

Tuyls, K., Omidshafiei, S., Muller, P., Wang, Z., Connor, J., Hennes, D., Graham, I., Spearman, W., Waskett, T., Steel, D., Luc, P., Recasens, A., Galashov, A., Thornton, G., Elie, R., Sprechmann, P., Moreno, P., Cao, K., Garnelo, M., et al. (2021). Game plan: What AI can do for football, and what football can do for AI. *Journal of Artificial Intelligence Research, 71*, 41–88. https://doi.org/10.1613/jair.1.12505

Walker, S. G., Mattson, S. L., & Sellers, T. P. (2020). Increasing accuracy of rock-climbing techniques in novice athletes using expert modeling and video feedback. *Journal of Applied Behavior Analysis, 53*(4), 2260–2270. https://doi.org/10.1002/jaba.694

Whitmore, J. (2009). *Coaching for performance: Growing human potential and purpose—The principles and practice of coaching and leadership* (4th ed.). Nicholas Brealey.

Wilson, B. D. (2008). Development in video technology for coaching. *Sports Technology, 1*(1), 34–40. https://doi.org/10.1080/19346182.2008.9648449

Part V
Fundamental Questions about AI in Coaching

Chapter 13
Why Coaching Needs Real Intelligence, Not Artificial

Tatiana Bachkirova

Abstract AI movement into the coaching arena continues to be steady and confident, meeting only rare and timid resistance. The progress of this movement can be explained by decades of technological advances, the entrepreneurial attitude of AI developers, and inherent peculiarities of the coaching business. The voices of caution are too quiet in "the noise of the progress". However, there are important reasons for coaching communities to be apprehensive about the ways this movement could change coaching as a service and what this means for all involved. In this chapter, I address potential problematic issues with the AI revolution in the context of a multitude of conceptual holes in coaching as a profession. I argue that dehumanising coaching under the guise of "enhancement by AI" undermines human intelligence, which is desperately needed while the discipline of organisational coaching remains in its early stages of development.

Keywords Organisational coaching · Artificial intelligence · Limitations of LLMs · Human intelligence · Ethics of coaching · Professionalisation of coaching · Coach education · Coaching supervision · Human dignity · Purpose of coaching

13.1 Introduction

I have argued elsewhere that the field of organisational coaching is full of conceptual holes (Bachkirova, 2024). By "conceptual holes" I mean those important characteristics of our service that should be identified, named, agreed upon, and committed to. As things stand, this is far from being the case and evidence of this can be found in many relevant sources in the conceptual literature of coaching (e.g. Garvey et al., 2010; Cavanagh, 2016; Bachkirova & Kauffman, 2009). Here are the examples of how these conceptual holes manifest in organisational coaching:

T. Bachkirova (✉)
International Centre for Coaching and Mentoring Studies, Oxford Brookes Business School, Oxford Brookes University, Oxford, UK
e-mail: tbachkirova@brookes.ac.uk

R. Wegener et al. (eds.), *Coaching in the Age of AI*, SpringerBriefs in Psychology, https://doi.org/10.1007/978-3-032-23332-5_13

- We avoid clarity about who the main recipient of organisational coaching is
- We are not specific about the purpose of our service that is commensurable to the means available to us
- We are not sufficiently clear about how our offer is different from other professional services, e.g. training, consultancy, therapy, AI coaching
- We do not own the serious ethical implications of our "unique set-up"
- We cannot provide clear guidance to less experienced coaches in terms of positioning their service in organisations in ethical ways
- As we are not clear about what we offer, we cannot be clear how to evaluate the quality of our service

In these conceptual "muddy waters" developers and enthusiasts of digital revolution are free to claim anything, from small and potentially useful technological adjustments to as far as pronouncing human coaching fully replaceable by AI chatbots. Without the industry's agreeing what the essential characteristics of organisational coaching are it is impossible to compare it with "AI coaching" and thus to explore if these strong claims have any legitimacy. To deal with the task of comparing human and AI coaching, in a recent paper (Bachkirova & Kemp, 2024) we have initiated a conversation by proposing six essential characteristics of organisational coaching and have argued that stand-alone AI coaching does not meet any of these criteria. As a result, we argued that AI intervention cannot be called coaching and suggested instead something like "digitally assisted self-coaching" as being more appropriate.

In this chapter, I am not arguing against any further development of AI "in coaching" as such, as AI could be a useful developmental device in the same way as working with a reflective diary can be useful. My main point is that we should not pretend that it is coaching as we know it being an interpersonal practice. There is no reason to think that AI could not be used as a supplement to human coaching, but as things stand it cannot, in principle, provide a stand-alone coaching service that is equivalent to human coaching. If we continue to do this pretending, we could pay a high price and undermine the potential of our profession to play an important role in developing people in organisations.

To build this argument, I would like first to highlight certain issues within the coaching field that I consider to be the conceptual "muddy waters" of organisational coaching (Bachkirova, 2024). I previously argued that the absence of conceptual clarity in the field of organisational coaching goes along with the lack of serious exploration of coaching's axiological dimension, which should set out the articulated purpose, values, and significance of coaching as a credible service. Exploration of this dimension involves answering questions such as:

- What is the purpose of organisational coaching?
- What problems does this service aim to solve?
- What is the balance between value and harm of such service to individuals, organisations, societies, and the planet?

Only when we have addressed these questions as fully as possible can we decide what qualifies as "quality" of this service. Only then the criteria of such quality can be established, against which we can assess if specific technological improvements add any value. However, AI developers have already identified coaching as a profitable enterprise and are not concerned about such abstract questions and long-term consequences of their innovations.

Lack of attention to these questions could be explained by the fact that the coaching industry is evidently solvent and seems to be growing. Moreover, it has survived multiple other popular adjustments, such as the exodus from physical rooms to online, the incorporation of various "beautiful ideas" (Bachkirova & Borrington, 2020) such as excessive use of mindfulness and knowledge from neuroscience, etc., so what further harm could mild "digital tweaking" do? However, it is possible that in this case the damage could be irreversible, and we need to be aware of what is at risk for the profession as a whole.

The difference is that these previous "innovations" did not impinge on the main feature of coaching—its *human* nature. The main interpersonal characteristics of coaching, such as "joint inquiry", appreciation of context, ethical foundation, and contract, remained intact. Most importantly, though, human intelligence has been at the heart and centre of the entire enterprise and this, I would argue, allows the coaching industry to thrive. It is human intelligence that enables the careful manoeuvring between multiple stakeholders; ensures flexibility and, at the same time, the ethical stance towards complex contextual issues; and helps repair ruptures in relationships. All of these might appear to be at the fringes of coaching but could easily undermine it if not intelligently managed. Of course, there is always a variation in terms of the degrees of intelligence available, even for human coaches, but I will argue that an "AI pseudo-coach" has no potential to be a person that matters in a coaching relationship.

In structuring this chapter, I will first discuss why human intelligence, however imperfect, has unique features that are fundamentally important for coaching. Second, I enlist support from philosophers of technology to demonstrate that AI does not have the kind of intelligence that matters in coaching. Third, I explore some implications that arise from putting too much faith into AI in the enterprise of coaching and the damage this might make for what organisational coaching as a profession stands. I finish with advocating an attitude to AI that might be more sensible for the various stakeholders of organisational coaching so as not to jeopardise the future of this service.

13.2 What Is It About Human Intelligence That Is So Important in Coaching

It is not my intention to provide a definition of intelligence. This is an enterprise that is notoriously fraught with difficulty as there are multiple possible variations that are context-specific for which different aspects matter to different extents and so can become central or marginal. My sole aim is to describe some features/aspects of human intelligence that demonstrate its relevance in the context of organisational coaching and at the same time help in distinguishing it from AI. Key amongst these features are the role of the body, meaning, and dialogue.

The first feature that drastically differentiates human intelligence from artificial is the way we perceive details important for understanding and action. Referring to Merleau-Ponty, Dreyfus (1972) argues that the human way to perceive and act is not through details, concepts, plans, etc. It is our *body* that grasps the gestalt and then acts. Humans respond to the world immediately rather than through the analysis of details. In grasping the complexity of clients' situations, this is how coaches identify patterns to reflect back to clients and to facilitate further exploration. AI cannot do this. Floridi (2023, p. 27), referring to this feature of intelligence, points out how CAPTCHA (the tool used by many websites to ensure that you are not a robot that was first developed as far back as 1997) remains an insurmountable task for AI. This gives some indication how little progress has been made in terms of the production of non-biological intelligence.

Body allows *an optimal grip of reality* through movement by interacting with objects of perception. Dreyfus called this ability "skilful coping" (1972). In essence, human intelligence is based on our physical embeddedness in the world. Because of this grip of reality, we make predictions and take risks, both being constituents of skilful coping. Because of the ability to create mental simulations, we can have "as-if" experiences and are thus able to understand situations we do not participate in. Our cognition is embodied: it happens not just in the brain. Emotions, for example, as an aspect of the whole body, are central to our thinking and action (e.g. Claxton, 2005, 2015). All of these allow humans to cope with imprecision, ambiguities, and metaphors. This is why talking one-to-one is far superior to messaging for understanding the intentions and responses of others as the voice, being part of the body, adds more nuanced information by its prosodic variables, such as intonation, pace, rhythm, etc. Computers do not have all the above qualities of the body and therefore cannot be intelligent in the way that humans are.

The controversial physicist David Bohm (1996) highlights further nuances of human intelligence that show how far AI is from emulating it. He argues that intelligence is what is not algorithmic and mechanical even in human thinking. It is the immediate perception of that which is false, which can happen through direct insight, that describes human intelligence. This happens because human intelligence is in our embodied ability to grasp *meaning*. As argued by Floridi (2023, p. 24), "…it is less about solving some problems and more about deciding which problems are worth solving, why, for what purpose, and acceptable cost, trade-offs, and consequences".

Intelligence particularly matters for ethical judgements that are constantly required in coaching situations. We arrive at moral evaluations not through solving logical puzzles but through consideration of what is irreducible in us: subjectivity, dignity, desire—all the things that AI doesn't have. This subjectivity is an important player when the meaning is co-constructed in the relationship with others, and this is why in coaching we deal with meaning tentatively and together as it emerges in relationship with clients.

Intelligence is also needed for understanding the client (Bakhtin, 1973). I have argued elsewhere that one of the most important values for coaching clients is a luxury of *being understood* in their unique and complex set of circumstances, with consideration of their personality, values, and attitudes and facing therefore a unique set of challenges in work and life (Bachkirova, 2024). Recognising such uniqueness does not foster self-inflation of the client or position them against others and the organisation. This understanding has no other agenda than being a prerequisite for productive *thinking together* (Stacey, 2012), essential for real working relationship. AI offers only a surrogate of such *responsive understanding*.

Intelligence allows meaning being shaped and developed in human interaction through dialogue or joint inquiry. Bakhtin (1973, p. 71) has argued that "human thought becomes genuine thought, i.e., an idea, only under the condition of living contact with another foreign thought, embodied in the voice of another person…". His even stronger argument is that human "life is dialogical by its very nature. To live means to engage in dialogue, to question, to listen, to answer, to agree, etc." (Bakhtin, 1979, p. 318). This view is echoed by Bohm (1996) writing how dialogue is a way of life in which one remains open to the Other, to difference, and to the possibility of new understanding, change, and personal growth. I would say that this is what is offered by another human in coaching and ensures the value of this service in the increasing complexity of current conditions of life and work by offering partnership in clients' inquiries. AI, however, cannot be that Other as it is not embodied, does not understand meaning, and only imitates dialogue.

It is important, of course, not to overstate the actual power of human intelligence in each particular case and recognise that the quality of intelligence in human coaches varies. However, they are equipped with the *necessary* conditions for delivering good quality coaching by virtue of being human. To create *sufficient* conditions, they do need, of course, much more than simply being human. It also requires quality of coach education, continuing development, ethical maturity, with all of these in the context of the appropriate governing of the coaching industry in organisations. Artificial coaches cannot have access to even the necessary conditions (Bachkirova & Kemp, 2024), a point further developed in the next section.

13.3 Why Technology and AI Are of Limited Help in Coaching

It is impossible to undervalue the role of technology in many areas of our life even if we have limited power to fully understand what is created and often limited control of every tool that is created. At the same time, we recognise that technologies are not neutral and therefore their "products" vary in terms of benefits and harms depending on how they are used. We gradually learn to take into account the cost of technological advances in terms of the resources they require and unpredictable consequences that may arise. However, it seems that this learning is currently weakened when presented with such an exciting innovation as AI, which entices with a promise of novelty, new powers, and benefits. Many authors address the concerns of such nature about AI in general (Beetham, 2024; Dennett, 2023; Dreyfus, 1972; Floridi, 2023). I will highlight only those that demonstrate limitations of AI in comparison to human intelligence in addition to those I already mentioned in the previous section.

Considering that it is in our nature to attribute human features to anything and everything, AI chatbots are most easily accepted as "humans-like" (Blut et al., 2021; Einola et al., 2023). They create a great impression of communicating and being able to think in ways that are easy to be convinced by. But are we being willingly deceived that we are communicating with a thinking "partner"? As an important characteristic of the coaching process is the collaborative activity of "thinking together" (Stacey, 2012), it matters if machines can really think. Interestingly, even the greatest authority in "machine thinking" Alan Turing (1950) said there was no way of answering the question of whether the *machine* can *think*, because both terms lack scientific definitions. It would be "meaningless to deserve discussion". Dijkstra (1984) was even more categorical about Turing's famous criteria to settle the question of whether Machines Can Think. He said that it is "a question of which we now know that it is about as relevant as the question of whether Submarines Can Swim". If the functioning of AI cannot be established as thinking, recognising it as intelligence is obviously even harder.

At the same time, even without an agreed definition of intelligence in principle, we can still discuss if AI can do what human intelligence can. Floridi (2023, p. 21), for example, is quite clear that the project of reproducing human intelligence has failed: "…as a branch of cognitive science interested in intelligence production, AI remains science fiction and has been a dismal disappointment. … AI does not merely underperform with respect to human intelligence. It has not yet even joined the competition". Similar arguments are made by Bender et al. (2021), who somewhat scornfully refers to large language models as "stochastic parrots" (Bender et al., 2021), a description which convincingly demonstrates that intelligence and linguistic capabilities do not go together.

This does not, however, mean that AI applications are not successful. They are, but not by replicating human intelligence. In fact, Floridi (2023) argued that they became much more successful when the developers stopped trying to simulate human intelligence. AI is not about reproducing any kind of biological intelligence; it is about doing *without it*. It solves problems in ways different to those employed by humans, bypassing the hard axiological problems of meaning, relevance, understanding, truth, intelligence, insight, etc. (Floridi, 2023). It is really up to us, then, to decide what it is that we need AI for and making sure that we are not beguiled into accepting them as a poor substitute for the things that really matter in the human realm. This is existentially relevant, not only to coaching, but to the experience of being a person in general. I cannot agree more with a humorous call for AI "to do my laundry and dishes so I can do art and writing, not for AI to do my art and writing so that I can do my laundry and dishes".

Floridi (2023) goes as far as suggesting that AI is an oxymoron. It is a new form of *agency,* not of intelligence (p. 6) and should be called AA (Artificial Agency). By suggesting "agency", he is utilising a minimalist definition, satisfying only three criteria (p. 10):

- Being able to receive and use data from the environment
- Taking action based on the input data autonomously to achieve goals
- Improving performance by learning from interactions

Whether this proposition by Floridi (2023, p. 208) is taken on board or not, I agree with his description of the most effective contribution from AI, which is inviting us "to reflect more seriously and less complacently on who we are, could be, and would like to become, and thus our responsibilities and self-understanding". Coaching is already a place where such things are addressed on a scale of individual projects, but the AI revolution brings these issues home with more urgency for coaching as a profession. By discussing meaning that matters, values that need to be affirmed, and the many assumptions that need to be questioned, we begin to properly fulfil what it is that coaching has the potential to contribute to the human condition. This is not a task that artificial intelligence has the capability to achieve.

13.4 What Is at Risk

As part of exercising human intelligence, it is important to recognise that the development and use of AI are not as benign as developers and AI advocates make it out to be. There are consequences, some of which may be damaging in a number of ways. The first such consequence starts from acknowledging that AI is successful, but not as the result of AI adapting to us and our world. Floridi (2023) argues that it is the other way around—*we* have been transforming the world into an increasingly AI-friendly environment. Every step that we take in digitising our environment and expanding the infosphere, we create an ecosystem in which AI systems become exponentially more useful and successful.

His warning is that the risk we are running is that our technologies and especially AI might shape our physical and conceptual environments. We already live in the infosphere (Floridi, 2023), but because of the exponential growth of computational power and speed of technological advancement, a significant part of our life now depends on it. So far coaching has been operating in more than infosphere, but the pressures, both implicit and explicit, to embrace AI into coaching push the discipline into this techno-environment in a persistently enculturating way. This risks coaching becoming a dry information exchange aimed solely towards mechanistically defined "goals" when values, meaning, desires, and full-scale subjectivity (the "axiological dimension") are being marginalised.

Without human encounter, even when it includes clashes of values and relational tensions, technology will continue to downgrade human interaction and human intelligence. Humans become part of the extended domain of the machines, e.g. working to improve the functioning of AI machinery, which at the same time leads to authentic human activity disappear by providing a poor substitute. The ethical concern here pertains to the moral worth of human dignity that was famously captured by Kant's categorical imperative to not treat humans as a means to an end. In coaching, this imperative is addressed through careful contracting to ensure that the "mutual use" of parties is fairly negotiated. It is a way to mitigate the unusual and complex ethical tension at the heart of organisational coaching (Bachkirova, 2024), where the quality of coaching depends on there being a trusting and confidential relationship between the client and coach, but coaches are paid by another party who has an invested interest in the outcome of this intervention. With exclusion, or at least minimisation, of the human coach, the coaching contract is compromised "upstream" to being an expression of what matters only to the organisation: a manoeuvre justified by the constraints of technology.

In this set up, the needs of organisations take considerably greater priority, thereby increasing the inequality already inherent in neo-liberal economies. Technologies are typically presented as a means of redistributing the power and freedom of users, but, as market forces dictate, they disproportionally benefit those who already have the resources that put them in the position of being able to take further advantage of these innovations (Schmachtenberger, 2024). This is why I think promoting AI "coaching" under the umbrella of "democratising coaching" is a highly disingenuous claim. Those in the position of power will continue using human coaching, while the rest are provided with a poor-quality substitute.

Another concern of a psychological nature is about what AI is doing not for us but to us, as argued by Susan Turkle (2015), on the grounds that our engagement with the world as interfaced through computers makes fundamental changes to who we are. In many ways we gradually remove ourselves from real events and by substituting our interactions with digital means we dehumanise the important elements of our life. For example, people become satisfied with "pretend empathy" and come to believe that this is what empathy is really like. An example of this kind of interpersonal category error is that of AI-assisted medical diagnosis which is already considered as providing more empathy than human doctors (NY Times, 2024). Turkle (2015) anticipates that people will start expecting from humans what they get from machines, describing real cases of "*artificial intimacy*" (e.g. children develop "friendship" with artificial friend and then expect this kind of empathy from real people). I believe this phenomenon is not dissimilar to the consequences of the "relationship" with pornography. In getting used to surrogates which are "easy", real human relationships might become too stressful or unpredictable and the availability of digital surrogates offering the illusion of interpersonal intimacy may promote degrees of narcissistic internalisation even more than is already troubling in Western society (Cushman, 1996).

Another important consequence of digitalising our life is losing trust in information in general because of LLM's tendency to "hallucinate" (Aladakatti & Senthil

Kumar, 2023; Athaluri et al., 2023). Daniel Dennett (2024) is very categorical about this danger:

> Because we won't know what we know, and we won't know who to trust, and we won't know whether we're informed or misinformed, we may become either paranoid and hyper-sceptical, or just apathetic and unmoved. Both of those are very dangerous avenues. And they're upon us. (Dennett, 2024)

Dennett (2023) is also quite radical in arguing that the creators of technology that results in such effects should be sued. He believes that this should be taken as seriously as molecular biologists developing the capability for biological warfare or atomic physicists paving the way for nuclear war. He calls it the "real code red".

In addition to the issue of losing trust in information because of this "hallucinatory tendency" as argued by Dennett (2024), I would question the use of this term in the first place. Naming chatbot disinformation as "hallucination" is more than a little misleading because first of all it assumes a human frailty as being naturally available to digitally organised information processing. Secondly and mainly, it implies that AI hallucinations are forgivable because in humans they are troublesome only to those who hallucinate. This could be seen as a clever strategy to deflect responsibility for the propagation of false information and camouflage the fact that consequences of hallucinations matter to all users of chatbots. Considering all of this, I would argue that according to the criteria set out by Harry Frankfurt (2005) in defining the phenomenon of "bullshitting", AI "hallucinations" should be called as such. Interestingly, Frankfurt argues that bullshitting is far more damaging than lying because a liar at least makes the conscious effort to lie as they know what the truth is and intentionally undertake to subvert it. On the other hand, the bullshitter simply does not care about truth, and this is what AI is.

Unfortunately, a clever misappropriation of AI is already happening. AI coaching is currently promoted as an intervention that is based on a proven method (questioning) thereby minimising biases the human coach might have. This sounds laudably like a commitment to objectivity and precision, but in reality, more mundane and cares mainly about reducing cost and improving the organisation's return on investment. Coaching, however, is about, and should be seen as being about, a different level of investment: the development of people, a process in which subjectivity and individualised approaches are essential elements. This development, in turn, arguably leads to higher productivity and justifies the investment in the longer term (Mayer, 2021). This discrepancy of intention might explain why some early reviews (Upwork, 2024) show how different the attitudes and responses are to the use of AI coaching between employers and employees: employers, being motivated by short-term cost-effectiveness, responding favourably at 96%, while employees seem considerably less impressed with 77% saying that AI decreases their productivity.

This disparity seems usefully supported by coaching clients who work in a "tech environment": "They want nothing to do with coachbots! Coaching is a refuge from the tech and a space where they can decompress with a human and be in relationship. Where empathy and thinking together is practised. A 'postmodern confessional' as Simon Western says" (Duhigg, personal communication, 2024).

13.5 Conclusion

It is clear that the digital revolution is inevitable and already makes a difference in our lives. Digital technology helps in solving many problems in a huge number of contexts, and it will continue to do so and do it well. The argument I have been making here, and will continue to make elsewhere, along with other authors (e.g. Beetham, 2024; Floridi, 2023) is that the use of this technology should be part of a *human project* utilised in service of directions in which *we* collectively wish to go, because it is only us (as human persons) who can see our world in terms of meaning and purpose. Just because technological advances demonstrate growing capabilities does not automatically entail that these should uncritically be put into practice without difficult conversations being had concerning possible consequences. In coaching, instead of being seduced by the fashionable allure of "shiny new things", it makes better sense to consider how to respond to questions such as these:

- Is coaching a job that should be kept human?
- Is the aggressive development of AI coaching in organisations worth it considering the price the rest of the world has to pay for it?
- What do we gain and what do we lose if even basic coaching becomes a province of AI?

In answering these questions, it might be useful to remember what Hubert Dreyfus (1972) wrote in relation to some technological advances: "The first man to climb a tree could claim tangible progress toward reaching the Moon—yet, actually reaching the Moon requires qualitatively different methods than tree-climbing." In offering people coaching services supplied by people, we already have a good method. Rather than invest in spoiling it, perhaps we would do better to invest our efforts in improving it in ways that increase its benefit to a wider clientele.

References

Aladakatti, S. S., & Senthil Kumar, S. (2023). Exploring natural language processing techniques to extract semantics from unstructured dataset which will aid in effective semantic interlinking. *International Journal of Modeling, Simulation, and Scientific Computing, 14*(01), 2243004. https://doi.org/10.1142/S1793962322430048

Athaluri, S. A., Manthena, S. V., Kesapragada, V. K. M., Yarlagadda, V., Dave, T., & Duddumpudi, R. T. S. (2023). Exploring the boundaries of reality: Investigating the phenomenon of artificial intelligence hallucination in scientific writing through ChatGPT references. *Cureus, 15*(4), e37432. https://doi.org/10.7759/cureus.37432

Bachkirova, T. (2024). The purpose of organisational coaching: Time to explore and commit. *International Journal of Evidence Based Coaching and Mentoring, 22*(1), 214–233.

Bachkirova, T., & Borrington, S. (2020). Beautiful ideas that can make us ill: Implications for coaching. *Philosophy of Coaching: An International Journal, 5*(1), 9–30.

Bachkirova, T., & Kauffman, C. (2009). The blind men and the elephant: Using criteria of universality and uniqueness in evaluating our attempts to define coaching. *Coaching: An International Journal of Theory, Research and Practice, 2*(2), 95–105.

Bachkirova, T. & Kemp, R. (2024). 'AI coaching': Democratizing coaching service or offering an ersatz? Coaching: An International Journal of Theory, Research and Practice, 18(1), 27–45. doi:https://doi.org/10.1080/17521882.2024.2368598.

Bakhtin, M. M. (1973). *Problems of Dostoevsky's poetics* (R. W. Rotsel, Trans.). Ardis.

Bakhtin, M. M. (1979). *The aesthetics of verbal creation* (W. Godzich, Trans.). S.G. Bocharov.

Beetham, H. (2024). *What price your 'AI-ready' graduates?* Substack https://helenbeetham.substack.com/p/what-price-your-ai-ready-graduates

Bender, E., Gebru, T., McMillan-Major, A., & Shmitchell, S. (2021). On the dangers of stochastic parrots: Can language models be too big? In *Proceedings of the 2021 ACM Conference on Fairness, Accountability, and Transparency* (pp. 610 623). Association for Computing Machinery. https://doi.org/10.1145/3442188.3445922

Blut, M., Wang, C., Wünderlich, N. V., & Brock, C. (2021). Understanding anthropomorphism in service provision: A meta-analysis of physical robots, chatbots, and other AI. *Journal of the Academy of Marketing Science, 49*(4), 632–658. https://doi.org/10.1007/s11747-020-00762-y

Bohm, D. (1996). *On dialogue*. Routledge.

Cavanagh, M. J. (2016). The coaching engagement in the twenty-first century: New paradigms for complex times. In S. David, D. Clutterbuck, & D. Megginson (Eds.), *Beyond goals* (pp. 151–184). Routledge.

Claxton, G. (2005). *An intelligent look at emotional intelligence*. ATL.

Claxton, G. (2015). *Intelligence in the flesh: Why your mind needs your body much more than it thinks*. Yale University Press.

Cushman, P. (1996). *Constructing the self, constructing America: A cultural history of psychotherapy*. Da Capo Press.

Dennett, D. C. (2023, May). *The problem with counterfeit people*. The Atlantic. https://www.theatlantic.com/technology/archive/2023/05/problem-counterfeit-people/674075/

Dennett, D. C. (2024). *Philosopher Daniel Dennett on artificial intelligence, consciousness and "counterfeit people"*. BBC Future. https://www.bbc.com/future/article/20240422-philosopherdaniel-dennett-artificial-intelligence-consciousness-counterfeit-people

Dijkstra, E. W. (1984). *The threats to computing science*. E. W. Dijkstra Archive, Center for American History, University of Texas at Austin. https://www.cs.utexas.edu/users/EWD/ewd0893.pdf

Dreyfus, H. L. (1972). *What computers can't do: The limits of artificial intelligence*. Harper & Row.

Einola, K., Khoreva, V., & Tienari, J. (2023). A colleague named Max: A critical inquiry into affects when an anthropomorphised AI (ro)bot enters the workplace. *Human Relations, 77*(11), 1620–1649. https://doi.org/10.1177/00187267231206328

Floridi, L. (2023). *The ethics of artificial intelligence: Principles, challenges and opportunities*. Oxford University Press.

Frankfurt, H. (2005). *On bullshit*. Princeton University Press.

Garvey, B., Stokes, P., & Megginson, D. (2010). *Coaching and mentoring: Theory and practice*. Sage Publications.

Mayer, C. (2021). The future of the corporation and the economics of purpose. *Journal of Management Studies, 58*(3), 887–901.

Schmachtenberger, M. (2024, May). *Moving from naïve to authentic progress: A vision for betterment [Podcast episode]*. The Great Simplification. https://www.thegreatsimplification.com/episode/126-daniel-schmachtenberger-7

Stacey, R. D. (2012). Comment on debate article: Coaching Psychology Coming of Age: The challenges we face in the messy world of complexity. *International Coaching Psychology Review, 7*(1), 91–95.
Turing, A. M. (1950). Computing machinery and intelligence. *Mind, 59*(236), 433–460.
Turkle, S. (2015). *Reclaiming conversation: The power of talk in a digital age*. Penguin Press.
Upwork. (2024). *From burnout to balance: AI-enhanced work models*. The Upwork Research Institute. https://www.upwork.com/research/ai-enhanced-work-models
Yong, E. (2024). *I'm a doctor. ChatGPT's bedside manner is better than mine*. The New York Times. https://www.nytimes.com/2024/10/05/opinion/ai-chatgpt-medicine-doctor.html

Chapter 14
Using the Five Maturities to Support the Co-Evolution of AI and Humans in Coaching

David B. Drake

Abstract AI has risen like a thunderstorm in the desert, bringing much-needed rain yet carrying the risk of flooding. The perspectives offered are based on the author's work in this space over the past 8 years, starting with the incorporation of his Narrative Coaching framework in an early-stage AI application and including his current work as Head of Ovida Labs (ovida.io). This chapter starts with an introduction which makes the case for thinking about coaching in new ways in the age of AI. The Five Maturities framework is offered as a guide for developing mature practitioners who are masterful in each of the five elements in the coaching process. A second table is offered which illustrates the roles AI can play in supporting the growth of coaches and clients. Five propositions are offered on the implications of the integration of AI in the coaching space. Tips for coaches, coach educators, and coaching bodies on how to ethically and effectively incorporate AI in their practice are provided. The Conclusion offers reflections and recommendations on what it will take to successfully address the AI storm and acknowledges the consequences of not rising to this momentous occasion.

Keywords AI integration · Five maturities · Coaching process · Maturity & mastery · Ethical responsibility · Conscious improvisation · Structured emergence · Human–AI partnership · Developmental growth · Social consciousness

> The pursuit of progress must never come at the cost of ethical responsibility.

D. B. Drake (✉)
The Moment Institute, Portland, OR, USA
e-mail: ddrake@narrativecoaching.com

R. Wegener et al. (eds.), *Coaching in the Age of AI*, SpringerBriefs in Psychology, https://doi.org/10.1007/978-3-032-23332-5_14

14.1 Introduction

> As sociologist Sherry Turkle notes, the very challenges that make relationships difficult or else that would make them meaningful. It's in moments of discomfort—when we navigate misunderstandings or repair after conflict—that intimacy grows these experiences, whether with therapists, friends, or partners, teach us how to trust and connect on a deeper level if we stop practicing these skills because AI offers a smoother, more convenient alternative we may erode our capacity to form meaningful relationships (Eyal, 2025).

Any ethical use of AI in the coaching process must bring out the best in and for humans as well as enhance the common good for humanity. This requires the concurrent development of a new paradigm and pedagogy from which to work. The Five Maturities framework (Drake, 2026) is offered as a robust resource for this purpose. Otherwise, we are just using the technology to perpetuate and accelerate the old paradigm: Consume more. Do more. Be efficient. Keep up. Get ahead. This keeps us trapped on the same treadmill, which means that we are adding to the very problems for which people come to coaching.

This is especially important given the urgent collective issues we face in terms of what defines and connects us as humans. In this sense, the application of AI in coaching is as much a social issue as it is a technological issue. This can be seen in recognizing that our well-being was for most of human history mediated through the community (e.g., through rituals and shamans, then shifted to the professional sphere (through pastors, therapists, and coaches), and is now shifted to the personal sphere (through AI-informed applications which can be accessed directly on our own)—though what is accessed is harvested from the communal and professional spheres. It prompts (pun intended) the question: *What is our role as humans and practitioners in this new world?*

What is already clear is that the world in which we are now coaching is not the world in which coaching was born. The ethical and effective use of AI will require coaching practitioners, educators, and associations to adapt themselves, their roles, and their approaches in significant ways. For example, in a world increasingly organized around scanning and skimming (superficial attention, horizontal engagement), how can we deepen our steeping and sensing (sustained attention, vertical engagement)? To make the most of AI, we need to see it as a catalyst for the reinvention of institutions not just a tool to get tasks done.

One of the first steps is to track how AI is making its way into the coaching process. It offers a golden opportunity to reimagine how coaching is conceptualized, delivered, and utilized in support of meaningful outcomes. This chapter draws on the Five Maturities framework (Drake, 2026) as a guide for leaders, educators, and practitioners in the coaching space who want to develop informed strategies and make wise choices in taking up this challenge. In so doing, we need to be aware of what we are giving up in exchange for what we are gaining, and to keep thinking about the long-term impacts not just the short-term gains. The conscious integration of AI in the coaching space requires preserving and enriching our sense of autonomy, agency, and accountability to enable all involved to grow.

14.2 Using the Five Maturities with AI in Coaching

I would argue that the effective use of our cognitive and applied skills *(mastery)* depends on our developmental depth and socio-emotional acuity *(maturity)*. Applying the Five Maturities framework in coaching enables coaches to develop the maturity to use their skills with discernment and for greater impact. It enables them to move from performative implementation to conscious improvisation. The use of AI in coaching is making this increasingly apparent. As such, there is a need for a more integrative approach to coach development, assessment, and practice. This will enable coaches to more holistically support their clients' growth as human beings so they can do the same for those they lead or serve.

The following chart (Table 14.1) illustrates a more integrative approach for developing coaches and advancing the practice of coaching (see Drake, 2026). It encompasses (1) the five key elements in a coaching conversation; (2) the five maturities; (3) the five masteries, with each one grounded in a corresponding maturity; and (4) the five iBEAM factors, based on Drake's (2019, 2021) meta-analysis of what impacts performance. This chart serves as a guide for how the grounded use of AI can inform the transition to what is next for coaching but also enrich practitioners' ability to step into these new roles.

14.2.1 What This Looks Like in Practice

14.2.1.1 People

A coach and a client recognize and acknowledge their struggle to handle a difficult interaction well *(Personal Maturity)*—and seek to increase their ability to hold space for the work to be done *(Capacity)* and increase their openness to what is present and calling for their attention *(Mindset)*.

14.2.1.2 Relationship

They work together to acknowledge their shared blindspot: the inability to track their somatic experience *(Spiritual Maturity)*—and seek to increase their ability to take on new perspectives *(Clarity)* and talk more honestly about why this issue is difficult for them and why that matters *(Aspiration)*.

Table 14.1 Support for each of the five elements in the coaching process

Coaching elements	People	Relationship	Skills	Process	Outcomes
Maturity	Personal	Spiritual	Professional	Social	Contextual
Mastery	Capacity	Clarity	Competency	Capability	Credibility
iBEAM factor	Mindset	Aspiration	Behavior	Environment	Identity

14.2.1.3 Skills

They focus together on their breathing to give them access to their somatic state *(Professional Maturity)*—and seek to increase their ability to self-regulate *(Competency)* and practice getting out of their head and into their body as they re-engage around the difficult interaction *(Behavior)*.

14.2.1.4 Process

They work together to understand what this experience is like for the other person *(Social Maturity)*—and seek to increase their ability to speak more authentically and accountably about their role in the difficulty *(Capability)* and invest in their trust of each other *(Environment)*.

14.2.1.5 Outcomes

They work together to reflect on what has changed for them in this process *(Contextual Maturity)*—and seek to increase their ability to articulate their inner states and what has changed *(Credibility)* and embody what has changed to deepen their working relationship *(identity)*.

Our ability to enrich the learning and growth from encounters in coaching, for those involved and for their working alliance, can be augmented through the selective use of AI as follows (Table 14.2).

For example, in using an AI-driven platform like Ovida (which we use in our Narrative Coaching program), a coach can:

1. Use AI to observe a recorded session and *frame* opportunities for their development, e.g., occurrences when they interrupted the client—enabling them to become more aware of their mindset at the time.

Table 14.2 Opportunities for the use of AI to support client's growth

Maturity I mastery	AI role	AI focus	Outcome
Personal capacity	Framing	Observe the conversation	Deepened awareness; shift in mindset
Spiritual clarity	Mirroring	Inquire and reflect on what emerges	Conscious attention; shift in aspiration
Professional competency	Focusing	Name the element to address	Grounded knowledge; shift in behavior
Social capability	Feedlooping	Do small intentional practices	Internalized changes; shift in environment
Contextual credibility	Anchoring	Determine a suitable new habit or nudge	Embodied responses; shift in identity

2. Use AI to guide their inquiry into the occurrence as a *mirror* through which to more fully see what is going on in this occurrence—enabling them to become more aware of their aspiration at the time.
3. Use AI to articulate the elements, grounded in expert knowledge, which are essential for greater mastery in these types of occurrences and choosing one to *focus* on—enabling them to take a manageable and meaningful first step.
4. Use AI to engage in small intentional practices (SIPs) as part of what I call a *feedloop* (moving between observing themselves and the impact of their experiments)—enabling them to internalize the desired change.
5. Use AI to support repeated practice to increasingly *anchor* the new behavior in their natural pattern of response when they would otherwise interrupt—enabling them to reflect on their progress and their updated identity.

Let us turn now to five key implications for coaching as a whole, each becoming more urgent and important as the technology evolves quickly. In the end, what matters most is who clients become and what they can do after they leave the session—and how the coaching process can best serve this purpose. AI can be a valuable ally for the coach, the coaching process, and the client to enable them to make the most of their engagement—regardless of the ratio of human/AI involvement.

14.3 Propositions for the Use of AI in Coaching

Proposition 1: The emergence of AI offers a golden opportunity and a set of resources to deconstruct coaching and reconstruct it in new forms for these times.

Implications include (a) decenter the session as the central feature in coaching; (b) provide more options in terms of how the contracted time is allocated; (c) align the structure of the coaching journey more closely with the research on outcomes; and (d) provide more AI-informed coaching-related resources along the way in sync with what the client needs most right now.

Proposition 2: The emergence of AI challenges us to expand how we think about knowledge—from a consumerist efficiency frame to a relational ethical frame.

Implications include (a) think about knowledge in broader terms in coach development and assessment; (b) draw on Bent Flyvbjerg's (2001) distinctions between *episteme:* knowledge that, *techne:* knowledge how, and *phronesis:* knowledge why (see Drake, 2011)—with a greater emphasis on the latter in support of "constant self-awareness as a moral actor" (Frank, 2004, p. 223); and (c) focus more on our subtle and somatic knowledge as humans.

Proposition 3: The emergence of AI offers valuable resources to enable coaches and clients to more effectively improve over time.

Implications include (a) move beyond competency models in developing and assessing practitioners, especially as they progress beyond novice levels; (b) focus more on studying masters than on scaling novices; (c) make use of the principle of *structured emergence* (Drake, 2021, 2022) rather than industrial era remnants such as agenda setting; and (d) support fewer, smaller, deeper actions done regularly.

Proposition 4: The emergence of AI invites us to rebalance our development efforts by deepening our social consciousness and ability to learn from our environment in real time.

Implications include (a) move beyond the traditional paradigm of learning than doing by offering practitioners more opportunities to learn in real time; (b) focus more on higher order skills such as cultural awareness, critical thinking, ethical decision-making, and emotional intelligence; and (c) pay more attention to how athletes and musicians learn through ongoing deliberate practice, immediate feedback, deeper self-awareness, and a sense of the whole not just the parts (see Beane, 2024).

Proposition 5: The emergence of AI challenges us to advance our maturity on pace with what it makes possible in terms of our mastery in service of the highest good.

Implications include (a) remain alert to the commercial and political realities around the (mis-)use of AI because naiveté here will not serve coaching or humanity well; (b) account for what we are giving up not just what we are gaining; and (c) be wary of outsourcing too much scaffolding for your learning and development or avoiding too much of the productive struggle necessary for the internalized mastery of coaching.

14.4 Developing Yourself as a Coach in the AI Era Using the Five Maturities.

In line with these five propositions, the Five Maturities offers a useful framework for articulating how coaches can develop themselves to ethically and effectively incorporate AI in their practice. Here are some tips for coaches:

- Personal Maturity | Capacity | Mindset
  - Deepen your self-awareness, self-trust, and grounding in an AI-enhanced landscape.
  - Get clear on your values, boundaries, and voice through reflexive and mindful practice.
  - Keep coming back to your own center as an authentic human being.
- Spiritual Maturity | Clarity | Aspiration
  - Develop and follow a strong code of ethics and continue to expand what you notice.
  - Sustain an existential, meaningful connection to the sacred, the whole, and the long view.
  - Be a steward of human dignity who stays rooted in meaning and purpose.

- Professional Maturity I Competency I Behavior
  - Make clear choices about how you will relate to AI, and learn what is essential to do so.
  - Become sufficiently skilled and integrate AI without compromising coaching integrity.
  - Advocate development of standards, safeguards, and models for AI-enhanced practice.
- Social Maturity I Capability I Environment
  - Enable clients to bring systemic change to their environment as well as to themselves.
  - Pay close attention to the spaces in which you are coaching for the good of the whole.
  - Stay aware of how AI is affecting your approach; remain alert to biases in AI resources.
- Contextual Maturity I Credibility I Identity
  - Embrace that AI is disrupting assumptions about what coaching is and how it's delivered.
  - Attune to shifting cultural, technological, and ecological landscape in which you coach.
  - Adapt your identities and roles to serve humans in an AI era and anticipate future needs.

14.5 Conclusion

> This AI 'moment' is forcing us to reclaim the tacit, embodied, and relational ways of knowing we sidelined. How to live meaningful lives in a world where we are no longer the smartest entities in it?
>
> Luis Lozano-Paredes

It is tempting to feel like coaching is a large ship and AI is a tugboat that has come along to push it in new directions. For me, this gives too much power and control to the tug, even as I can recognize and appreciate the nudges which AI offers in the coaching space. We are at risk of exchanging depth and dexterity for speed and efficiency and of exchanging long-term and collective well-being for immediate and individual gains. The questions then become, "How can we mindfully, proactively, and productively engage with AI resources to not only improve coaching practice and coaching outcomes but to also help us reimagine coaching itself?"

This is important because technological innovations often necessitate trade-offs. As such, we need to attend to the broader impact of technologies such as AI as part of our ethical considerations. Otherwise, AI will—like all technologies—create new challenges in the course of addressing current challenges and the net gain will at best be nil. This dynamic is heightened and accelerated with AI given the speed at which it is advancing—both in terms of its capabilities and its reach. This is why digital, AI, research, and ethical literacies should become mandatory as part of the development and assessment of coaches in terms of their maturity and mastery.

In the end, I believe coaching will transform into a hybrid model that leverages the strengths of AI and humans in coaching. This partnership will enable coaches to blend what AI and humans each do best into a new form of practice. It will enable coaching to become a more truly client-centered practice—one in which practitioners can operate with greater depth (not just greater speed) to help develop better humans and a better world. As such, I believe that (1) coaching will move to become a descriptive adjective not a boxed noun, (2) the word "coach" will return to sports, and (3) new types of practitioners will emerge who could be seen as "developmental guides" who use their maturity (wisdom) and mastery (expertise) to guide clients in gaining what they need to evolve and serve in an increasingly challenged world.

What Kai-Fu Lee (2021) writes about education in the future can be readily applied to the future of what we once knew as coaching:

There will still be plenty for teachers to do. Teachers will play two important roles: First, they will be human mentors and connectors for the students. Human teachers will be the driving force behind stimulating the students critical thinking, creativity, empathy, and teamwork. The teacher will be a clarifier when a student is confused, a confronter when the student is complacent, and a comforter when the student is frustrated. In other words, teachers can focus less on the rote aspects of imparting knowledge and more on building emotional intelligence, creativity, character, values, and resilience, in students. The second role that teachers will play is to direct and program the AI teacher and companion in ways that will best address the students' needs. They will do this based on their experience, wisdom, and in-depth understanding of the students' potential and dreams (Kai-Fu Lee, 2021, p. 119).

Just as we need to stop sending changed people back into unchanged environments, we need to stop sending unchanged processes back into changed environments. In this regard, AI is neither our master nor our slave—an outdated frame we need to transcend at many levels—but rather as an ally that we can use at all levels. This calls for diligence in ensuring that AI does not add to the non-sustainable patterns and systems at the core of postmodern society—e.g., by masking larger issues, such as isolation—but instead is used to challenge us to create healthier forms of societies. Rather than just giving us yet another reason to stare endlessly at our phones, what if we consciously and courageously curated how we use AI such that it freed us to mature as individuals and as a species?

References

Beane, M. (2024). *The skill code: How to save human ability in an age of intelligent machines*. HarperBusiness.

Drake, D. B. (2011). What do coaches need to know? Using the Mastery Window to assess and develop expertise. *Coaching: An International Journal of Theory, Research & Practice, 4*(2), 138–155. https://doi.org/10.1080/17521882.2011.596486

Drake, D. B. (2019). Using integrative development to create a coaching culture in a professional services firm. In R. G. Hamlin, A. D. Ellinger, & J. Jones (Eds.), *Evidence-based initiatives for organizational change and development* (pp. 506–514). IGI Global.

Drake, D. B. (2021). Rethinking our work with leaders: Using developmental threshold zones in coaching. *Journal of Leadership Studies, 14*(4), 50–59. https://doi.org/10.1002/jls.21714

Drake, D. B. (2022). Using developmental threshold zones to accelerate clients' growth. *The Coaching Psychologist, 18*(1), 37–43.

Drake, D. B. (2026). *The Five Maturities: Transforming How We Work in a World Beyond Coaching*, The Moment Institute.

Eyal, M. (2025, July). *I'm a therapist, and I'm replaceable. But so are you.* TIME: Ideas. https://time.com/7261110/ai-therapy-human-connection-essay/

Flyvbjerg, B. (2001). *Making social science matter: Why social inquiry fails and how it can succeed again.* Cambridge University Press.

Frank, A. W. (2004). Asking the right question about pain: Narrative and phronesis. *Literature and Medicine, 23*(2), 209–225. https://doi.org/10.1353/lm.2005.0003

Lee, K.-F. (2021). *AI 2041: Ten visions for our future.* Penguin Random House.

Chapter 15
The Value of Standards and Ethical Use of AI in Coaching: Creating Trust in Technology

Joel A. DiGirolamo

Abstract The application of artificial intelligence (AI) in the coaching profession is very new. We are currently applying it in a very rudimentary manner and in just a few of the many possible application areas. Since the concepts in current AI architectures and the methods of using them are so new, it is helpful to provide education to stakeholders within a schema or model that the stakeholders already know. This will facilitate a more rapid understanding of how the technology works and how each stakeholder can apply it. The presence of standards for AI coaching products can provide a useful schema and can help to raise awareness of important elements within the technology, as well as what to look for in a product available for purchase. Since software product developers are usually focused on the technology, they may not have experts in the human element of the product functionality. These experts may be coaching professionals, social scientists, or both. The human experts can put standards to good use by following the framework set out in the standards and develop appropriate test use cases and evaluating live beta tests within that framework. Some of the most important considerations for high-quality AI coaching applications are data privacy, data use beyond the overt application uses, transparency of algorithms, and methods to minimize bias. Coaches, clients, and purchasers of AI technology must educate themselves on standards and how the technology works, explore AI tools and vendors, and ultimately get experience with AI systems.

Keywords Artificial intelligence in coaching · AI coaching standards · Ethics of AI · Data privacy in coaching · Data security in coaching · Bias in AI · Professional coaching standards · Trust in technology · Hybrid human–AI coaching · Coach training

J. A. DiGirolamo (✉)
International Coaching Federation, Lexington, KY, USA
e-mail: joel.digirolamo@coachingfederation.org

R. Wegener et al. (eds.), *Coaching in the Age of AI*, SpringerBriefs in Psychology, https://doi.org/10.1007/978-3-032-23332-5_15

15.1 Introduction

In order to put our exploration of ethics, standards, and the use of artificial intelligence (AI) in coaching into perspective, let's go all the way back to our primal roots of ethical behavior. Consider an example from one of our ancestors, the bonobos:

> In 2016, Tokuyama observed the highest-ranking male in the PE group, Snare, repeatedly harassing a female. Subsequently, three females started to violently attack him, and he fell from the tree on his own and escaped. Then, he disappeared from the group. After about 20 days, Snare showed up in the group from time to time, but he always stayed at the periphery. He no longer had the same social status that he did in the past (Furuichi, 2019, p. 80).

In this example, Snare behaved unethically and the females of the group were not going to accept his behavior. This is an example of how ethical behavior is subconsciously woven into our primal and current social fabric. Ethical behavior is at the core of human social behavior, likely due to the evolutionary advantage of cooperation and collaboration. As an extension to this, we expect the machines we interact with to behave in similar ethical ways, especially ones that purport to be "intelligent."

15.2 Ethics

As ancient philosophers honed their cognitive skills with logic and critical thinking, ethics became more conscious, detailed, and nuanced. In one sense, standards can be considered codification of ethical norms or at least desired norms as well as frameworks for communication within a given knowledge or development domain.

Aristotle (2009) believed that all individuals are capable of deliberate voluntary action and therefore that virtuous action is within everyone's power. Further, Immanuel Kant felt that each of us has an obligation or duty to behave morally (Kant, 1785/2012; Kranak, 2022). Virtuous and moral behavior leads to trust in an individual. As we trust that other people will behave ethically, we desire to translate that trust to feeling that machines must also behave ethically. It is important to consider ethical human behavior first since we have thousands of years of human experience and consideration, which provides a rich backdrop against which to contrast ethics of AI systems.

In the domains of coaching and psychology, many ethical codes exist, including ones from the American Psychological Association (APA, 2017), the European Federation of Psychologists' Associations (Lindsay et al., 2025), the European Mentoring and Coaching Council (EMCC, 2018), and the International Coaching Federation (ICF, 2024a). While these codes primarily address human-to-human behavior, recent versions address machine or technology behavior and interaction as well, and some, such as the Ethics Guidance for Providers of Coaching, Mentoring and Supervision Using Technology and AI by the EMCC (2023), focus solely on practice involving the use of technology. This EMCC guidance includes elements of data protection and transparency or disclosure on when technology will be used in the practice. The most recent version of the ICF code of ethics now includes language specifically calling out confidentiality and legal compliance, "through any technology systems I may utilize (i.e. technology-assisted coaching tools, databases, platforms, software, and artificial intelligence)" (ICF, 2024a, p. 7). These ethics codes apply to varying degrees in situations such as when using AI coaching platforms such as chatbots, when a coach augments their work with a client by using AI, or when using AI tools in training and coaching supervision.

No matter what type of AI technology a coach or organization uses, Dignum (2019) provides an excellent framework for consideration of the AI ethics involved:

- Ethics in design, that is, being mindful of the potential uses and consequences of the tools being developed
- Ethics by design, that is, the ultimate behaviors of the developed system
- Ethics for designers, that is, standards and certifications built for reference purposes

Norton et al. (2024) highlight the need for social scientists such as consulting psychologists to be integrated into AI development teams, bringing awareness of human risks as well as efficacy considerations into the product design. Further, these scientists can provide insights into possible downstream effects or behaviors of specific algorithms such as undesirable bias and low efficacy.

When an AI system has a lapse in ethical behavior such as when an AI chatbot exhibits bias, our first instinct may be to blame the system rather than considering more deeply who designed the system and the rigor of the development process. Dignum feels that AI tools are simply artifacts, and that with, "… tools built for a given purpose, responsibility can never lie with the AI system because as an artefact, it cannot be seen as a responsible actor" (Dignum, 2019, p. 2). Extending this paradigm, Dignum compares an algorithm to a cooking recipe and that it is the creator of the recipe, or algorithm that is responsible, and not the recipe or algorithm itself (Dignum, 2019). Standards and certifications in a given field signify maturity in that field, and this has begun in the domain of AI in coaching, which will be discussed in the next section.

Transparency is linked to ethical leadership and high transparency can promote trust in a leader or team integrity (Bennis et al., 2008; Norman et al., 2010; Palanski et al., 2011). Similarly, trust in the AI machine, regardless of whether it is working interactively or in the background, means that it must be transparent about the why and what of decisions and actions, where data is stored and who has access to it, efficacy, biases, where it might be used, and system reliability (Hendrycks, 2025; ICF, 2019).

An aspect of coaching that is seldom discussed but has significant ethical implications is what is provided in a coaching session—whether human-to-human or via an AI coaching platform. The ICF defines coaching as "partnering with clients in a thought-provoking and creative process that inspires them to maximize their personal and professional potential" (ICF, n.d.). As provided in the ICF Core Competencies (2019), coaching is a non-directive process where coaches facilitate client growth by fostering new insights or awareness without providing specific direction. However, human coaches and AI coaching platforms such as chatbots and AI coaching augmentation may combine the coaching skills with domain knowledge to provide a higher level of efficacy for the client. Working in this manner requires an enhanced level of skill, however, since the human coach or AI coaching platform must first uncover the client motivations and goals before offering pertinent domain knowledge (DiGirolamo et al., 2025; DiGirolamo & Berman, 2025). Ethically, what is very important is for the human coach, AI chatbot, or AI coaching augmentation platform to describe specifically what they will be offering so that it meets the client's needs and expectations.

15.3 Standards

As noted above, the existence of standards created by a community of domain experts indicates a significant level of maturity in that domain. Fundamentally, standards foster consistency (e.g., reliability and predictability) and trust. Looking at standards from another angle, multiple reasons for them include:

- Interoperability, e.g., language, networking protocols, electrical plugs, and outlets
- Quality and safety, e.g., food safety and housing
- Human rights, e.g., maximum number of working hours per day or week, worker age limits
- Economies of scale, e.g., in manufacturing

Standards groups may form in a multitude of professions and with a plethora of technologies, while several global standards organizations have a cross-geography impact, including the International Organization for Standardization (ISO), the Institute of Electrical and Electronics Engineers (IEEE), and the European Union (EU). One of the most recent and impactful standards came from the European Union (EU), the General Data Protection Regulation (GDPR; European Parliament, 2016). This standard laid a foundation and paradigm for ethical use and protection of individual data. The EU Artificial Intelligence Act extends protections to ethical behavior of AI systems (European Parliament, 2024) and allows for a phased-in approach culminating in full compliance after August 2, 2027.

In early 2021, the ICF convened a group of four AI coaching developers and two experienced coaches, the ICF AI Coaching Standards Working Group, to begin work on AI coaching standards. The goal of that development process was to create AI coaching standards that could be used in a fashion similar to human-to-human coaching standards. The standards were intended to provide legitimacy for AI coaching products and indicate a commitment to excellence in coaching by the AI coach developer.

The Working Group developed multiple iterations of draft documents and solicited public feedback in order to gather opinions from a diverse audience. The final ICF Artificial Intelligence Coaching Framework and Standards document was publicly released in November 2024 (ICF, 2024b). These standards were developed with multiple audiences in mind, including:

- Software developers (providers)
- Organizations who purchase AI coaching tools
- Coaches
- Coaching clients
- Coaching education and training organizations
- Coaching supervisors

The standards cover multiple types of applications, including scheduling (time-related activities), data processing, interactive (over an extended period of time, such as for habit formation or in training), and conversational (in real time, such as chatbots, coaching augmentation systems, or coaching supervision). While such a wide variety of applications leads to a more complicated set of standards, it brings more value to the profession through a comprehensive approach. The requirements contained in the standards include content (information for clients, coaches, and purchasers), functionality or system capabilities, actions the system may need to take, and validation or quality and performance standards.

The ICF AI Coaching Standards cover many aspects of system transparency, such as how underlying algorithms work, why specific decisions were made, potential biases, where data is stored, and who has access to it. The Standards largely follow the ICF Core Competencies (2019) with additions for AI-powered client reinforcement such as growth-tracking, coaching reliability measures, assurance and testing, security, privacy, and system resilience and accessibility.

15.4 Example Ethical Challenges

Fundamentally, AI can be applied in three ways in the coaching process, as illustrated in Fig. 15.1: in strictly human coaching, when AI is integrated as a tool in real time in the human coaching process (a hybrid approach), and in a standalone AI coaching scenario. In a hybrid scenario, the AI coaching tool could be handling real-time administrative tasks such as monitoring and displaying potential client topics and goals, relieving the coach of these cognitive tasks, and thus allowing them to follow the client more dynamically into deeper areas of motivations, values, and beliefs. For the strictly human coaching and hybrid scenarios, an AI client can be used for human client simulation and potential evaluation.

Consider that in the hybrid and AI coaching scenarios human clients are divulging potentially very confidential information about themselves, work colleagues, friends, and their employer to the AI systems. In cases where an employer is paying for the coaching services, they may request access to the coaching session recordings or transcripts. In all cases, a human coach using the AI technology as a complement to their human coaching may request access to similar client data. Ethically, it is extremely important that all parties involved, including the AI provider, the

Fig 15.1 Conceptual applications of AI in coaching

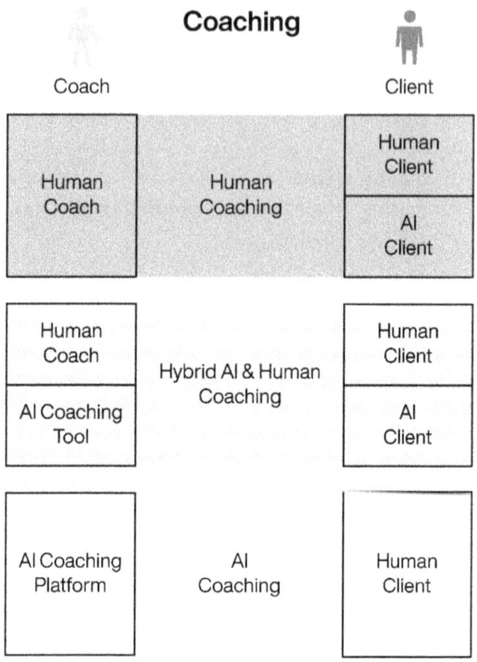

purchaser, the coach, and the client understand and have written agreements very clearly defining what data in what format will be accessible to any party, including employees of the AI provider.

15.5 Conclusion

While human ethical behavior has primal roots, behaviors can be perceived differently by each individual human, resulting in a complicated tapestry of thoughts and emotions by the receiver. As we overlay the human ethical framework onto artificial intelligence machines and set out a desire for similar ethical behavior, the challenge can seem daunting.

However, we can consider ethical use of AI in all types of systems such as the necessity to keep user data private and secure and to be transparent about who may have access to the data. Consider, for example, when an AI platform is used by an employee of an organization and their superior or an HR professional wants access to the data. Is access authorization transparently disclosed to all parties with capability to opt out? How is training and testing data gathered and processed in order to minimize bias and updated when biases may be uncovered? How is the system monitored to assess bias at frequent intervals?

Considering AI chatbots specifically, they may feel very human, and therefore are they transparent in notifying and reminding users that they are not human? Do they explain what they are capable of and offer options for the way they will work with clients?

When a human coach augments their work with an AI system, are they transparent in disclosing this to the client and other stakeholders? How do the coaches assess bias and efficacy in the AI system?

In what ways do the providers of AI coach training and supervision tools report efficacy, system limitations such as coaching model used, and the gamut of capability? Considering how large the breadth of concepts arising in coach training and coach supervision is, the AI tool may easily find itself beyond its range of understanding.

And so, while AI has dramatically shifted how coaches may work, it is incumbent on all parties involved to understand, identify, and communicate all limitations of the AI tools before they are deployed in production.

15.5.1 Questions for Future Consideration

In what ways should the user of an AI coaching platform such as a chatbot be able to report unethical or biased behavior of the chatbot?

Given that tools such as AI chatbots learn and adjust how they respond as they are used, in what ways might the bias of the system change over time?

In what ways would you find it useful for your clients to use an AI coaching chatbot between your human-to-human coaching sessions?

When considering who might have access to sensitive client data in an AI coaching system, in what ways do you feel system providers may be able to provide assurances of privacy?

References

American Psychological Association. (2017). *Ethical principles of psychologists and code of conduct*. https://www.apa.org/ethics/code/ethics-code-2017.pdf

Aristotle. (2009). *The Nicomachean ethics* (D. Ross, Trans.). Oxford University Press (Original work published ca. 350 B.C.E.)

Bennis, W., Goleman, D., & Biederman, P. W. (2008). Creating a culture of candor. In W. Bennis, D. Goleman, J. O'Toole, & P. W. Biederman (Eds.), *Transparency: How leaders create a culture of candor* (pp. 1–43). Jossey-Bass.

DiGirolamo, J. A., & Berman, B. (2025, April). Specialty coaching: Integration of coaching skills with domain knowledge [Master tutorial]. In *Society for industrial and organizational psychology annual conference, Denver, CO, United States*.

DiGirolamo, J. A., Barney, M., Tkach, J. T., & Yousufzai, A. G. (2025). *What is coaching? Exploring the application of coaching skills in multiple domains* [Manuscript in preparation].

Dignum, V. (2019). *Responsible artificial intelligence: How to develop and use AI in a responsible way*. Springer.
European Mentoring and Coaching Council. (2018). EMCC code of ethics.
European Mentoring and Coaching Council. (2023). *Ethics guidance for providers of coaching, mentoring and supervision using technology and AI (Version 1.0 July 2023)*. European Mentoring and Coaching Council. https://emccdrive.emccglobal.org/api/file/download/u7xOUK5c7JhpjZinckAUW6OoX4kG1Hcq8FSwVnR5
European Parliament. (2016). Regulation (EU) 2016/679 of the European Parliament and of the Council of 27 April 2016 on the protection of natural persons with regard to the processing of personal data and on the free movement of such data, and repealing Directive 95/46/EC (General Data Protection Regulation). *Official Journal of the European Union, 59*, 1–88. https://eur-lex.europa.eu/eli/reg/2016/679/oj
European Parliament. (2024). Regulation (EU) 2024/1689 of the European Parliament and of the Council of 13 June 2024 laying down harmonised rules on artificial intelligence and amending Regulations (EC) No 300/2008, (EU) No 167/2013, (EU) No 168/2013, (EU) 2018/858, (EU) 2019/2144 and (EU) 2019/881 and Directives 2014/90/EU, (EU) 2016/797 and (EU) 2020/1828 (Artificial Intelligence Act). *Official Journal of the European Union, L 168*, 1–161. https://eur-lex.europa.eu/legal-content/EN/TXT/PDF/?uri=OJ:L_202401689
Furuichi, T. (2019). *Bonobo and chimpanzee: The lessons of social coexistence*. Springer.
Hendrycks, D. (2025). *Introduction to AI safety, ethics, and society*. Taylor & Francis.
International Coaching Federation. (2019). *Updated ICF core competency model*. https://coachingfederation.org/core-competencies
International Coaching Federation. (2024a). *ICF code of ethics*. International Coaching Federation. https://coachingfederation.org/resource/icf-code-of-ethics/
International Coaching Federation. (2024b). *The International Coaching Federation artificial intelligence coaching framework and standards*. https://coachingfederation.org/research/coalition-technology-in-coaching
International Coaching Federation. (n.d.). *ICF definition of coaching*. Retrieved May 8, 2026, https://coachingfederation.org/about
Kant, I. (1785/2012). *Groundwork of the metaphysics of morals* (M. Gregor & J. Timmermann, Trans.). Cambridge University Press.
Kranak, J. (2022). Kantian deontology. In G. Matthews (Ed.), *Introduction to philosophy: Ethics* (pp. 53–64). Rebus Community.
Lindsay, G., Øvreeide, H., & Koene, C. (2025). *Ethics for European psychologists* (2nd ed.). Hogrefe.
Norman, S. M., Avolio, B. J., & Luthans, F. (2010). The impact of positivity and transparency on trust in leaders and their perceived effectiveness. *The Leadership Quarterly, 21*(3), 350–364. https://doi.org/10.1016/j.leaqua.2010.03.002
Norton, L. W., Howell, A. W., DiGirolamo, J. A., & Hayes, T. L. (2024). Using artificial intelligence in consulting psychology. *Consulting Psychology Journal: Practice and Research, 76*(2), 137–162. https://doi.org/10.1037/cpb0000274
Palanski, M. E., Kahai, S. S., & Yammarino, F. J. (2011). Team virtues and performance: An examination of transparency, behavioral integrity, and trust. *Journal of Business Ethics, 99*, 201–216. https://doi.org/10.1007/s10551-010-0650-7

Chapter 16
Coaching and Human Development in the Context of Science, Technologies, and Business

Adina Tarry

Abstract This chapter explores how coaching and human development evolve in the context of science and digital technology, which strongly impact society and business. The introduction of AI in many organisational activities, to democratise access to coaching for large numbers of people, is a reality and is to be embraced. The chapter also introduces the Co-Me-Su-Tra® Model of Models as a framework that highlights where the limitations of AI vs. human coaching are, to the net advantage of humans, highlighting what human coaching at mastery level has to offer, by no means threatened by technology in the foreseeable future. Embracing digital transformation by upgraded skills and higher order capabilities is the adaptive approach to reality as it is to increase agency and empower the coaching community to face the future with a unique and human-specific level of competence and hope.

Keywords Cross-disciplinary · AI · Coaching · Mentoring · Supervision · Dialectic · Digital · Co-Me-Su-Tra® · SOCIETALByDesign® · SUSTAINABLEByDesign® · Development

16.1 Technology, Business, and Human Development

Change is a natural aspect of evolution and usually occurs either by an accumulation of events and modifications to the status quo or by revolutions, which pushed an entire existing order, onto a completely new trajectory. Science and technology are such factors that by three industrial revolutions of the last 200 years (1765: steam; 1870: electricity; 1969: electronics) have led us to a safer, healthier, and more comfortable existence with impacts on the natural social, economic, and political landscape and the lives of millions. The difference it makes can be seen in regions where electricity, transportation, sanitation, infrastructure, mechanisation, health care, and education are missing with dire results.

A. Tarry (✉)
Deep Tech Innovation Centre (DTIC), University of Warwick, Coventry, UK

R. Wegener et al. (eds.), *Coaching in the Age of AI*, SpringerBriefs in Psychology, https://doi.org/10.1007/978-3-032-23332-5_16

Because of its benefits technology continues to evolve unstoppably and the Internet has enabled mass access to what it has to offer.

Today, on the cusp of the fourth revolution the electronics of 1969 have been digitised and evolved into robotics, automation, artificial intelligence (AI), virtual reality (VR), augmented reality (AR), nanotechnology, quantum computing, biotechnology, the Internet of Things (IoT) and the industrial Internet of Things (IIoT), 3D printing, and autonomous vehicles.

The recent COVID-19 pandemic of 2020 and the release of ChatGPT in 2023, under tabloid type headlines such as "AI is going to take away your job", have also both democratised the powerful and seductive technology of artificial intelligence (AI) and normalised hybrid working, online social connectivity, and training and education, including the human resources (HR) function in business, which have used technology since 2000.

At the same time, the world has become—according to definitions by academics and governments—volatile, uncertain, complex, ambiguous, turbulent, novel, brittle, anxious, non-linear, incomprehensible, rapid, unpredictable, paradoxical, and tangled. A world of contradictions, challenges and opportunities, ethical questions, and forced rapid adaptation that stresses individuals, society, business, and governance, faced with finding answers on the run and little time to make sense and find meaning in how reality unfolds.

But human civilisation is a history of adaptation to change learning and skilling up, use of tools to human advantage, moving away from monotonous, repetitive, or risky work and instead utilising human ingenuity for social cohesion, shared prosperity, access, and opportunity, and achieving personal and collective fulfilment.

And coaching, mentoring, supervision, and training are all practices that serve precisely individual and collective learning and development, ideally positioned to mediate in times of transition and change, contributing to the widest of human aspirations to achieve.

16.2 Coaching and AI in the Digital Age

In this context, the role and appeal of coaching (on the rise since the 1990s with strong support from business) as a practice that is steeped in human learning between individuals and within groups and society and a catalyst for realising human potential and based on positive emotions, role modelling, rapport building, chemistry, presence, empathy, sympathy, and transfer of wisdom could not be stronger.

Professionalised at some pace since 2002 and diversified to include executive, team, personal, career, and wellness types of coaching—to name just a few—coaching remains deeply steeped in the relations between human beings; coaching is rapidly moving from a place of tech fear to a place of understanding its role and opportunities, around what its real value is, and what it can do to use technology as a helpful tool for its own evolution, as it reflects the times (Tarry, 2018).

With AI being able to deliver speed, precisions, scale, and volume of prescribed automated process-driven activities, AI can make an excellent administrative assistant: schedule, monitor, correct, find, recall, and summarise content or imitate and create content if given a model, template, or examples to follow, and instructions on what it needs to do, very precisely, by using natural language in the shape of prompting sentences.

AI can be used on both sides of the coaching process for clients and practitioners, alike. For the benefit of clients, the opportunities for AI and automation in the coaching process include the following—and not only—aspects.

AI can be used to automate and democratise access to a number of coaching process-based models such as GROW, ACHIEVE, LASER, ACE, EGAN, STIR and PIE, ABCDE, and PERMA: all acronyms that stand for the respective steps used in the model.

AI can be used to perform gap analysis against competencies and capabilities and suggest personalised learning, training, and development recommendations on the basis of competencies frameworks, performance monitoring, and psychometric assessments including MBTI, PF16, and Bar-On EQ.

Overall such applications of AI elicit answers and provide ranking exercises, goal-setting paths and maps with tracking of milestones, analysis of resources, objectives setting and action planning, time management, and gamification strategies that all converge to enable clients' self-directed, independent developmental work to take place, at their convenience and by direct online use of technology. They cover a wide range of coaching diversified from business and management to career, self-development, wellness, and life coaching, which have also added a new retail market for individuals to enjoy independent technology-enabled access. Such applications also use the technique of questioning, which—just as in coaching—enable focus and awareness of self, others, and context and self-reflection with informative, formative, and potentially transformative outcomes which serve in enabling talent to overcome obstacles, fulfil potential, achieve objectives, and ultimately contribute to society and business as a whole.

For coaching practitioners, AI's offerings depend on the type of work coaches do. For internal coaches and associate coaches, the technology tools will be given to them by the employers or clients/tech providers. For all coaches who use globally adopted office and work suites of applications—such as Microsoft, Google, and Apple—the access to admin and task-focused apps is already provided in the package, either free or by subscriptions.

But developing people in business contexts goes beyond the individual, to groups and teams, by design and delivery of programmes for change, transformation, restructuring, learning, and development on a large scale across the entire organisation. The magnitude of number of participants and speed of project delivery become a challenge which automation, AI, gamification, or virtual reality can overcome.

Technology can deploy online applications to countless individuals, based on constructs, principles, models, frameworks, methodologies, and standard, from multidisciplinary sources such as academic disciplines (psychology, sociology, philosophy, ethics, neuroscience, anthropology), business schools and management science, and high-performing business practices developed typically in blue-chip corporations.

For example, surveys related to:

- Leadership traits and style-based models (charismatic, heroic, competent, servant, enabler, etc.)
- Types of organisational culture and structure (hierarchical, distributed, solar system, etc.)
- Dimensions of national cultures (the models of Hofstede, Trompenaars, the GLOBE project).
- Analysis of types of followers, etc.

Or practice-based methodologies, industry standards, gold standards, and best practices that have emerged from learning organisations, such as:

- Standards: ISO 9001, ISO4000-1, Capability Maturity Model—CMM, Investors in People.
- Waterfall and Agile project management.
- Just in time, Six Sigma, and lean optimisation methods.
- Kai Zen and total quality management (TQM).
- Problem-solving fishbone root cause analysis (Ishikawa diagram), brainstorming, affinity diagrams.
- Design thinking, etc.

Technology can be effectively used as a first-line scaling up method to profiling, surveying, data collecting, informing, educating, assessing, evaluating, and making personalised recommendations for a large number of people on a company-wide scale.

However both at individual level and collective level, when it comes to integrating multidisciplinary cross-functional information from different assessment sources for one individual or aligning individuals in a team and the team to the organisation as a whole, this becomes a complex task that AI cannot perform.

Integrating complex sets of information, from multiple disconnected sources, involves the real qualitative jump and value added of human intelligence with its seamless flexibility, adaptability, transferability, heuristics, filling out information gaps, integrating feedback, making sense, and finding meaning in real time and the emergent space of human, ethically informed, reflective, and reflexive dialogue.

These are not within the current AI capability and remain a distant aspiration for the future general artificial intelligence (GAI) that is yet to be developed some decades away, if ever. Therefore, the current best approach seems to be based on gaining advantages from use in a hybrid model of both technology/AI and the complex capabilities of human practitioners.

16.3 Using the Unified Co-Me-Su-Tra® "Model of Models" to Differentiate and Bridge AI and Human Coaching

The Unified Co-Me-Su-Tra® Model and Theory positioned for coaching, mentoring, supervision, and training has been developed to differentiate the respective contributions and limitations of AI and human practitioners at a time of rapid emergence of AI applications that open both challenges and opportunities to human development practices. This is an integrative cross-disciplinary framework that offers a "Model of Models" with constructs applicable for coaching and other developmental practices, presented as levels and dimensions for practical applications in dialogical interactions. The model's architecture is scalable, multidimensional, hierarchical, inter- and transdisciplinary, dynamic, evolving, and dialectic (Tarry, 2025).

The five levels (L) and seven dimensions (D) constructs of the Unified Co-Me-Su-Tra® Model (Fig. 16.1) are interconnected and map stages of constructs and (personal) development over time (biological age).

The five (construct) levels relate to both nature and nurture and are as follows: L one: personality, L two: values and beliefs, L three: behaviour and communication, L four: learning and skills, L five: spirituality self-actualisation. The seven (constructs) dimensions are as follows: D one: age, D two: feelings, D three: motivation, D four: awareness, D five: identity, D six: functionality, D seven: creativity, innovation. Together they cover most if not all aspects of human development (emotional, cognitive, spiritual, behavioural, etc.) and allow related sets of concepts to exist

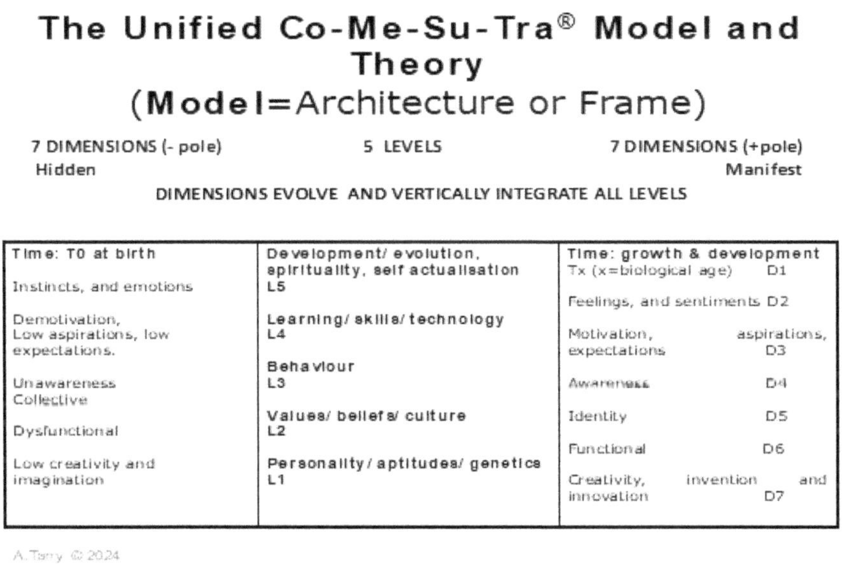

Fig. 16.1 The Co-Me-Su-Tra® Model

within. All levels and dimensions naturally evolve as a result of the passing of time and gained work and life experience. They can be used at any point in time and repeatedly over time, as a roadmap to guide enquiry, dialogue, and reflection around specific objectives, facilitated by dialogical practices such as coaching, mentoring, supervision, and training.

Such developmental interactions may be initiated by the need or desire to focus on a particular aspect of one's personal profile and by the objectives set either by organisations in talent development programmes or by individuals in a private capacity (retail markets).

In practice, human coaches in conjunction with their clients decide what aspects of the customised coaching journey may benefit from a deeper exploration aided by instruments available online. For example, initially focus on L four: skills and D six: functionality, and explore L one: personality, aptitudes and D three: motivation, aspirations, with relevant existing online tools, e.g. MBTI, V&B, job performance, gap analysis, performance reviews, and 360 questionnaires. The first level of information can be collected by the client/s independently by use of technology and AI and can be scaled up to teams and groups, as described in the previous section.

Next, clients and coaches engage in a skilled human coach led qualitative dialogue along the seven guiding principles of the Co-Me-Su-Tra® Model and Theory, namely sense making, meaning-making, adequacy, congruence, alignment, assessment by numbers, and helical iterations. This dialogue helps to leverage existing and new learning, refine a client-specific action plan, and meet pre-set—but also new or emerging—objectives or lines of enquiry, achieving a successful way of delivering a hybrid human and technology-enabled coaching.

This qualitative process cannot be exercised by AI alone and needs human mastery to support clients' transformation and transcendence to another level of personal and professional self-actualisation.

Developing complex evolving and adaptive humans and human systems cannot be done by AI. This complex integrative process requires skilled coaches, mentors, and supervisors delivering learning and development support at high and mastery level of practice, using evolved human intelligence, knowledge, wisdom, competencies, and capabilities currently not replicated by machines. Adapting, applying, and adopting complex streams of information requires intelligent human intervention and practitioners enabled by a cross-disciplinary learning mind-set and a multi-skilled coaching capability beyond models, with an effective professional flow, in real time. These complex capabilities are not currently afforded by narrow AI.

Apart from helping in the demarcation line between automation and human intervention, the Unified Co-Me-Su-Tra® Theory and Model of Models is all inclusive; it allows and welcomes complementary use of many existing or developing models, frameworks, and principles from other disciplines and practices, all seen as of equal value, particularly when deployed in the best-of-breed approach, customised to every individual, team, or organisation client.

It is human coaching that brings the qualitative refocusing and leveraging of individual or team learning through technology to embody the conversion of technology-informed resources back to human appreciation and deployment in the actual real-world settings of the clients' contexts. And it is humans (coaches and HR specialists) that provide the final evaluation of the success that arises from such talent and organisation change and development imperatives.

The role of AI is to assist with data collection, metrics, reports, summaries, and process steps and provide tangible materials useful for the human to human value adding conversations which in themselves support individuals or teams—in their respective roles—to be prepared, motivated, empowered, and resourced to make their expected contributions in business and civil society by their involvement in change, decision-making, project implementation, legislation, and governance. As a result, practitioners' presence in the developmental co-created space becomes a richer resource and a stronger role model, in the success of technology-assisted developmental interactions, for all sides.

Technology is not human in nature but presents a range of tools made of aluminium and iron, plastics, and glass, hungry for rare metals, mined at great cost to nature and surrounding human settlements, and using energy, which currently remain mostly produced by polluting fossil fuels. And whilst we may be seduced by our own desire to anthropomorphise animals or objects because of the benefits that they bring us and may become attached to pets, robots, and AI companions, it is our dreams and desires to build beneficial and long-lasting relationships with other humans that energise and feed our aspirations as we first experienced them, when nurtured by humans in our early years. Expanded with time, growth, and maturity they scale up into our desire to connect with and protect nature and society, contribute to shared prosperity, and celebrate life in all its forms (Tarry, 2023).

16.4 Embracing Technology in Coaching as a Solution and Not a Problem

The proof that technology works with developmental practices since 2015 for delivering better outcomes—in combination with human intelligence and the human touch—is already here in models and tools that support empowered self-directed learning whilst remaining connected to professionalised human practitioners who provide qualitative emotional and relational touch to motivation, self-actualisation, and practical personal and professional goals.

By embracing the way the world is now, understanding the wider forces that impact society and the role of technology is a professional development duty. Opening up the habitual inward-looking lenses to much wider and more cross-disciplinary and integrative view of these developmental practices in the context of science, technology, business, and society will elevate not only the quality of professional services delivered to others, but also thinking and cognitive competence, self-worth, and agency of the practitioners themselves.

16.5 Concluding with Hope and Optimism

Technology defines human civilisation and rejecting technology is impossible unless we aspire to return modern society back to life in caves as hunters and gatherers. Leveraging the many advantages of this age, and embracing this digital reality, is the better option than daunting defeat in the face of unavoidable changes of the twenty-first century.

Digital technologies and AI are the latest expression of science and human innovation and are here to stay, as tools in the service of our higher aspirations and to be used alongside our human empathy, creativity, ethics, ambition, intentions, and potential. Rejecting technology due to fear instead of enjoying the significant interdisciplinary resources available may in fact defeat the purpose and cause us to miss out on an exceptional opportunity to prevail, enjoy our times, and thrive. Until and unless AI evolves to GAI and becomes a proper imitation of the highlights of human intelligence, devoid of its numerous biases, and evolved into a sustainable version that is kind to nature, AI will continue to deliver—under the watchful human eye—its specific benefits, just like all other technologies and evolve and improve by ongoing corrective iterations, not as a replacement but as a complement to what—for now—only humans can do.

References

Tarry, A. (2018). *Coaching with careers and AI in mind: Grounding a hopeful and resourceful self fit for a digital world* (1st ed.). Routledge. https://doi.org/10.4324/9780429451553

Tarry, A. (2023). *Nine things AI can't do for your future career but you can.* Fractal Publications.

Tarry, A. (2025). *Practicing coaching, mentoring, supervision & training in complex human systems with AI and ChatBots: The new order at the edge of chaos 2.0.* Fractal Publications.

Part VI
Conclusion

Chapter 17
Concluding Chapter: Navigating the Future of Coaching and Artificial Intelligence

Robert Wegener, Tamara Garcia, Nicky Terblanche, and Till Grossrieder

Abstract This concluding chapter synthesizes key insights from the book's exploration of the evolving relationship between coaching and artificial intelligence (AI). Four major themes are highlighted: AI as a tool to augment human coaching; the potential replacement of coaching by AI systems; the role of AI in coach education and supervision; and the ethical, societal, and professional challenges arising from this technological shift. While some applications demonstrate how AI can enhance coaching practice through personalization, analytics, and reflection support, others raise concerns about the loss of relational depth and ethical complexity. The chapter argues that the future of coaching is not a binary choice between human and machine but a dynamic interplay of both. It calls for hybrid models in which AI supports, rather than replaces, the human elements of coaching. Ultimately, this chapter emphasizes the importance of shaping AI's role in coaching through intentional design, professional standards, and a clear commitment to human dignity and development.

Keywords Artificial intelligence · Coaching research · Human–AI collaboration · Ethical principles · AI-based coaching effectiveness · Generative AI applications in coaching · Coach training and supervision analytics · Algorithmic bias in AI coaching · Hybrid human–machine intelligence · Future research on AI-enabled coaching

---

R. Wegener
Fachhochschule Nordwestschweiz FHNW, Hochschule für Soziale Arbeit, Olten, Schweiz
e-mail: robert.wegener@fhnw.ch

T. Garcia · T. Grossrieder (✉)
Institute of Applied Psychology, ZHAW Zurich University of Applied Sciences, Zürich, Switzerland
e-mail: tamara.garcia@zhaw.ch; till.grossrieder@zhaw.ch

N. Terblanche
Stellenbosch Business School, Cape Town, South Africa
e-mail: nickyt@sun.ac.za

R. Wegener et al. (eds.), *Coaching in the Age of AI*, SpringerBriefs in Psychology, https://doi.org/10.1007/978-3-032-23332-5_17

The exploration of artificial intelligence and coaching across the chapters of this book reveals a field in transition, one that stands at the intersection of profound technological innovation and deeply human practice. Coaching, historically rooted in dialogue, reflection, and relational presence, is now confronted with a set of tools and systems capable of mimicking certain cognitive functions, offering personalized insights, and scaling interactions in ways previously unimaginable. This book approached this convergence from multiple angles: conceptual, empirical, ethical, and developmental and, taken together, it paints a nuanced picture of both promise and complexity. This concluding chapter draws these threads together and offers four insights.

The first insight is the vision of coaching as a fundamentally human practice that can be significantly expanded and improved through the use of artificial intelligence. Several authors have depicted scenarios in which AI operates not as a replacement for the coach, but as a quiet co-pilot, a presence in the background that augments human capability without supplanting it (e.g., Diller & Smith, Geißler, Isaacson in this book). The metaphor of a coach wearing a discreet earpiece, receiving subtle prompts from an AI system during sessions, encapsulates this idea: an intelligent companion that helps the coach listen more deeply, frame more incisive questions, and track subtle patterns in client narratives that might otherwise go unnoticed. Such augmentation is not merely theoretical. As discussed in chapters by Geißler and by Mai and Richert, prototypes already exist in the form of coaching chatbots, sentiment analysis tools, and AI-driven prompt generators that enhance reflection and focus. These tools promise to reduce cognitive load, provide real-time analytics, and even suggest evidence-based interventions aligned with established coaching frameworks such as GROW or cognitive-behavioral coaching.

What makes this vision compelling is not just efficiency. At its heart lies the possibility of personalization at scale—AI systems that learn the client's goals, adapt to their communication style, and support the coach in crafting interventions that are uniquely resonant. This aligns with broader trends in other helping professions where AI is used to tailor therapy protocols or educational plans. In coaching, the potential is similarly transformative: real-time dashboards that track micro-progress toward goals, digital "memory" of prior sessions, and predictive insights that help both coach and client anticipate challenges ahead. However, this augmentation model also highlights the limits of current AI. Despite advances in natural language processing and large language models, AI lacks the capacity for true empathy, embodied presence, and contextual sensitivity, qualities that remain at the heart of the coaching relationships. The chapters that explored this augmentation theme consistently cautioned against overreliance on technology, noting that the power of coaching often lies not in providing answers but in co-creating meaning. AI can provide structure and information, but the relational depth and trust that enable transformative learning remain profoundly human.

A second, more provocative insight threaded through the book is the prospect of coaching as a practice that could, at least in theory, be completely replaced by artificial intelligence. This vision conjures images of humanoid robots or fully autonomous digital coaches capable of conducting sessions indistinguishable from those of a human practitioner. Such ideas, once the realm of science fiction, have gained traction with the rise of generative AI systems. As Terblanche and others have observed, empirical studies already show AI coaching chatbots performing comparably to human coaches on certain outcome measures such as goal attainment, at least in short-term interventions. If narrow AI can match human coaches in structured, outcome-focused domains, some argue it is only a matter of time before broader relational competencies follow.

The chapters exploring this possibility do not shy away from its disruptive implications. The efficiency and cost-effectiveness of fully automated coaching could democratize access, bringing developmental support to populations and contexts where human coaching is currently unaffordable or unavailable. In corporate settings, AI coaches could be deployed at scale, offering personalized development pathways for thousands of employees simultaneously. However, the notion of total replacement also raises existential questions for the profession. If coaching can be reduced to algorithms and data, what remains of the human craft? Does the coaching relationship, long celebrated for its relational alchemy and co-created meaning, become something qualitatively different when mediated entirely by machines?

Several chapters take a cautious stance, emphasizing that while AI can simulate aspects of empathy and insight, it does not possess consciousness, moral reasoning, or the embodied presence that underpins trust in human relationships. Bachkirova's reflections are particularly salient here, warning against conflating "artificial" with "authentic" intelligence. Even as AI grows more sophisticated, there may remain an irreducible human dimension to coaching such as the felt experience of being deeply seen and heard by another person that technology cannot replicate. Nonetheless, the allure of full replacement, particularly in high-volume or low-cost contexts, cannot be dismissed, and this possibility challenges the profession to articulate more clearly what makes coaching uniquely human.

A third insight, and one of the most practically promising, is the role of AI in coach education, training, and supervision. Here, AI is not positioned as the coach itself, but as a tool for developing coaches. Several chapters, notably by Malafronte and by Haitoglou and colleagues, describe emerging applications where AI enhances learning for trainee coaches. These include AI-driven video analysis that provides objective feedback on coaching micro-skills, natural language processing tools that analyze session transcripts for patterns of questioning or reflective listening, and simulation environments where trainees can practice with AI-generated "difficult clients" in psychologically safe conditions. The value proposition is compelling: AI can deliver immediate, data-rich feedback at scale, accelerating learning curves and supplementing human mentorship.

The potential extends beyond initial training into ongoing professional development and supervision. AI could assist supervisors by flagging themes across multiple coaching sessions, identifying potential blind spots, or even ensuring ethical compliance by monitoring language for risk indicators. In contexts where access to experienced supervisors is limited, AI could provide a baseline level of oversight, ensuring that new coaches do not practice in isolation. Importantly, this does not diminish the role of human supervisors but rather augments it, allowing them to focus their attention on the nuanced, relational aspects of supervision that AI cannot address. The chapters in this section underscore the need for careful design to avoid over-mechanizing coach education, emphasizing that AI should support, not replace the reflective, dialogic processes through which coaches internalize their professional identity.

The final insight emerging across the chapters concerns the broader ethical and societal questions raised by the integration of AI into coaching. Ethical considerations permeate every aspect of this discourse: from data privacy and informed consent to algorithmic bias and the potential commodification of human development. Authors such as Rutschmann and DiGirolamo highlight the tension between innovation and precaution, calling for robust ethical frameworks that can guide both practitioners and technology developers. Questions of data ownership loom large: who controls the sensitive information generated during AI-supported coaching sessions? How can clients be assured that their personal narratives will not be exploited for commercial gain or inadvertently used to train algorithms without their consent?

Bias is another pressing concern. AI systems are only as fair as the data on which they are trained, and historical inequities embedded in datasets can perpetuate or even amplify systemic biases. In coaching, where issues of identity, culture, and power are often central, such biases could have significant harm if left unaddressed. The chapters advocate for transparency in algorithm design, continuous auditing for fairness, and the inclusion of diverse perspectives in the development process. Beyond technical ethics, there is also a philosophical dimension: as AI takes on roles traditionally reserved for humans, what does this mean for concepts like agency, autonomy, and relational authenticity in coaching?

These ethical questions intersect with broader societal issues. The rise of AI coaching poses challenges for professional identity and accreditation. How should credentialing bodies like the ICF or EMCC respond to AI-mediated coaching? Will new competencies be required, such as AI literacy or ethical technology management? The democratizing potential of AI, its ability to make coaching accessible to those previously excluded, sits uneasily alongside concerns about a widening digital divide, where those without technological access or literacy are left further behind. Several authors call for proactive engagement by the coaching profession in shaping policy and standards, lest these be dictated solely by technology companies whose priorities may not align with coaching's humanistic ethos.

Across these four insights, a unifying thread emerges: the relationship between AI and coaching is not binary but dialectical. The chapters collectively resist simplistic narratives of utopia or dystopia. Instead, they invite us to inhabit the tensions between augmentation and replacement, efficiency and empathy, innovation and ethics. They challenge coaches, researchers, and educators to engage with AI not as a distant future but as a present reality already reshaping practice. Indeed, the arrival of generative AI has accelerated this timeline dramatically. Only a few years ago, the idea of conversational agents capable of nuanced coaching dialogues seemed remote; today, such tools are publicly accessible and widely used, even if still imperfect.

The path forward will require ongoing dialogue between technologists and coaching practitioners, as well as between researchers, ethicists, and policymakers. Hybrid intelligence where human intelligence and artificial intelligence complement rather than compete may offer the most viable and ethically sound approach. In such a model, AI handles tasks of analysis, pattern recognition, and scalable feedback, while humans bring relational presence, moral reasoning, and the capacity to co-create meaning. This vision aligns with the broader trajectory of the helping professions, many of which are moving toward blended models that harness the strengths of both human and machine.

As we conclude this volume, we do so not with definitive answers but with a richer set of questions. How will coaching evolve as AI systems become more sophisticated and more deeply embedded in organizational and personal development contexts? What new skills will coaches need to remain relevant and effective in an AI-augmented world? How will ethical frameworks adapt to ensure that the dignity, privacy, and autonomy of clients are protected amid rapid technological change? And perhaps most fundamentally, what does it mean to be human and to engage in human development when machines can increasingly replicate aspects of our intelligence?

This book offers early, thoughtful responses to these questions, grounded in both empirical research and reflective practice. As the profession of coaching stands on the threshold of the remarkable technology disruption, this synthesis affirms that the future of coaching will not be determined by technology alone. It will be shaped by the choices of coaches, educators, organizations, and clients about how to integrate AI in ways that honor the relational, ethical, and transformative essence of coaching. The task ahead is to harness the extraordinary capabilities of artificial intelligence while remaining steadfast in our commitment to human flourishing. In doing so, we may find that the partnership between human and machine does not diminish coaching's humanity, but deepens it, inviting us to become not less human, but more fully so.

GPSR Compliance
The European Union's (EU) General Product Safety Regulation (GPSR) is a set of rules that requires consumer products to be safe and our obligations to ensure this.

If you have any concerns about our products, you can contact us on

ProductSafety@springernature.com

In case Publisher is established outside the EU, the EU authorized representative is:

Springer Nature Customer Service Center GmbH
Europaplatz 3
69115 Heidelberg, Germany

www.ingramcontent.com/pod-product-compliance
Ingram Content Group UK Ltd.
Pitfield, Milton Keynes, MK11 3LW, UK
UKHW020648021026
476200UK00001B/75

9783032233318